HARRY POTTER
and the WITHDRAWN
ORDER OF THE COURT

The J.K. Rowling Copyright Case and the Question of Fair Use

I.C.C. LIBRARY

Mr. Want is an attorney and editor. He is publisher of NationsCourts.com, which reports on new cases in copyright and other areas of the law.

Harry Potter & the Order of the Court offers commentary on the fair use doctrine as presented in a copyright case filed by J.K. Rowling. There is no affiliation with Ms. Rowling or the *Harry Potter* books.

TABLE OF CONTENTS

INTRODUCTION 1

J.K. ROWLING LITIGATION 3
- Plaintiffs' Complaint.. 5
- Fair Use Project at Stanford University 7
- Order of the Court 9
   1. Plaintiffs' Arguments Supporting Preliminary Injunction 10
   2. Defendant's Arguments Opposing.................................... 12
   3. Plaintiffs' Response 14
   4. The Trial... 15
   5. Judge Patterson's Opinion 18

THE FAIR USE DOCTRINE 23
- What is Fair Use? 24
   1. Comment and Criticism.. 25
   2. Parody... 25
- Measuring Fair Use: the Four Factors 26
   1. Purpose and Character of Use....................................... 26
   2. Nature of Copyrighted Work.. 27
   3. Amount of Portion Taken.. 27
   4. Effect of Use on Potential Market................................. 28
   5. "Fifth" Fair Use Factor.. 28
- Additional Considerations 29
- Summaries of Fair Use Cases 31
   1. Cases Involving Text... 31
   2. Artwork and Audiovisual Cases 32
   3. Parody Cases 34
   4. Music Cases 36
   5. Internet and Software Cases 37
- Disagreements over Fair Use 38
- Fair Use in the Internet Age... 39

COURT DOCUMENTS 41
- Plaintiffs' Complaint 42
- Declaration of J.K. Rowling... 62
- Plaintiffs' Memorandum Supporting Preliminary Injunction 66
- Defendant's Memorandum Opposing 84
- Plaintiffs' Reply Memorandum.. 101
- Declaration of J.K. Rowling... 108
- Defendant's Answer to Plaintiffs' Complaint 113
- Transcript of J.K. Rowling Trial Testimony.......................... 127
- Judge Patterson's Opinion 163

INTRODUCTION

The adventures of wizard-in-training Harry Potter may have ended, but the drama continues. In the latest episode, the central locale has shifted from the stately halls of Hogwarts to the stately halls of federal court in Manhattan. In Manhattan, however, there are no wizards in sight, only muggles (ordinary people) including among them a judge and attorneys who must deal with the issues presented in a lawsuit brought by *Harry Potter* author J.K. Rowling.

The case is of interest not only to Harry Potter fans but to much of the general public. *Potter & the Order of the Court* discusses the case, including the court's decision and its broader implications.

The trial was highlighted by J.K. Rowling taking the witness stand, her first time appearing in a courtroom. Her dramatic testimony -- offering insights into her creative process and her emotional attachment to the *Harry Potter* series -- is included, both direct examination and cross-examination.

Beyond the star presence of Ms. Rowling, the case is of general interest because it involves an important but little understood aspect of copyright law, the doctrine of "fair use." Fair use refers to situations where one may use material from a copyrighted work without seeking permission from the author. The doctrine has taken on added importance in this Internet Age where almost all of us "publish" in one form or another -- be it through creating web pages, writing blogs, or uploading content. Copyright law applies not only to what we write on paper but also to what we publish online, in the form of text, graphics, sounds, or video. And as authors or publishers (the Internet tends to blur the distinction), we often feel the need to quote, closely paraphrase, or otherwise use material others have created. This is where fair use comes in, and it is an important concept to be familiar with, understanding the privileges it offers as well as its limitations.

The Copyright Act says uses may be considered "fair" when they are done for such reasons as criticism, comment, news reporting, teaching, or scholarship and research. The act states further that in determining whether fair use applies in a given situation, courts are to consider whether the use is of a commercial nature or for nonprofit educational purposes. Also to be considered is the portion used in relation to the copyrighted work as a whole and the effect of the use on the potential market for the original work.

The distinction between what is a fair use and what constitutes infringement is often unclear and not easy to define. When confronted with the fair use issue, courts must closely examine the particular facts of the case before them, as did the judge in the J.K. Rowling case. We will look at specific examples where the courts have found fair use, and examples where they have not.

We begin our discussion of fair use by taking a close look at the issue as it presents itself in the recently concluded J.K. Rowling case. In the lawsuit, Ms. Rowling sought to prevent the publication of an encyclopedia based on her copyrighted *Harry Potter* material. The publisher of the proposed encyclopedia characterized it as a literary reference guide that he had every right to publish under the fair use doctrine. The case is important given the enormous popularity of the *Harry Potter* books and their legion of fans around the world. These fans are generating extensive commentary and scholarship on all things Harry Potter on innumerable fan websites, and in print as well. Also the case speaks to the issue of the extent to which reference guides and other compilations of copyrighted material are permissible under copyright law.

After discussing the specifics of the J.K. Rowling case, we will examine the broader implications of the fair use issue as it affects many of us in our day-to-day writing activities, both online and off. We will go over specific examples as to how courts have ruled on the issue in different factual situations.

In addition to Ms. Rowling's testimony, we have included selected court documents filed in the litigation, including the court decision. Perhaps because the case involves one of the most popular fictional series of all time, these court documents make for fairly compelling reading, rather like a novel one cannot put down.

J.K. ROWLING
FAIR USE LITIGATION:

Does a reference guide (an encyclopedia) to the *Harry Potter* series violate author J.K. Rowling's copyright in the series? That is the issue boiled down to its essentials. Ms. Rowling gave impassioned testimony at trial in the affirmative. Still, the judge said the issue in the case before him was a close call, and his decision reflects that. We will discuss that decision and its implications below. But first some background.

The J.K. Rowling fair use case that is the subject of this commentary began on October 31, 2007, when Ms. Rowling and Warner Bros. Entertainment filed suit in federal court in Manhattan against the planned publication of a book billed as an unofficial encyclopedic companion to the *Harry Potter* series. Ms. Rowling owns the copyright to the *Harry Potter* books; and through a license granted by Ms. Rowling, Warner Bros. owns production rights to the *Harry Potter* films.

While the case is officially known as *Warner Bros. Entertainment et al v. RDR Books et al* (U.S. District Court for Southern New York, #07-cv-09667-RPP), the lead plaintiff is, in fact, J.K. Rowling. Ms. Rowling made the decision to initiate the case – though she says she did so reluctantly -- and, as we shall see, she played an active role in the litigation.

J.K. Rowling needs no introduction. As almost everyone knows, Ms. Rowling is the author of the *Harry Potter* books, which through seven editions have cast a worldwide spell. Rowling says the idea for the books came to her while riding on a train from London to Manchester, England, in 1990. At the time, she was divorced and living on public assistance in Edinburgh, Scotland, while preparing to resume her teaching career.

Ms. Rowling attended Exeter University, in the south of England. Her degree was in French, though she took courses in Greek and Roman mythology as well. After graduation, she embarked on a career as a bilingual secretary. But it did not take her long to realize that this was not the career path she was cut out for. She has said that she lacked the organizational skills to be a secretary and found it difficult to remain attentive during meetings, preferring to write story ideas rather than take notes as her job required.

In 1991, the 26 year-old Ms. Rowling moved to Portugal to be an English teacher, though continuing to work on an emerging story idea she had about a "wizard." In Portugal, she met and married a journalist (he was Portuguese). In 1993 a daughter, Jessica, was born. Shortly thereafter, the marriage ended in divorce and Rowling and her infant daughter moved back to the UK, settling in Edinburgh where she was determined to continue work on her novel. She recently disclosed that during this period she suffered from depression and sought medical help.

As plots and characters began to take form, she drafted her manuscripts in longhand at an Edinburgh coffee shop while her daughter slept. Early on, she was told these manuscripts were uncommercial, overlong, and wouldn't sell. But she persisted. And the rest is history, recent history. The first book was published in 1997; the seventh and final book in the series, ten years later. It has been reported that the books have sold well over 325 million copies worldwide and have been translated into more than 65 languages.

The series tells the story of an orphaned boy named Harry Potter. Harry lives a normal enough life, sleeping in a tiny room under the stairs in the home of his hated Aunt Petunia, Uncle Vernon, and cousin Dudley, all of whom are "Muggles" (humans without magical abilities). On his eleventh birthday he begins to receive letters from the Hogwarts School of Witchcraft & Wizardry, which he is invited to attend. Harry learns that his parents did not die in a car crash but in fact were wizards who were killed by Voldemort, the Lord of Darkness, and that he, Harry, is famous in the world of wizardry.

Each of the seven books covers one of Harry's seven years at Hogwarts. Over the course of these books, Harry learns many new things, makes new friends, travels, and has many adventures. He learns to hone his wizarding skills, cast spells, make portions and play new games, including "Quidditch," a game invented by Ms. Rowling that has some elements of soccer and rugby but the two teams fly on broomsticks and try to score points by getting balls through goals that are suspended in mid-air.

Given the huge popularity of the *Harry Potter* series of books and films, it is not surprising that many imitations have emerged. And it is not surprising that Ms. Rowling should try to protect her legal rights to the fantastical world she had created. On her behalf, her attorneys have brought actions around the world to try to prevent unauthorized translations and adaptations that borrow heavily from *Harry Potter's* world of characters and events. Sometimes she has been successful; sometimes not. For example, her attorneys have not been successful in their attempt to halt publication in Russia of a series of books about an 11-year-old girl named Tanya Grotter who, like Harry Potter, is an orphan, wears glasses and has a mole on her nose. And like the *Harry Potter* books, the Grotter series is full of fanciful magic words that set spells in motion. The Russian publisher refused Ms. Rowling's request that the Grotter series be withdrawn, saying they are completely independent of *Harry Potter* and rooted in Russian culture and folklore.

The Harry Potter versus Tanya Grotter allegations have not been litigated in the Russian courts. A court in the Netherlands found in Ms. Rowling's favor, but its decision applies only in that county. Were the case to be heard by an American court, the Russian publisher, in order to prevail, would need to convince the court that its version of wizardry and magic spells adds substantial new material to the genre and thus does not infringe on Ms. Rowling's copyright. As the matter now stands, both Harry Potter and Tanya Grotter can be found side-by-side on Russian bookshelves and both are very popular.

Ms. Rowling has not always been the plaintiff in court actions involving *Harry Potter*. Several years ago, she found herself in the role of defendant in a copyright infringement lawsuit brought in federal court in Philadelphia by American author Nancy Stouffer. Ms. Stouffer claimed that Rowling had stolen material from her own children's books, including stories about a boy named "Larry Potter." The court could find no factual basis for the allegations and dismissed the suit (*Stouffer v. Scholastic Inc. et al*, U.S. District Court for Eastern Pennsylvania, #00-cv-01201-HH, September 8, 2000).

While most parents and educators appreciate that the *Harry Potter* books have encouraged young people to read, some have objected to what they see as an "anti-Christian" message in the books (which Ms. Rowling strongly denies). In a recently filed lawsuit, a library assistant who is a Southern Baptist claims that the City of Poplar Bluffs, MO, fired her because her religious beliefs prohibited her from working on "Harry Potter Night" at the library. She says her religious beliefs prevent her from being involved in the promotion of worship of the occult, particularly when it is directed at children (*Smith v. City of Poplar Bluffs (MO)*, U.S. District Court for Eastern Missouri, #08-cv-00094, June 20, 2008).

Plaintiffs' Complaint

In the J.K. Rowling lawsuit (*Warner Bros. Entertainment et al v. RDR Books*), Ms. Rowling claims that a 400-page reference book -- *The Harry Potter Lexicon* ("Lexicon") originally scheduled for released by RDR Books in November 2007 -- has infringed on her copyright through widespread misappropriation of her fictional characters and universe, including "list after list of spells and potions, imaginary places, fantastic creatures and invented games."

Ms. Rowling said in her suit that the Lexicon – described by its author as an encyclopedia of all things *Harry Potter* -- was a "derivative" work and thus an infringement of her copyright. Under copyright law, a holder of a copyright not only has the right to make and distribute copies of the original material – in this case the *Harry Potter* books – but also the right to create derivative works – adaptations -- based on the original. For example, translations based on the original material are considered derivative works, as are screenplays and computer games. Only if the author of the translation or screenplay or computer game has added substantial new material might it be found not to infringe on the original material. Note that the *Harry Potter* films are derivative works based on the books. Ms. Rowling granted a license to Warner Bros. to produce the films. Had she not done so, Warner Bros. would have created a derivative work in violation of Rowling's copyright.

Ms. Rowling argued that the Lexicon was not an original work of authorship but rather one that borrowed extensively from her own copyrighted material. Explaining her decision to bring the action against RDR Books, Rowling issued the following statement:

> As is now widely known, a complaint has been filed in the name of Warner Bros. and myself against the publisher of a proposed Lexicon, written by Steven Vander Ark. This decision was reached, on my part, with immense sadness and disappointment, and only because direct appeals for a reasonable solution failed. I never dreamed, in the light of our previous good relations – including giving the [online version of the] Lexicon a Fansite Award – that this situation would ever arise.

> From what I understand, the proposed book is not a criticism or review of Harry Potter's world, which would be entirely legitimate – neither I nor anybody connected with Harry Potter has ever tried to prevent such works being published. It is, we believe, a print version of the website [www.hp-lexicon.com], except now the information that was freely available to everybody is to become a commercial enterprise.

> It is not reasonable, or legal, for anybody, fan or otherwise, to take an author's hard work, re-organize their characters and plots, and sell them for their own commercial gain. However much an individual claims to love somebody else's work, it does not become theirs to sell.

The complaint claimed that the Lexicon drew extensively from the *Harry Potter* series, including "list after list of spells, potions and imaginary creatures; fictional characters such as wizards, ghosts and Muggles, as well as invented games and made-up places, such as Hogwarts School of Witchcraft & Wizardry, Diagon Alley, and the governmental Ministry of Magic, all of which regurgitate Ms. Rowling's original creative expression with minimal additional commentary."

The complaint argued further that the Lexicon contained synopses of the major plots and story lines of the *Harry Potter* books, descriptions of the history and personalities of the major characters, and detailed catalogues of the fictional creatures and magical elements that constitute the "heart" of the books. In making its case for copyright infringement, the complaint stated that "these descriptions, character details and plot points comprise stories created and owned by Ms. Rowling, who has the sole right to control their distribution and who did not give permission to the defendant to publish a book that stands to make millions of dollars off the back of Ms. Rowling's creativity."

In Ms. Rowling's complaint, her attorneys offered details on the creative process behind the *Harry Potter* series and provided, from plaintiff Rowling's perspective, a comprehensive analysis of the legal issues involved. For both Harry Potter fans and those interested in the legal issues, the complaint -- and other material filed in the case -- make for fairly compelling reading. This material is included in the "Court Documents" section beginning on page 41 below.

Responding to plaintiffs' charges, the publisher of the Lexicon, RDR Books, said in a statement that the encyclopedia drew material and inspiration from the *Harry Potter* books but was an entirely new piece of work. "It is a companion to Rowling's work, not a substitute for it. No one is going to buy the Lexicon instead of a *Harry Potter* book, or instead of seeing a *Harry Potter* film."

The Fair Use Project at Stanford Law School

The filing of the J.K. Rowling lawsuit appeared to set in motion a David and Goliath confrontation. The Goliath in this scenario is clearly the plaintiffs' side: Ms. Rowling, a billionaire author with legions of fans around the world, and Warner Bros., a billionaire corporation that produces and distributes major motion pictures (the *Harry Potter* films alone have thus far taken in over $4 billion in worldwide receipts). The David in the lawsuit is the defendant, RDR Books, a small independent publisher based in Muskegon, Michigan (www.rdrbooks.com).

However, in a plot twist worthy of a *Harry Potter* novel, the David-Goliath analogy was pushed aside by a surprise announcement that signaled a more level playing field. On December 4, 2007, the Fair Use Project at Stanford Law School's Center for Internet & Society (cyberlaw.stanford.edu) said that it had signed on to aid the defense of RDR Books. The Fair Use Project is well known for its crusading efforts against what it considers overly-aggressive attempts by publishing and media companies to control the use of their copyrights. The project argues for more flexibility in the enforcement of copyright law. In making the RDR Books announcement, the Fair Use Project issued a statement saying that the proposed Lexicon is protected by copyright fair use rules that have long given people "the right to create reference guides that discuss literary works, comment on them and make them more accessible." The project said that the Lexicon is a reference work based on more than seven years of research by a distinguished volunteer team of librarians and academics, and that fair use protects scholars' rights to create such companion guides. Their arguments are further considered below.

Stanford's Center for Internet & Society was founded in 2006 by Stanford Law Professor Lawrence Lessig. Mr. Lessig is one of the nation's foremost authorities on copyright law. He has long argued that the powers of copyright holders have grown enormously over the past half-century, in duration, reach, and force; and this, he says, has upset the balance intended in the U.S. Constitution between owners of intellectual property and the public.

Mr. Lessig maintains that copyright law is often used as a club against talented and well-meaning creators of content, particularly in digital formats that allow for the innovative remixing of material, such as mash-ups in which two or more kinds of copyrighted works are mixed to create something new. He is critical, for example, of what he calls punitive lawsuits filed by the recording industry against school kids who downloaded music to their MP3s, and media companies who aggressively limit user generated content of copyrighted material on such sites as YouTube when in fact this content may qualify as fair use. Mr. Lessig sites a recent case where a mother posted a video on YouTube of her baby dancing to Prince's song "Let's Go Crazy" – and Universal Music promptly demanded the removal of the video on the basis of copyright infringement.

Mr. Lessig is an advocate for the Creative Commons Project in which copyright holders can voluntarily limit the scope of their copyrights (creativecommons.org), for example, by signing a license allowing others to copy their material for noncommercial purposes or allowing their copyright duration to end (and thus their material to become part of the public domain) in less than the allowed copyright term of life of the author plus 70 years. In one voluntary action, the company that owns the Beatle's catalog has given hip-hop labels permission to use samples of Beatle songs in hip-hop recordings.

Concerning remixing of copyrighted material, an excellent study on the subject has recently been published (January 2008) by American University's Center for Social Media. The study, *Recut, Reframe, Recycle: Quoting Copyrighted Material in User-Generated Video*, argues that many uses of copyrighted material in current online videos are eligible for fair use consideration. A copy of the study is available on the center's website, www.centerforsocialmedia.org.

Order of the Court

The first order of business for the court hearing the J.K. Rowling case, the U.S. District Court in Manhattan, was to consider and then rule on plaintiffs' motion for a preliminary injunction. A preliminary injunction would prevent defendant RDR Books from publishing its Lexicon while the case was being litigated on its merits. (The judge had previously issued a temporary restraining order.)

A ruling in plaintiffs' favor on the preliminary injunction would not mean the plaintiffs had "won" the case; but it would provide an indication as to which way the court was leaning, as no court would take the punitive step of enjoining publication – a restraint on freedom of the press -- unless it felt plaintiffs had presented in strong case and were likely to succeed on the merits of the case.

Also, for the court to grant a preliminary injunction, the plaintiffs must show that they would suffer "irreparable injury" should the court allow the book to be published while plaintiffs' claims of copyright infringement were being considered. There is further discussion of these legal issues below.

The case was being heard not before a judge and jury but (as per agreement of the parties) before a judge only. The judge is U.S. District Judge Robert B. Patterson Jr.

Judge Patterson has had a long, distinguished career on the federal bench in Manhattan. At 85 years-of-age (federal judges receive lifetime appointments), he is thin, gravel-voiced and gray-haired. He was named to the federal bench in 1988 by President Reagan. Mr. Patterson's father, Robert B. Patterson Sr., had served on the same court, appointed to the bench by Franklin Delano Roosevelt.

Though named to the court by Ronald Reagan, a president known for his conservative outlook, Robert B. Patterson Jr. had long been considered a fairly liberal fixture in New York's legal establishment. Prior to his appointment, he served as director of the New York Legal Aid Society and was chairman of Prisoners Legal services, which provides legal counsel to inmates. As a federal judge, he has often shown sensitivity to First Amendment rights of freedom of speech and political expression. In 1990 he ruled that proposed federal restrictions on access to telephone-pornography services were unconstitutional.

In 1998, in a right-to-protest case, Judge Patterson ruled that the Mayor Giuliani administration was violating the First Amendment rights of taxi drivers by preventing them from protesting regulations that the city was seeking to impose on their industry. In 2006 when gay demonstrators from around the world announced plans to march past the United Nations, some wanted to walk up Fifth Avenue as well, and sued when the city denied the request. Judge Patterson ruled that the city could limit the marchers to a single route, but he also criticized the city, saying that it had not allowed the protesters enough of a forum to express their views.

While Judge Patterson's sensitivity to freedom of expression claims might indicate that defendant's arguments in the J.K. Rowling case would resonate with him, he has also shown a willingness to be influenced less by ideology than by the facts of the particular case before him. This was certainly the situation in the J.K. Rowing case under discussion here.

Judge Patterson's opinion is discussed below, beginning on page 18. But first, we will look at the arguments presented by the adversaries in the case. Both the plaintiffs and defendant submitted briefs to the court, arguing their respective positions on plaintiffs' motion for a preliminary injunction. Their arguments presented in the briefs go to the merits of the case as well.

1. Plaintiffs' Arguments in Support of Preliminary Injunction

As indicated, for J.K. Rowling's attorneys to prevail on their motion for a preliminary injunction, they must show (1) the likelihood that they will prevail on the merits and (2) irreparable injury if the Lexicon is allowed to go ahead.

In their memorandum to the court in support of their motion for a preliminary injunction, the plaintiffs argued that they are likely to succeed on the merits of their claim of copyright infringement because of the defendant's extensive copying from the *Harry Potter* books. The plaintiffs' said that defendant's attempt to justify its infringement as "scholarship" and thus qualify as fair use under copyright law is nothing less than a sham. Defendant's book is not, plaintiffs argued, a scholarly critique or reference guide but merely a mass-market work that lifts whole chunks of Ms. Rowling's text and places them in alphabetical order, in effect "rearranging the furniture" that Ms. Rowling created, and that this rearrangement "lacks any originality or invention." The plaintiffs claimed that the Second Circuit (the federal appeals court whose rulings govern the Manhattan district court where the case was being heard) has expressly stated that such works are not fair use but rather copyright infringements warranting injunctive relief.

One of the principal cases cited by plaintiffs in their memorandum was *Castle Rock Entertainment v. Carol Publishing Group*, a decision handed down by the U.S. Court of Appeals for the 2nd Circuit in 1998. The case involved a challenge to a quiz book based on the *Seinfeld* TV show that included hundreds of questions involving minute details from the show. The court did not find fair use in that case and, plaintiffs argued, the court should not find fair use in the current case, where the facts were even more favorable to a fair use determination.

The plaintiffs maintained that the current availability of the contents of defendant's book on the "The Harry Potter Lexicon" website (hp.lexicon.org) did not change the result; there is a world of difference between permitting a free fan site to operate and allowing RDR Books to commercialize this material. A contrary rule, plaintiffs claimed, would also harm the fan community by necessitating more monitoring and restriction of an activity by copyright owners afraid of compromising their rights against infringers.

The plaintiffs further argued that injunctive relief was particularly appropriate given the evidence of defendant RDR Books' bad faith in proceeding with its planned publication despite having strong reason to believe that its conduct was unlawful. Steven Vander Ark, owner of the Lexicon website and the book's "author," had long been aware of Ms. Rowling's plan to write a *Harry Potter* encyclopedia of her own, the plaintiffs claimed. Vander Ark even stated in a "smoking gun" e-mail that it would be "illegal" to sell such a work without Rowling's permission and that she had reserved her rights in the *Harry Potter* series. Plaintiffs noted that Vander Ark had sought employment as a co-author of Rowling's planned encyclopedia, but his services were declined.

Concerning the question of irreparable injury, plaintiffs argued that in copyright infringement actions such as this that feature extensive copying, there was a presumption of irreparable injury. Further, if publication were allowed to go ahead, Ms. Rowling would effectively be "scooped" by her own work and deprived of the exclusive right to be the first to create a definitive encyclopedia of the *Harry Potter* series, as well as the right to exercise quality control over derivative works based on the series. Moreover, the plaintiffs said, when Rowling publishes her own guide she might find herself in the absurd position of defending a claim that she infringed RDR's copyright in its unauthorized derivative work based on *her* creation.

For a further presentation of plaintiffs' arguments, in the "Court Documents" section below, see "Plaintiffs' Complaint" (beginning on page 42) and "Plaintiffs' Memorandum Supporting Preliminary Injunction" (beginning on page 66).

2. Defendant's Arguments Opposing Preliminary Injunction

In presenting its arguments against a preliminary injunction, defendant RDR Books -- represented as indicated by a team of attorneys under the leadership of the Stanford Fair Use Project -- said that J.K. Rowling was seeking to claim a monopoly on the right to publish literary reference guides relating to her own fiction, and that this was a right no court had ever recognized.

If such a right were recognized, RDR Books argued, it would dramatically extend the reach of copyright protection, and eliminate an entire genre of literary supplements: third party reference guides to fiction which for centuries have helped readers better access, understand and enjoy literary works. By extension, RDR said, it would threaten not just reference guides, but encyclopedias, glossaries, indexes, and other tools that provide useful information about copyrighted works. "Ms. Rowling's intellectual property rights simply do not extend so far and, even if they did, she has not shown that the publication of *this* reference guide [encyclopedia] poses a sufficient threat of irreparable harm to justify an injunction. Her preliminary injunction motion should be denied."

RDR Books noted that Ms. Rowling claimed the right to be the "first to publish" a companion book to the Potter series. But it is, RDR said, far too late for that as nearly 200 Harry Potter companion guides have already been published, many of which incorporate A to Z listings in a manner that closely resembled the Lexicon's:

> Unique or not, the Lexicon is a serious book -- a reference guide that is the product of eight years work by Vander Ark and his staff. ...[L]exicons like this one have an important and distinguished place in the literary world. Indeed, the value and importance of this lexicon is evident from its contents. It organizes a tremendous amount of information into a concise and readable form with citations to the scores of original sources it draws upon. At the same time, it provides a significant amount of original analysis and commentary concerning everything from insights into the personality of key characters, relationships among them, the

meaning of various historical and literary allusions, as well as internal inconsistencies and mistakes in the novels.

RDR Books argued that J.K. Rowling cannot show a likelihood of success on the merits of her copyright claim, a basic requirement for a preliminary injunction. As noted, one of the principal cases plaintiffs relied on in their motion for a preliminary injunction was *Castle Rock Entertainment v. Carol Publishing Group*, where the court did not grant fair use status to a quiz book based on the *Seinfeld* TV show that included hundreds of questions involving minute details from the show. But the analogy of the Lexicon to *Castle Rock* was misguided, RDR said. At issue there was a 132-page book containing 643 trivia questions and answers about the events and characters in *Seinfeld*. The court found that the trivia questions could not be used to research *Seinfeld* and did not contain any commentary or analysis about *Seinfeld*:

> The Lexicon, by contrast, is a valuable research tool, and contains significant commentary about the Harry Potter Works, as well as analysis of the nature and names of characters, places and things that appear in them, along with extensive citations to original sources. Moreover, its contents are drawn not simply from the Harry Potter Works, but scores of other sources, including other references books and many interviews with J.K. Rowling. The Lexicon, therefore, does much more than simply pose trivia questions.

On the question of "irreparable injury," RDR Books maintained that Ms. Rowling's encyclopedia, whenever it is published, would be "distinctive" and thus not harmed by the publication of defendant's reference guide. Further, as noted, almost 200 guides have already been published, so Rowling cannot claim that the publication of defendant's Lexicon would deny her the right to be first.

The Copyright Act gives authors the right to published "derivative works" based on their original material. Examples of derivative works include: translations, musical arrangements, dramatizations, fictionalizations, motion picture versions, art reproductions, abridgments or other forms in which a work may be recast or adapted. Defendant RDR Books argued that a reference guide to copyrighted works (e.g., the Lexicon being the reference guide and the *Harry Potter* books being the copyrighted work) is not among the examples listed, and does not recast or adapt copyrighted works in comparable ways. RDR referred to the decision of the U.S. appellate court in Chicago in the case *Ty, Inc. v. Publ'ns Int'l Ltd.*, where the court held that a collector's guide to Beanie Babies was not a derivative work and thus qualified as a fair use. If anything, defendant argued, the Lexicon was a "supplementary" work the purpose of which was "explaining . . . commenting upon [and] assisting in the use of" the *Harry Potter* Works.

RDR Books further maintained that even if the Lexicon were a "derivative work," J.K. Rowling would still have to show substantial similarity between the Lexicon and the *Harry Potter* series in order to defeat a finding of fair use. "Ms. Rowling cannot do that under the traditional 'ordinary observer' or 'total concept and feel' tests, or under the quantitative/qualitative test applied in *Castle Rock Entertainment, Inc. v. Carol Publishing Group, Inc.* On the contrary, *Castle Rock* itself acknowledged that a secondary work may cease to be substantially similar if it transforms the original sufficiently." And that transformation, RDR argued, was precisely the case here.

For a further presentation of RDR Book's arguments, see "Defendant's Memorandum Opposing Preliminary Injunction" beginning on page 84 below.

3. Plaintiffs' Response

Responding to RDR Books' arguments against a preliminary injunction, plaintiffs J.K. Rowling and Warner Bros. said that RDR's counsel, the Stanford Fair Use Project, had mischaracterized the nature of the Lexicon to advance its political agenda of "extend[ing] the boundaries of fair use." The plaintiffs said that both the facts and the law showed that the Lexicon simply did not qualify as fair use in its current form, and therefore must be enjoined.

Plaintiffs said that RDR Book's reliance on *Ty, Inc.* to make the case that the Lexicon constituted a fair use was misplaced. "The court there found that 'textual portions of a collector's guide' (*e.g.,* release dates, retirement dates, prices) were critical and evaluative rather than a mere recasting of the underlying dolls. In contrast, RDR Books' [Lexicon] is nothing more than a recast of Ms. Rowling's original text."

Plaintiffs argued that the Lexicon's undisputed commercial nature weighed against a finding of fair use. Further, they said, RDR Book's characterization of the Lexicon as "transformative" was wrong because it did not create "new information, new aesthetics, new insights and understandings." RDR's implausible claim that the Lexicon was a "serious book" filled with scholarly commentary and analysis was merely an attempt to excuse blatant infringement, plaintiffs said.

For a further presentation of plaintiffs' arguments, see "Plaintiffs' Reply Memorandum," beginning on page 101 below.

4. The Trial

The nonjury trial before Judge Patterson began on April 14, 2008, and lasted three days. Judge Patterson said at the trial that he would "fast-track" the case and decide at the same time both the merits of case and the motion for preliminary injunction (that is, the issue of copyright infringement and that of motion to injoin publication) since they were closely entwined. In doing so, the judge acted to shorten litigation that would have been more drawn out had he opted to decide the injunction issue first and then hear the case on the merits.

In a nutshell, the issue before Judge Patterson: Was the Lexicon that defendant sought to publish a "fair use" of copyrighted *Harry Potter* material? In their opening statements, lawyers for both sides highlighted for the court the major points set forth in the memoranda previously submitted (see above). Defendant RDR Books argued yes, it was a fair use because the Lexicon offered a comprehensive presentation that "transforms" the original material. Plaintiff J.K. Rowling said no, that it was simply a regurgitation of the facts, offering little in the way of analysis.

Making the opening argument for Ms. Rowling was Dale M. Cendali. Ms. Cendali, an attorney with the law firm of O'Melveny & Myers, said that the Lexicon purported to be a reference guide to the *Harry Potter* series but was in fact composed of quotations and "sporadic, qualitatively meaningless" phrases lifted directly from Rowling's work.

Ms. Cendali thoroughly detailed the four factors that courts consider in ruling on questions of fair use -- the purpose and character of the use, the nature of the copyrighted work, the amount of the work copied, and the effect on the market -- arguing that all of these factors came down against a finding of fair use. She focused on the third factor -- the amount copied -- repeating several times the phrase that the Lexicon "takes too much and does too little." She said that unlike other Harry Potter companion books on the market, the Lexicon adds nothing new or original but merely "rearranges the furniture of Rowling's novels." There is not the creativity for the fair use exemption to come into play, Ms. Cendali argued.

Presenting the opening argument for defendant RDR Books was Anthony Falzone of the Stanford Fair Use Project. Mr. Falzone defended the Lexicon as a reference guide, calling it a legitimate effort "to organize and discuss the complicated and very elaborate world of Harry Potter." He said that RDR was not contesting that the encyclopedia infringes on Rowling's copyright but rather arguing that it is a fair use allowable by law for reference books. He suggested that Ms. Rowling was trying to exert a bit of the dark arts herself, by testing whether she "has the power to make the Lexicon disappear from our world." The power Rowling asserts over her fictional characters, he said, does not translate into power she can assert over companion guides written by others.

The first day of the trial was the most dramatic, with J.K. Rowling appearing on the witness stand to argue her case. It was the first time Ms. Rowling had testified in a courtroom and she admitted to being somewhat nervous, facing a packed gallery of fans and print media (federal courts do not allow televised trials). Rowling said she felt compelled to testify because she felt so strongly about someone else turning 17 years of her labor on the *Harry Potter* series into an encyclopedia. The thought of such an outcome, she said, had caused great "stress and heartache" and had all but paralyzed her normal writing life.

See transcript of Ms. Rowling's testimony-- both direct examination and cross examination -- beginning on page 127 below.

The *New York Times*, in describing Ms. Rowling's testimony, said she stoically held back tears as she talked about the Potter books as if they were her children.

Ms. Rowling said she had read the Lexicon and saw it as a copyright infringement and little more than an alphabetical form of plagiarism. She claimed the author of the encyclopedia lifted large chunks of her own language without quotation marks. "I believe that it is sloppy, lazy, and that it takes my work wholesale verbatim," she testified. She said the book would compete unfairly with an encyclopedia she had been planning to create since 1998, the profits of which she intended to donate to a British charity.

But what Ms. Rowling denounced as copyright infringement, the attorneys for RDR Books defended as literary scholarship and an invaluable tool for Harry Potter readers, similar to a Shakespeare concordance, the Encyclopedia Britannica, the dictionary and other reference works.

Much of Ms. Rowling's testimony focused on her contention that the encyclopedia in question was not very good, although she conceded under cross-examination from David Hammer, the lead attorney for RDR Books, that it was unusually comprehensive. Still, Ms. Rowling held her ground, responding to Mr. Hammer: "Is that the best you can say for the Lexicon? That it has text? She added, "An alphabetical rearrangement is the easiest and laziest way to re-sell my work."

The defense found it ironic that the same website she was now denigrating was the very one she had admitted using herself on numerous occasions to check facts. Ms. Rowling responded that she never wanted to censor the site. She said that if she loses the lawsuit, other authors will conclude that they need to exercise more control over fan websites, unlike J.K. Rowling who "was an idiot. She let it all go."

Ms. Rowling testified for about three hours. She spent breaks in the proceedings in the seclusion of a jury room, away from fans all too eager to engage her in conversation or perhaps obtain an autograph. On Ms. Rowling's performance as a witness, the *Wall Street Journal* quoted Columbia University copyright professor Tim Wu: "She was the definition of a star witness. It was hard for [the defense] to get anything out of her."

The next day, Steven Vander Ark, author of the contested Lexicon, took the stand. The 50-year-old, mild-mannered librarian (who resembles Harry Potter) called Ms. Rowling his idol, noting that he had spent years studying the books and indexing their content online. One day, he testified, Ms. Rowling was singling out his Harry Potter Lexicon website for praise, out of "hundreds of thousands" of Potter fan sites on the Web; the next, she was accusing him of plagiarism for wanting to turn it into a book. Mr. Vander Ark said he and his website staff members, including a teacher of Greek and Latin and two other librarians, had compiled the alphabetical Lexicon as a "ready reference" for Potter fans, because the books had no index or glossary.

If Ms. Rowling stoically held back tears during her testimony, as observers described her as doing, Mr. Vander Ark showed no such restraint. On the stand he wiped away tears and at times could barely speak when asked to reflect on what the case has done to his relationship with the community of Harry Potter fans. "It's been difficult because there has been a lot of criticism, obviously, and that was never the intention." He acknowledged, under cross-examination, that he, too, had substantial concerns all along about whether publishing an encyclopedia based on the Harry Potter universe would constitute copyright infringement. He said he was talked into doing it by RDR Books.

The third, and final day, of the trial was highlighted by Judge Patterson's urging the parties to settle the dispute out of court, and Ms. Rowling offering an olive branch herself. The judge said the case was a legal close call, involving unresolved areas of American law, and was almost certain to end in years of appeals. "I think this case, with imagination, could be settled," he said. Judge Patterson said that he loved literature, reminding the parties that in Dickens' "Bleak House" the character Miss Flite faithfully attends every day of the trial and dies before the litigation ends. "A very sad story," he said. "Litigation isn't always the best way to solve things."

For her part, Ms. Rowling echoed a conciliatory tone upon being called to the witness stand for a second time. The *New York Times* reported that she seemed clearly wounded after the previous day's testimony by Mr. Vander Ark, who said he had once been one of her biggest fans but now felt cast out of the "Harry Potter community" by her lawsuit. Ms. Rowling said she had been misunderstood. "I never ever once wanted to stop Mr. Vander Ark from doing his own guide – never, ever. Do your own book, but please, change it so it does not take as much of my own work."

In spite of the judge's comments and Ms. Rowling's olive branch, the lawyers for both sides came on strong in their closing arguments. For the plaintiffs, Ms. Cendali reiterated her main theme: that the Lexicon "takes too much and does too little." She also emphasized the marketing aspect, saying the Lexicon could hurt Ms. Rowling's ability to sell books and Warner Brothers' interest in marketing movies and merchandise related to Harry Potter.

For the defense, Mr. Falzone who had not spoken since his opening statement, responded to Ms. Rowling's argument that the Lexicon was poorly put together and full of errors. He said that under the law, what mattered was not the quality of the book but whether it transformed Rowling's material in some way. The Lexicon, he said, "organizes, synthesizes and distills" thousands of pages and this is what makes it "transformative." "Quality shouldn't matter," he said. If the Lexicon is lousy, the answer is not to suppress it but for Rowling to write her own.

After the trial, the parties were able to reach a settlement on one of plaintiffs' claims, that of false advertising. Under the settlement, neither J.K. Rowling's name nor her quote endorsing the online version of Vander Ark's Harry Potter Lexicon would appear on the cover of the book version, should it ever be published. But the copyright infringement issue and the question of fair use – the essence of the case – remained to be decided.

5. Judge Patterson's Opinion

Judge Patterson announced his decision on September 8, 2008. He ruled in favor of plaintiffs and permanently enjoined defendant RDR Books from publishing its Lexicon. (He also awarded the plaintiffs $6,750.00 in damages, a minimal fine the judge said since the Lexicon had not been published.) He said plaintiffs had established copyright infringement against defendant and that defendant had failed to establish its defense of fair use. "Plaintiffs have shown that the Lexicon copies a sufficient quantity of the Harry Potter series to support a finding of substantial similarity between the

Lexicon and Rowling's novels," the judge said in this thorough and closely-reasoned opinion.

It was a hard-fought victory for J.K. Rowling, a victory achieved after almost a year of litigation and a 3-day trial

At the conclusion of the trial, Judge Patterson had said his decision could go either way. When one reads the opinion (the court's order and opinion begin on page 163 below), the initial impression is that the judge is leaning toward defendant's position. But then he veers off in the other direction and in the end, after a finely-tuned balancing act, comes down firmly in Ms. Rowling's corner. In his opinion, he characterized some of Rowling's impassioned testimony at trial as "overstated." (She had compared the taking of her work to "plundering.") Yet the judge seemed swayed by the passionate way in which she expressed herself on behalf of her literary creation, referring to her evocative language several times in the course of his decision.

In this case, Judge Patterson sided with J.K. Rowling, the copyright holder. But in so doing he said he tried to balance the interests expressed by both sides in the controversy: the incentive to create original works which copyright protection fosters and the freedom to produce secondary works which monopoly protection of copyright stifles -- both interests benefiting the public. The judge said reference guides to works of literature serve a useful purpose (such as the Lexicon's making an elaborate imaginary world searchable, item by item) and should be encouraged. But the Lexicon, he ruled, copied too much from the original, taking a troubling amount of direct quotation or close paraphrasing of Ms. Rowling's original language, and offered too little in added commentary.

For example, in the entry for "armor, goblin made," the Lexicon uses Rowling's poetic language nearly verbatim without quotation marks. The original language from *Harry Potter and the Deathly Hallows* reads:

Muggle-borns," he said. "Goblin-made armour does not require cleaning, simple girl. Goblins' silver repels mundane dirt, imbibing only that which strengthens it."

The Lexicon entry for "armor, goblin made" reads in its entirety:

Some armor in the wizarding world is made by goblins, and it is quite valuable. According to Phineas Nigellus, goblin-made armor does not require cleaning, because goblins' silver repels mundane dirt, imbibing only that which strengthens it, such as basilisk venom. In this context, "armor" also includes blades such as swords.

In another example, Judge Patterson noted that a number of Lexicon entries copy Ms. Rowling's artistic literary devices that contribute to her distinctive craft as a writer. For example, the Lexicon entry for "brain room," uses Rowling's evocative literary device in a very close paraphrase.

The original language from *Harry Potter and the Order of the Phoenix* reads:

> For a moment it seemed suspended in midair, then it soared toward Ron, spinning as it came, and what looked like ribbons of moving images flew from it, unraveling like rolls of film.

The Lexicon entry reads in part:

> . . . When Summoned, the brains fly out of the tank, unspooling ribbons of thought like strips of film, which wrap themselves around the Summoner and cause quite a bit of damage . . . .

In his full opinion, Judge Patterson offers many more examples of what he believes clearly demonstrative excessive copying by defendant.

While Ms. Rowling eventually won the war over fair use, she lost the battle in her argument that the Lexicon was a derivative work along the lines of a translation or dramatization and thus subject under copyright law to her control. Judge Patterson ruled that a work is not derivative simply because it is "based upon" the original work, in this case the original work being the *Harry Potter* series. "By condensing, synthesizing, and reorganizing the preexisting material in an A-to-Z reference guide, the Lexicon does not recast the material in another medium to retell the story of *Harry Potter*, but instead gives the copyrighted material another purpose."

RDR Books did not prevail, however, on the issue at the heart of its case: that the Lexicon, though admittedly copying extensively from *Harry Potter*s, was nonetheless permissible under the doctrine of fair use.

Copyright law provides that courts shall consider (though not be limited to) the following four factors in determining whether a particular use is a fair use:

(1) the purpose and character of the use, including whether such use is of a commercial nature or is for nonprofit educational purposes;

(2) the nature of the copyrighted work;

(3) the amount and substantiality of the portion used in relation to the copyrighted work as a whole, and

(4) the effect of the use upon the potential market for or value of the copyrighted work.

Judge Patterson said in this opinion that most critical to the inquiry under the first fair-use factor – the purpose and character of the use -- is whether and to what extent the new work is "transformative," i.e., creates something new with a different purpose or different character. The Lexicon is transformative, he finds, as it uses material from the series for the practical purpose of making information about the intricate world of *Harry Potter* readily accessible to readers in a reference guide. Thus this factor, the judge said, weighs in favor of defendant and a finding of fair use.

The second fair use factor looks at the nature of the copyrighted work and generally gives creative and fictional works stronger protection than fictional works. This factor thus favors plaintiffs and runs against a finding of fair use, Judge Patterson wrote.

The third fair use factor -- the amount and substantiality of the portion used in relation to the copyrighted work as a whole – weighs most heavily against defendant in its fair use claim, Judge Patterson said. The Lexicon's verbatim copying of highly descriptive expressions raises a significant question, he said, as to whether such extensive copying was necessary for the purpose of creating a useful reference guide.

The fourth factor considers the effect of the use upon the potential market for the copyrighted work. Judge Patterson appears to weigh this factor in defendant's favor. He said the Lexicon would not affect the market for the *Harry Potter* books (people would not buy the Lexicon *instead* of the books) and Ms. Rowling had no right to complain that sales of the Lexicon would interfere with the potential market for the encyclopedia she intended to publish. Since the Lexicon is not a derivative work, the judge said, competing with Rowling's planned encyclopedia is permissible.

Thus, in coming to a decision in the case, Judge Patterson was confronted with balancing the fair use factors. In striking the balance between the property rights of original authors and the freedom of expression of secondary authors, he said that reference guides to works of literature should generally be encouraged by copyright law as they provide a benefit to readers and students. But using Ms. Rowling's "overstated" language, the judge said they should not be able to "plunder" the works of original authors.

Judge Patterson's opinion makes it clear that it was the third fair use factor -- the amount of material copied – that tipped the balance in Ms. Rowling's favor and ultimately defeated RDR Book's fair use argument.

The opinion is significant because it confirms the importance of reference guides while at the same time stating clearly that one cannot merely copy extensively from an author's work without adding to it and still be protected from copyright infringement under the exemption provided by the fair use doctrine.

Anthony T. Falzone, one of RDR Book's attorneys, put the best face on what must have been a disappointing outcome. "We are encouraged by the fact that the court recognized that as a general matter authors do not have the right to stop the publication of reference guides and companion books about literary works. As for the Lexicon, we are obviously disappointed with the result." He said RDR was considering its options, including the possibility of an appeal. But the chances of success on appeal would doubtless be slim, as Falzone himself characterized Judge Patterson's decision as "thoughtful and meticulous."

Steven Vander Ark, author of the Lexicon, said he wished he could now come to a resolution with Ms. Rowling that would allow him to proceed with the encyclopedia. He said that his latest project was a book entitled *In Search of Harry Potter* that was soon to be published (Methuen Publishing Ltd., London). He described the book as a memoir of his travels to locations similar to the ones mentioned in the *Harry Potter* series, adding that as a travel memoir it was unlikely to raise any red flags.

Since J.K. Rowling started the whole proceedings with her lawsuit, perhaps it is only fitting that she has the last word. In a statement after the court's ruling, she said "Many books have been published which offer original insights into the world of Harry Potter. The Lexicon is just not one of them."

We will in the next section look at the fair use doctrine in a broader context and examine in more detail the four fair use factors discussed above. Also, we will see why the doctrine has become an increasingly hot issue in recent years, particularly with the emergence of the Internet.

THE FAIR USE DOCTRINE

Under the fair use provisions of copyright law, an author may make limited use of another author's work without asking permission. In the J.K. Rowling case discussed above, the issue before the court was whether the defendant's Harry Potter Lexicon could be judged a reference guide that qualified as a fair use. If it could be so characterized, then permission from Ms. Rowling was not necessary. But as we saw, the court determined otherwise.

In this section, we will broaden the scope of our inquiry into fair use and consider the matter in terms of other issues – issues we are likely to encounter in our day-to-day writing activities, both in print and online. Consider the following:

- In putting together a newsletter on his home computer, someone reprints an editorial he likes from his daily newspaper.
- An historian quotes from several unpublished letters and diaries written by his subject.
- A freelance writer closely paraphrases two paragraphs from the *Encyclopedia Britannica* in an article she's writing.
- A poet quotes a line from a poem by T.S. Eliot in one of her own poems.
- A comedian performs a parody of the famous song "Blue Moon" which he then uploads to YouTube.

Do the people in the above examples need permission from the author or copyright owner to use the material? The answer is probably not, thanks to the fair use doctrine, which is based on the proposition that the public is entitled to freely use portions of copyrighted materials for certain purposes. These purposes -- as set forth in federal copyright law (title 17, U.S. Code) and expanded on by the courts – are as follows:

- **Criticism and comment** -- quoting or excerpting a work in a review or criticism for purposes of illustration or comment. For example, if you wished to criticize a novelist, the fair use exception of comment and criticism would likely give you the freedom to quote a portion of the novelist's work without asking permission. Absent this freedom, copyright owners could stifle any negative comments about their work.
- **News reporting** -- for example, summarizing an article, with brief quotations, in a news report.

- **Research and scholarship** -- for example, quoting a short passage in a scholarly, scientific, or technical work for illustration or clarification of the author's observations.
- **Nonprofit educational uses** -- for example, the photocopying of limited portions of written works by teachers for classroom use.
- **Parody** -- a parody is a work that ridicules another, usually well-known work by imitating it in a comic manner.

In these situations, you are justified in feeling confident that your use would be a fair use and permission would not be needed. In other situations, the case might not be so clear, and you would be risking a lawsuit to copy without the author's permission. This is what happened in the J.K. Rowling litigation. Ms. Rowling argued that the defendant copied extensively from her *Harry Potter* series and thus fair use did not apply. The court agreed.

As we saw in the J.K. Rowling case, the court had to engage in a finely-tuned balancing act to come to a decision. The distinction between fair use and infringement is often unclear. The only guidance copyright law gives the courts in deciding the issue is provided by a set of fair use factors. These factors, which are discussed below, are analyzed in each case to determine whether a particular use qualifies as a fair use. For example, one important factor is whether a use will deprive the copyright owner of income.

The fair use analysis presented in this section is reproduced, with slight revision, from the book, *Getting Permission: How to License & Clear Copyrighted Materials Online & Off*, by Richard Stim, attorney and legal editor at Nolo, and is used by permission. Visit Nolo (www.nolo.com) for information on their titles in intellectual property (copyright, patent and trademark) and other areas of the law.

What is Fair Use?

In its most general sense, a fair use under copyright law is any reproduction of copyrighted material done for a limited and "transformative" purpose, such as to comment upon, criticize or parody a copyrighted work. Such uses can be done without permission from the copyright owner.

So what is a "transformative" use? If this definition seems ambiguous or vague, be aware that millions of dollars in legal fees have been spent attempting to define what qualifies as a fair use. There are no hard-and-fast rules, only general guidelines and varying court decisions. That's because the judges and lawmakers who created the fair use exemption did not want to limit the definition of fair use. They wanted fair use -- like free speech -- to have an expansive meaning that could be open to interpretation. In spite of this built-in vagueness, however, one can gain general insights as to uses that likely constitute fair use and those that likely do not.

While the J.K. Rowling case involved fair use in the context of a reference guide (encyclopedia), most court analysis on the issue falls into two categories: (1) commentary and criticism and (2) parody. Both of these and other fair use issues will be examined below. For a discussion of fair use as it relates specifically to the reproduction of copyrighted works by educators and librarians, see Copyright Office Circular 21 (www.copyright.gov -- click on "Circulars and Brochures"). Also, for educational fair use in a multimedia context, see guidelines issued by the Consortium of College & University Media Centers (www.ccumc.org).

1. Comment and Criticism

If you are commenting on or critiquing a copyrighted work -- for instance, writing a book review -- fair use principles allow you to reproduce some of the work to achieve your purposes. Some examples of commentary and criticism include:

- quoting a few lines from a Bob Dylan song in a music review,
- summarizing and quoting from a medical article on prostate cancer in a news report,
- copying a few paragraphs from a news article for use by a teacher or student in a lesson, or
- copying a portion of a Sports Illustrated magazine article for use in a related court case.

The underlying rationale of the comment and criticism exemption is that the public benefits from your review, which is enhanced by including some copyrighted material to make its point.

2. Parody

A parody is a work that ridicules another, usually well-known work, by imitating it in a comic way. Judges understand that by its nature, parody demands some taking from the original work being parodied. Unlike other forms of fair use, a rather extensive use of the original work is permitted in a parody in order to "conjure up" the original.

Parody and other fair use examples are given under "Summaries of Fair Use Cases," beginning on page 31 below.

Measuring Fair Use: The Four Factors

If you are looking for a definitive answer on a fair use question, you probably won't get one. Unfortunately, the only way more or less definitive answers come about is when someone brings a federal lawsuit alleging copyright infringement (copyright law is litigated at the federal level, not the state). This is what J.K. Rowling did.

Under copyright law, judges as indicated use four factors in resolving fair use disputes. It is important to understand that these factors are only guidelines and the courts are free to adapt them to particular situations on a case-by-case basis. In other words, a judge has a great deal of freedom when making a fair use determination and the outcome in any given case can be hard to predict.

The four factors courts consider are the:

(1) the purpose and character of the use, including whether such use is of a commercial nature or is for nonprofit educational purposes;
(2) the nature of the copyrighted work;
(3) the amount and substantiality of the portion used in relation to the copyrighted work as a whole, and
(4) the effect of the use upon the potential market for or value of the copyrighted work.

1. The Purpose and Character of the Use: The Transformative Factor

In a 1994 case, the U.S. Supreme Court emphasized this first factor as being a primary indicator of fair use. The Court characterized the principal issue as whether the material has been used to help create something new, or merely copied verbatim into another work. When taking portions of a copyrighted work (whether the material is from a print or online source or whether you plan to use it in print or online), ask yourself the following questions:

• Has the material you have taken from the original work been transformed by adding new expression or meaning?
• Was value added to the original by creating new information, new aesthetics, new insights and understandings?

If you can answer, yes, to both questions, then what you have done likely constitutes fair use. Consider the following:

EXAMPLE: Roger borrows several quotes front the speech given by the CEO of a logging company. Roger prints these quotes under photos of old-growth redwoods in his environmental newsletter. By juxtaposing the quotes with the photos of endangered trees, Roger has transformed the remarks from their original purpose and used them to create a new insight. The copying would probably be permitted as a fair use.

2. The Nature of the Copyrighted Work

Because the dissemination of facts or information benefits the public, you have more leeway to copy from factual works such as biographies than you do from fictional works such as plays or novels. This was an important consideration in the J.K. Rowling case.

In addition, you will have a stronger case for fair use if the material copied is from a published work rather than an unpublished work (such as the unpublished letters of an author). The scope of fair use is narrower for unpublished works, because authors have the right to control the first public appearance of their expressions.

3. The Amount and Substantiality of the Portion Taken

The less you take, the more likely that your copying will be excused as a fair use. However, even if you take a small portion of a work, your copying will not be a fair use if the portion taken is considered the "heart" of the work. In other words, you are more likely to run into problems if you take the most memorable aspect of a work. For example, it would probably not be a fair use to copy the opening guitar rift and the words "I can't get no satisfaction" from the Rolling Stone song "Satisfaction."

This rule -- less is better in terms of fair use -- is not necessarily true in parody cases. In a parody, the parodist is borrowing in order to comment upon the original work. A parodist is permitted to borrow quite a bit, even the heart of the original work, in order to conjure up the original work. That is because, as the Supreme Court has acknowledged, "the heart is also what most readily conjures up the [original] for parody, and it is the heart at which parody takes aim." (*Campbell v. Acuff-Rose Music*, 510 U.S.569 (1994).)

4. The Effect of the Use Upon the Potential Market

Another important fair use factor is whether your use deprives the copyright owner of income or undermines a new or potential market for the copyrighted work. One of the surest ways to attract a lawsuit is to create the possibility that a copyright owner may be deprived of income. This is true even if you are not competing directly with the original work.

> **EXAMPLE:** In one case an artist used a copyrighted photograph without permission as the basis for wood sculptures, copying all of the elements of the photo. The artist earned several hundred thousand dollars selling the sculptures. When the photographer sued, the artist claimed his sculptures were a fair use because the photographer would never have considered making sculptures. The court disagreed, stating that it did not matter whether the photographer had considered making sculptures; what mattered was that a potential market for sculptures of the photograph existed. (*Rogers v. Koons*, 960 F.2d 301 (2d Cir. 1992).)

Parody is given a slightly different fair use analysis with regard to the impact on the market. It is possible that a parody may diminish or even destroy the market value of the original work. That is, the parody may be so good that the public can never take the original work seriously again. Although this may cause a loss of income, it is not the same type of loss as when an infringer merely appropriates the work. As one judge explains, "The economic effect of a parody with which we are concerned is not its potential to destroy or diminish the market for the original -- any bad review can have that effect -- but whether it fulfills [e.g., supplants] the demand for the original." (*Fisher v. Dees*, 794 F.2d 432 (9th Cir. 1986).)

5. The "Fifth" Fair Use Factor: Are You Good or Bad?

There is an "unwritten" fair use factor as well. When you review fair use cases the courts have considered, you may find that they sometimes seem to contradict one another or conflict with established rules of thumb. Fair use involves subjective judgments and is often affected by factors such as a judge or jury's personal sense of right or wrong. Despite the fact that the Supreme Court has indicated that offensiveness is not a fair use factor, you should be aware that a morally offended judge or jury may have this consideration in the background while it rationalized the case on the basis of the four fair use factors discussed above.

For example, in one case a manufacturer of novelty cards parodied the successful children's dolls, the Cabbage Patch Kids. The parody card series was entitled the Garbage Pail Kids and used gruesome and grotesque names and characters to poke fun at the wholesome Cabbage Patch image. Some copyright experts were surprised when a federal court considered the parody an infringement, not a fair use. (*Original Appalachian Artworks Inc. v. Topps Chewing Gum Inc.,* (642 F. Supp.1031 (N.D. Ga. 1986).)

Additional Considerations

Too Small For Fair Use: The De Minimis Defense

In some cases, the amount of material copied is so small (or "de minimis") that the court permits it without even conducting a fair use analysis. For example, in the motion picture *Seven*, several copyrighted photographs appeared in the film, prompting the copyright owner of the photographs to sue the producer of the movie. The court held that the photos "appear fleetingly and are obscured, severely out of focus, and virtually unidentifiable." The court excused the use of the photographs as "de minimis" and a fair use analysis was not required. (*Sandoval v. New Line Cinema Corp.*, 147 F.3d 215 (2d Cir. 1998).)

As with fair use, there is no bright line test for determining a de minimis use. For example, in another case, a court determined that the use of a copyrighted poster for a total of 27 seconds in the background of the TV show, "Roc" was not de minimis. What distinguished the use of the poster from the use of the photographs in the *Seven* case? The court stated that the poster was clearly visible and recognizable with sufficient observable detail for the "average lay observer " to view the artist's imagery and colorful style. (*Ringgold v. Black Entertainment Television Inc.* 126 F.3d 70 (2d Cir. 1997).)

What If You Acknowledge the Source Material?

Some people mistakenly believe it's permissible to use a work (or portion of it) if an acknowledgment is provided. They believe, for example, that it is okay to use a photograph in a magazine as long as the name of the photographer is included. This is not true. Acknowledgment of the source material (such as citing the photographer) may be a consideration in a fair use determination, but it will not always protect against a claim of copyright infringement. In some cases, such as advertisements, acknowledgments can backfire and create additional legal claims, for example a violation of the right of publicity. When in doubt as to the right to use or acknowledge a source, the most prudent course may be to seek permission of the copyright owner.

While you may be able to successfully claim fair use without acknowledging your sources, it is always advisable to do so; not to acknowledge might leave you open to a charge of plagiarism. Such an accusation may not result in damages in court but it may damage your reputation.

Does It Help to Use a Disclaimer?

A disclaimer is a statement that "disassociates" your work from the work that you have borrowed. For example, if you write an unauthorized biography of Mickey Mouse, you may decide to include a disclaimer such as "This book is not associated with or endorsed by the Walt Disney Company." Will it help your position if you use a disclaimer? In close cases where the court is having a difficult time making a fair use determination, a prominently placed disclaimer may have a positive effect on the way the court perceives your use.

However, a disclaimer by itself generally will not help. That is, if the fair use factors weigh against you, the disclaimer won't make any difference. For example, in a case involving a "Seinfeld" trivia book (which was cited in the J.K. Rowling decision), the publisher included a disclaimer that the book "has not been approved or licensed by any entity involved in creating or producing Seinfeld." Despite the disclaimer, the court held that the use of the "Seinfeld" materials was an infringement, not a fair use.

The Question of Plagiarism

The term plagiarism is often confused with copyright infringement. But one may engage in plagiarism without infringing on another's copyright. Suppose, for example, that you have written a novel about the Wild West, including extensive accounts as to how cowboys and Indians clashed and coexisted during this period. And that you have paraphrased selected material taken from copyrighted history books on the subject but did not acknowledge this borrowing as source material. If the borrowing was not too extensive, it may not constitute copyright infringement but rather qualify as fair use, since you have presumably created something new and different, that is, your use has been transformative. But you have plagiarized: you have taken from another's work and passed it off as your own. This may not prompt a copyright lawsuit under federal law, but it may expose you to accusations of unethical conduct and, in some instances, liability under state law.

The ease of cut and paste plagiarism in the Internet Age is all too tempting and (we can always hope) no one will notice. Still, common decency if nothing else should be reason enough to give credit where credit is due.

Summaries of Fair Use Cases

As discussed above, fair use is a subjective matter, and it is difficult to come up with hard and fast rules. The best way to get a feel for what probably would be allowed in a particular situation, and what probably would not, is to review actual cases decided by the courts.

1. Cases Involving Text

- **Not a fair use**. An author copied more than half of an unpublished manuscript to prove that someone was involved in the overthrow of the Iranian government. **Important factors:** A substantial portion was taken (half of the work) and the work had not yet been published. (*Love v. Kwitny*, 772 F. Supp. 1367 (S.D. N.Y. 1989).)

- **Fair use**. A biographer of Richard Wright quoted from six unpublished letters and ten unpublished journal entries by Wright. **Important factors:** No more than 1% of Wright's unpublished letters were copied and the purpose was informational. (*Wright v. Warner Books Inc.*, 953 F.2d 731 (2d Cir. 1991).)

- **Not a fair use**. A biographer paraphrased large portions of unpublished letters written by the famed author J.D. Salinger. Although people could read these letters at a university library, Salinger had never authorized their reproduction. In other words, the first time that the general public would see these letters was in their paraphrased form in the biography. Salinger sued – successfully -- to prevent publication. **Important factors:** The letters were unpublished and were the "backbone" of the biography -- so much so that without the letters the resulting biography would probably not have been a commercial success. In other words, the letters may have been taken more as a means of capitalizing on the interest in Salinger than in providing a critical study of the author. (*Salinger v. Random House*, 815 F.2d 90 (2d Cir. 1987).)

- **Not a fair use**. *The Nation* magazine published excerpts from ex-President Gerald Ford's unpublished memoirs. The publication in *The Nation* was made several weeks prior to the date of serialization of Mr. Ford's book in *Time* magazine. *The Nation* argued that they had taken only 300 words in a 3000-word manuscript. **Important factors:** Though only a short excerpt was copied, the copied material dealt with Mr. Ford's pardon of Richard Nixon – the "heart of the book" according to the court – and thus affected the marketability of the *Time* article and the book on which it was based. (*Harper & Row v Nation Enters.*, 471 U.S. 539 (1985).)

• **Not a fair use**. A company published a book entitled *Welcome to Twin Peaks: A Complete Guide to Who's Who and What's What*, containing direct quotations and paraphrases from the television show "Twin Peaks" as well as detailed descriptions of plot, character and setting. **Important factors**: The amount of the material taken was substantial and the publication adversely affected the potential market for authorized books about the program. (*Twin Peaks v. Publications Int'l Ltd.*, 996 F.2d 1366 (2d Cir. 1993).)

• **Not a fair use**. A company published a book of trivia questions about the characters of the "Seinfeld" TV series (a case cited by plaintiffs in J.K. Rowling litigation). The book included questions based upon characters in 84 "Seinfeld" episodes and used actual dialogue from the show in 41 of the book's questions. **Important factors:** As in "Twin Peaks" (see above), the book affected owner's right to make derivative "Seinfeld" works such as trivia books. (*Castle Rock Entertainment v. Carol Publ. Group*, 150 F.3d 132 (2d Cir. 1998).)

• **Fair use**. Publisher Larry Flynt made disparaging statements about the Reverend Jerry Falwell on one page of *Hustler* magazine. Rev. Falwell made several hundred thousand copies of the page and distributed them as part of a fund-raising effort. **Important factors:** Rev. Falwell's copying did not diminish the sales of the magazine (since it was already off the market) and would not adversely affect the marketability of back issues. (*Hustler Magazine Inc. v. Moral. Majority Inc.*, 606 F. Supp. 1526 (C.D. Cal. 1985).)

2. Artwork and Audiovisual Cases

• **Fair use**. It was a fair use, not an infringement, to reproduce Grateful Dead concert posters within a book. **Important factors:** The court focused on the fact that the posters were reduced to thumbnail size and reproduced within the context of a timeline. (*Bill Graham Archives v. Dorling Kindersley Ltd.*, 448 F.3d 605 (2d Cir. 2006).)

• **Not a fair use**. The district court found that a Google search engine infringed a subscription-only website featuring nude models by reproducing thumbnails of the models in a Google search request. **Important factors:** the adult website made money from the thumbnails by selling them for use on mobile phones. In other words, the infringement could deprive the plaintiff site of income. (*Perfect 10 v. Google Inc.*, 456 F. Supp. 2d 828 (C.D. Cal, 2006).) **Note:** This decision was recently overturned on appeal. See next entry.

• **Fair use**. The *Perfect 10* case above was appealed and the Ninth Circuit Court of Appeals in San Francisco reversed, holding that the thumbnail images reproduced as part of search results did indeed constitute a fair use under copyright law. **Important factors:** The court considered Google's use of thumbnails as "highly transformative," noting that a search engine transforms the image into a pointer directing a user to a source of information (versus the image's original purpose: entertainment, aesthetics, or information). This transformative use outweighs any commercial factors regarding Google's ability to earn money from placement of ads on the search results page. The court's reasoning – that "a search engine provides an entirely new use for the original work" – re-affirmed the principles established in the Ninth Circuit's *Kelly v. Arriba Soft* decision, noted below (*Perfect 10 v. Amazon.com*, 487 F. 3d 701 (9th Cir. 2007).)

• **Not a fair use**. A television news program copied one minute and 15 seconds from a 72-minute Charlie Chaplin film and used it in a news report about Chaplin's death. **Important factors**: The court felt that the portions taken were substantial and part of the "heart" of the film, (*Roy Export Co. v. CBS Inc.*, 672 F.2d 1095 (2d Cir. 1982).)

• **Fair use**. The makers of a movie biography of Muhammad Ali used 41 seconds from a boxing match film in their biography. **Important factors:** A small portion of film was taken and the purpose was informational. (*Monster Communications Inc. v. Turner Broadcasting Sys. Inc.*, 935 F. Supp. 490 (S.D. N.Y. 1996).)

• **Not a fair use**. A television station's news broadcast used 30 seconds from a four-minute copyrighted videotape of the 1992 Los Angeles beating of Reginald Denny. **Important' factors:** The use was commercial, involved the heart of the work and affected the copyright owner's ability to market the video. (*Los Angeles News Service v. KCAL-TV Channel 9*, 108 F. 3d 1119 (9th Cir. 1997).)

• **Fair use**. In a lawsuit commonly known as the *Betamax* case, the Supreme Court determined that the home videotaping of a television broadcast was a fair use. This was one of the few occasions when copying a complete work (for example, a complete episode of the "Kojak" television show) was accepted as a fair use. Evidence indicated that most viewers were "time-shifting" (taping in order to watch later) and not "library-building" (collecting the videos in order to build a video library). **Important factors:** The Supreme Court reasoned that the "delayed" system of viewing did not deprive the copyright owners of revenue. (*Universal City Studios v. Sony Corp.*, 464 U.S. 417 (1984).)

• **Not a fair use.** A poster of a "church quilt" was used in the background of a television series for 27 seconds. **Important factors:** The court was influenced by the prominence of the poster, its thematic importance for the set decoration of a church and the fact that it was a conventional practice to license such works for use in television programs. (*Ringgold v. Block Entertainment Television Inc.*, 126 F.3d 70 (2d Cir. 1997).)

• **Fair Use.** A search engine's practice of creating small reproductions ("thumbnails") of images and placing them on its own website (known as "inlining") did not undermine the potential market for the sale or licensing of those images. **Important Factors:** The thumbnails were much smaller and of much poorer quality than the original photos and served to index the images and help the public access them. This is one of the cases relied on in the *Perfect 10* appeals court ruling above. (*Kelly v. Arriba-Soft*, 336 F. 3d Cir. (9th Cir. 2003).)

3. Parody Cases

• **Fair use.** The rap group 2 Live Crew borrowed the opening musical tag and the words (but not the melody) from the first line of the song "Pretty Woman' ("Oh, pretty woman, walking down the street "). The rest of the lyrics and the music were different. **Important factors:** The group's use was transformative and borrowed only a small portion of the "Pretty Woman" song. The 2 Live Crew version was essentially a different piece of music and the only similarity was a brief musical opening part and the opening line. (**Note:** the rap group had initially sought to pay for right to use portions of the song but were rebuffed by the publisher who did not want "Pretty Woman" used in a rap song.) (*Campbell v. Acuff-Rose Music*, 510 U.S. 569 (1994).)

• **Fair use.** The composers of the song, "When Sunny Gets Blue," claimed that their song was infringed by "When Sonny Sniffs Glue, " a 29-second parody that altered the original lyric line and borrowed six bars of the song. A court determined that the parody was excused as a fair use. **Important factors:** Only 29 seconds of music were borrowed, not the complete song. (*Fisher v. Dees*, 794 F.2d 432 (9th Cir. 1986).) **Note:** As a general rule, parodying more than a few lines of a song lyric is unlikely to be considered a fair use. Performers such as Weird Al Yankovic, who earn a living by humorously modifying hit songs, generally seek permission of the songwriters before recording their parodies.

• **Fair use.** Comedians on the late-night television show "Saturday Night Live" parodied the song "I Love New York" using the words "I Love Sodom." Only the words "I Love" and four musical notes were taken from the original work. **Important factors:** The "Saturday Night Live" version of the jingle did not compete with or detract from the original song. (*Elsmere Music Inc. v. National Broadcasting Co.*, 482 F. Supp. 741. (S.D. N.Y.), aff'd 632 F.2d 252 (2d Cir. 1980).)

• **Not a fair use.** An author mimicked the style of a Dr. Seuss book while re-telling the facts of the O.J. Simpson murder trial in *The Cat NOT in the Hat! A Parody by Dr. Juice.* The court held that the book was a satire, not a parody, because the book did not poke fun at or ridicule Dr. Seuss. Instead, it merely used the Dr. Seuss characters and style to tell the story of the murder. **Important factors:** The author's work was nontransformative and commercial. (*Dr. Seuss Enterprises v. Penguin Books USA Inc.*, 109 F.3d 1394 (9th Cir.1997).)

• **Fair use.** A movie company used a photo of a naked pregnant woman and superimposed the head of actor Leslie Nielsen. The photo was a parody using similar lighting and body positioning of a famous photograph taken by Annie Leibovitz of the actress Demi Moore for the cover of *Vanity Fair* magazine. **Important factors:** The movie company's use was transformative because it imitated the photographer's style for comic effect or ridicule. (*Leibovitz v. Paramount Pictures Corp.*, 137 F.3d 109 (2d Cir. N.Y. 1998).)

• **Not a fair use.** An artist created a cover for a *New Yorker* magazine that presented a humorous view of geography through the eyes of a New York City resident. A movie company later advertised their film "Moscow on the Hudson" using a similar piece of artwork with similar elements. The artist sued and a court ruled that the movie company's poster was not a fair use. **Important factors:** Why is this case different than the previous case involving the Leslie Nielsen/Annie Leibovitz parody? In the *Leibovitz* case, the use was a true parody, characterized by a juxtaposition of imagery that actually commented on or criticized the original. "The Moscow on the Hudson" movie poster, on the other hand, did not create a parody; it simply borrowed the New Yorker's parody (that being the typical New York City resident's geographical viewpoint as New York City as the center of the world). (*Steinberg v. Columbia Pictures Industries Inc.*, 663 F. Supp. 706 (S.D. N.Y. 1987).)

4. Music Cases

• **Not a fair use**. The courts have refused to recognize the downloading of songs as a fair use. A woman was sued for copyright infringement for downloading 30 songs using peer-to-peer file sharing software. She argued that her activity was a fair use because she was downloading the songs to determine if she wanted to later buy them. **Important factors:** Since numerous sites, such as iTunes permit listeners to sample and examine portions of songs without downloading, the court rejected this "sampling" defense. *BMG Music v. Gonzalez*, 430 F.3d 888 (7th Cir. 2005).

• **Fair use**. A person running for political office used 15 seconds of his opponent's campaign song in a political ad. **Important factors:** A small portion of the song was used and the purpose was for that of political debate. (*Keep Thomson Governor Comm. v. Citizens for Gallen Comm.* 457 F. Supp. 957 (D. N.H. 1978).)

• **Fair use**. A television film crew, covering an Italian festival in Manhattan, recorded a band playing a portion of a copyrighted song "Dove sta Zaza." The music was replayed during a news broadcast. **Important factors:** Only a portion of the song was used, it was incidental to the news event, and it did not result in any actual damage to the composer or to the market for his work. (*Italian Book Carp, v. American Broadcasting Co.*, 458 F. Supp. 65 (S.D. N.Y. 1978).)

• **Fair use**. In a recent decision handed down in Manhattan federal court, Yoko Ono, widow of John Lennon, lost her bid to prevent the movie documentary "Expelled" – which tries to make the point that academia discriminates against people who espouse "intelligent design" theory as an alternative to evolution – from using 15-second clip of Lennon's song "Imagine." **Important factors:** The court noted the brevity of the clip and its transformative nature in that it's purpose was to criticize the "anti-religious" message of the song. Further, the court noted that no evidence was presented to indicate that the clip would harm the market for licensing the song for traditional uses. (*Lennon et al v. Premise Media Corp. et al.* U.S. District Court for Southern New York, #08-cv-03813-SHS, June 2, 2008.)

5. Internet and Software Cases

• **Not a fair use.** Entire publications of the Church of Scientology were posted on the Internet by several individuals without Church permission. **Important factors:** Fair use is intended to permit the borrowing of portions of a work, riot complete works. (*Religious Technology Center v. Lemma*, 40 U.S.P.Q. 2d 1569 (E.D. Va. 1996).)

• **Fair use.** The Washington Post used three brief quotations from Church of Scientology texts posted on the Internet (see previous case). **Important factors:** Only a small portion of the work was excerpted and the purpose was for news commentary. (*Religious Technology Center v. Pagliarina*, 908 F. Supp. 1353 (E.D. Va. 1995).)

• **Not a fair use.** The Los Angeles County Sheriff's Department purchased 3,663 licenses to use a software program, but installed the software onto 6,007 computers. Although the software was installed on 6,007 computers, the computers were configured such that the total number of workstations able to access the installed software did not exceed the total number of licenses the Sheriff's Department purchased. **Important factors:** The installation of the software onto nearly all of the Sheriff's office computers was not transformative, did not promote an advancement of the arts, and was commercial in nature. (*Wall Data Inc. v. Los Angeles County Sheriff's Department*, 447 F.3d 769 (9th Cir. 2006).

• **Fair use.** Displaying a cached website in search engine results is a fair use and not an infringement. A "cache" refers to the temporary storage of an archival copy -- often a copy of an image of part or all of a website. With cached technology it is possible to search web pages that the website owner has permanently removed from display. An attorney/author sued Google when the company's cached search results provided end users with copies of copyrighted works. The court held that Google did not infringe. **Important factors:** Google was considered passive in the activity---users chose whether to view the cached link. In addition, Google had an implied license to cache web pages since owners of websites have the ability to turn on or turn off the caching of their sites using HTML tags and code. In this case, the attorney/author knew of this ability and failed to turn them off. (*Field v. Google Inc.*, 412 F. Supp. 2d 1106 (D. Nev. 2006).)

Disagreements Over Fair Use: When Are You Likely to Get Sued?

The difficulty in claiming fair use is that there is no predictable way to guarantee that your use will actually qualify as a fair use, should litigation result. You may believe that your use qualifies – and you may be right -- but if the copyright owner disagrees, the courts may ultimately have to decide. Even if the court ultimately upholds your position, the expense and time involved in litigation may well outweigh any benefit of using the material in the first place.

> **EXAMPLE:** Sam quotes from four pages of a biography in his documentary film about the poet Allen Ginsberg. He believes that his use qualifies as a fair use and he does not seek permission from Barbi, the author of the biography. Barbi does not think that Sam's copying is a fair use and wants to be paid for having her work used in his film. She sues Sam for copyright infringement, and Sam is forced to hire a lawyer to defend him in the lawsuit. Sam won the case but incurred lawyer fees totaled over $20,000, exceeding by far any profits he earned from the film.

Because of the uncertainty surrounding fair use, there is never a guarantee that your use will qualify as such. The fair use doctrine has been described as a murky concept in which it is often difficult to separate the lawful from the unlawful. Two types of situations are especially likely to cause legal problems:

- Your work causes the owner of the original work to lose money. For example, you borrow portions of a biology text for use in a competing biology text.
- The copyright owner is offended by your use. For example, you satirize the original work and your satire contains sexually explicit references or other offensive material.

Remember, this discussion of fair use and the cases presented will not determine whether you will prevail in a fair use lawsuit -- it simply indicates how a particular court has ruled on the particular facts presented. And remember, when you use someone 's work and deprive them of money or offend them, the chances of a lawsuit increase.

And just as there are situations that are more likely to provoke a lawsuit, there are steps you can take that may lower the risk:

- You use a very small excerpt, for example, one or two lines from a news report or of a factual work, and your use is for purposes of commentary, criticism, scholarship, research or news reporting.
- You diligently tried to locate the copyright owner but were unsuccessful, and after analyzing the fair use factors, you became convinced that your use would qualify as a fair use.

Fair Use in the Internet Age

When the U.S. Constitution was written in 1787, the framers took care to include a copyright clause (Article I, Section 8) stating that "The Congress shall have Power...To promote the Progress of Science and useful Arts, by securing for limited times to Authors...the exclusive Right to their...writings." Although fair use was not mentioned in early laws affecting copyrights, the doctrine was developed over the years through court decisions. In 1976 fair use was codified in Section 107 of the Copyright Act as the "four factors" discussed above. Still, as we have seen, fair use remains a vague concept that the courts must deal with on a case-by-case basis.

The framers of the Constitution could not, of course, imagine the technological advances that would so greatly impact copyright, and for the past 100 years or so both the courts and Congress have had to play catch-up in adapting copyright law to what was happening in the real world -- from sound recordings to motion pictures to computers, and now, the Internet.

The Internet has greatly broadened the reach of copyright law. In the age of the Internet all most all of us are "publishers" in the sense that websites we create, including text files, artwork and photographs, sound recordings and video, are subject to copyright protection (emails as well receive copyright protection, though fair use issues rarely arise in this context). Similarly, when we publish blogs on our own website or the websites of others. Or when we upload material to such sites as YouTube or MySpace. The Internet may make copying someone's material easier than ever, but it does not make it legal. It is legal to copy someone's copyrighted material only when you have permission or when fair use applies.

And, as we have seen, fair use applies in the online world just as it does in the physical. Further, it has been pointed out that individuals who copy for noncommercial purposes have much greater fair use rights than those who copy for commercial reasons. (In the J.K. Rowling case, Ms. Rowling did not object to the online lexicon, which was free, but to the proposed print version, which was a commercial project.)

Thus it is likely a fair use to download a copy of an article from the online edition of *The New York Times* and store it on your computer for future (noncommercial) use. Also, you have an *express right* to email a copy of the article to others, as the *Times* site specifically allows you to do so once you register (www.nytimes.com). As in the physical world, it is also likely a fair use when you quote portions of an online article: (1) in connection with commentary on the article, (2) in the course of news reporting, (3) for teaching purposes, (4) as part of scholarship or research activity, or (5) for use in a parody.

When you use material of others, whether in print or online, the more "transformative" the use is the more likely it would be considered a fair use. As previously discussed, a use is transformative when the material copied is used to create a new and different work, not simply an adaptation that closely follows the original. When the latter occurs, the adaptation is considered to be a derivative work, and the right to create derivative works lies with the copyright holder.

In addition to making authors and publishers out of a large segment of the population, the Internet has engaged the creative talents of young people all over the world through editing tools that allow the easy remixing of music and videos, often involving mixing copyrighted works with original material. Such mixing frequently takes the form of parody, as a visit to YouTube amply demonstrates, and thus in many instances – when the use of copyrighted material is not too extensive -- may well quality as a fair use. For example, when a video lampooning Comedy Central's popular TV series the "Colbert Report" was posted on YouTube, Viacom, owner of Comedy Central, complained and demanded that the show be removed on the basis of copyright infringement. YouTube complied. But a fair use complaint filed against Viacom by Stanford's Fair Use Project convinced the company to relent and YouTube was allowed to restore the clip.

It is to encourage the creative energies made possible by the Internet and new technologies that such groups as the Fair Use Project (cyberlaw.stanford.edu) and the Creative Commons (creativecommons.org) advocate a freer use of copyrighted material.

Finally, in this time of proliferating online content, the doctrine of fair use is seen to take on added importance. We must constantly deal with such questions as: When can I use the copyrighted content of others without seeking their permission? And, conversely, when can someone use content I have created without seeking my permission? That is, when are such uses likely to constitute fair use under the copyright law? While fair use doctrine provides no definitive answers -- one must closely look at the facts of each situation -- it is hoped that the discussion here offers some guidelines and assistance in dealing with questions as they arise.

COURT DOCUMENTS:
J.K. ROWLING LITIGATION

This section includes selected material filed in the copyright action brought by J.K. Rowling, and a transcript of Ms. Rowling's trial testimony. The material offers background information on Ms. Rowling and the *Harry Potter* series and details on the legal issues presented in the case. The documents have been edited for clarity, including the exclusion of footnotes. The complete documents, as well as other material filed in the case, are available from the federal court in Manhattan, New York (*Warner Bros. et al v. RDR Publishing Co. et al.* U.S. District Court for Southern New York, #07-cv-09667-RPP).

Plaintiffs' Complaint 42
Declaration of J.K. Rowling 62
Plaintiffs' Memorandum Supporting Preliminary Injunction 66
Defendant's Memorandum Opposing 84
Plaintiffs' Reply Memorandum 101
Declaration of J.K. Rowling 108
Defendant's Answer to Plaintiffs' Complaint 113

Transcript of J.K. Rowling Trial Testimony 127

Judge Patterson's Opinion 163

PLAINTIFFS' COMPLAINT (AMENDED)

WARNER BROS. ENTERTAINMENT INC. AND
J.K. ROWLING,

                    Plaintiffs,

        -against-

RDR BOOKS and DOES 1-10

                    Defendants.

Case No. 07-09667 (RPP)   Filed: October 31, 2007 (Amended 1/15/08)

PLAINTIFFS' FIRST AMENDED COMPLAINT

Plaintiffs Warner Bros. Entertainment Inc. ("Warner Bros.") and J. K. Rowling, by their undersigned counsel, for their First Amended Complaint, hereby allege, on knowledge as to their own conduct and otherwise on information and belief as follows:

NATURE OF THE ACTION AND RELIEF SOUGHT

1. This action arises out of Defendant RDR Books' willful and blatant violation of Plaintiffs' respective intellectual property rights in the highly-acclaimed *Harry Potter* series of children's books (the *"Harry Potter* Books") and films (the *"Harry Potter* Films") (collectively the *"Harry Potter* Works") and the misuse of Ms. Rowling's name in advertising materials without her consent in violation of the Copyright Act, the Lanham Act, and New York state law. Defendant, being fully aware of Plaintiffs' rights in and to the *Harry Potter* Works, seeks to misappropriate those rights by publishing a 400-page book entitled the *"Harry Potter Lexicon"* (the "Infringing Book") which is comprised of widespread misappropriation of Ms. Rowling's fictional characters and universe. While Defendant has attempted to characterize the Infringing Book as a work of "scholarship," the Infringing Book merely compiles and repackages Ms. Rowling's fictional facts derived wholesale from the *Harry Potter* Works without adding any new creativity, commentary, insight, or criticism. Defendant's attempt to cloak the Infringing Book in the mantle of scholarship is merely a ruse designed to circumvent Plaintiffs' rights in order to make a quick buck. If this behavior was not egregious enough, Defendant has designed the cover of the Infringing Book to mislead consumers into believing that Ms. Rowling endorses and approves the book when she clearly opposes it.

2. The Infringing Book is particularly troubling as it is in direct contravention to Ms. Rowling's long and repeatedly stated intention to publish her own companion books to the series and donate proceeds of such books to charity, as she already has done in the past with respect to the first two companion guides she authored, *Quidditch Through the Ages* and *Fantastic Beasts and Where to Find Them* (the "Companion Books"). These guides helped raise more than $30 million for charity so far. Ms. Rowling has only authorized limited derivative works of her series and has never authorized a companion guide to engage in such wholesale misappropriation of her work.

3. Both Defendant and Steven Vander Ark, the author of the Infringing Book, were well aware of Ms. Rowling's intentions and that any efforts to publish an unauthorized companion book based on the *Harry Potter* Works would be a violation of Ms. Rowling's rights.

4. Plaintiffs did everything they could prior to filing this lawsuit to engage in a substantive dialogue with Defendant only to be rebuffed and treated rudely. Over the course of six weeks just prior to the time Defendant indicated that the Infringing Book would be published, Plaintiffs contacted Defendant numerous times in an effort to discuss the issues arising from Defendant's publication of the Infringing Book. While claiming not to have the ability or time to respond to Plaintiffs' multiple "cease and desist" letters because of a family tragedy, Defendant instead was hawking the foreign publishing rights to the Infringing Book in Germany. Moreover, Defendant had the audacity to accuse Warner Bros. of violating the purported copyrights of the Infringing Book's author in a timeline based on the *Harry Potter* Books -- a complete fabrication apparently intended to deflect Plaintiffs' complaints -- but which merely serves to highlight the hypocritical nature of Defendant's conduct.

5. Defendant's main excuse for its blatant conduct is to argue that the Infringing Book is merely a print version of Mr. Vander Ark's free-of-charge *Lexicon* Website. Even if this were the case --which it most certainly is not -- there is a significant difference between giving the innumerable *Harry Potter* fan sites latitude to discuss the *Harry Potter* Works in the context of free-of-charge, ephemeral websites and allowing a single fan site owner and his publisher to commercially exploit the *Harry Potter* Books in contravention of Ms. Rowling's wishes and rights and to the detriment of other *Harry Potter* fan sites. In any event, the Infringing Book is a 400-page dictionary taken from the world of *Harry Potter* that does not include any of the vibrant fan art, graphical interfaces, fan fiction or discussions from the 700+ Internet page *Lexicon* Website and thus is not a mere print copy of the website.

6. Plaintiffs had no choice but to file this lawsuit seeking injunctive relief and damages that they have suffered as a result of Defendant's activities. Plaintiffs intend to donate any monetary award that may result from Defendant's activities prior to an injunction being entered to charity. Specifically, Plaintiffs' claims against Defendant include copyright infringement under the Copyright Act of 1976, 17 U.S.C. §§ 101 et seq., federal trademark infringement under the Lanham Act, 15 U.S.C. § 1114(1), false endorsement, false designation of origin and unfair competition under the Lanham Act, 15 U.S.C. § 1125(a)(1)(A), false advertising under the Lanham Act, 15 U.S.C. § 1125(a)(l)(B), deceptive trade practices under § 349 of the General Business Law of New York; violation of Ms. Rowling's right of privacy under §§ 50-51 of the Civil Rights Law of New York and unfair competition under the common law of New York. Moreover, Warner Bros. seeks a declaratory judgment pursuant to 28 U.S.C. § 2201 (a) that its "Hogwarts Time Line" does not infringe any purported rights Defendant or anyone else claims to have in a *Harry Potter*-related time line from either the Infringing Book or the *Lexicon* Website.

PARTIES

7. Ms. Rowling is an individual residing in Edinburgh, Scotland. Ms. Rowling is a highly respected, world-famous author. She is and, at all times material herein, was engaged in the business of, among other things, creating literary works, including the *Harry Potter* Books, and licensing the right to create derivative works based on her literary works, including the copyrighted elements of those works, to others for exploitation.

8. Warner Bros. is a Delaware corporation with its principal place of business at 4000 Warner Boulevard, Burbank, California 91522. Warner Bros. has offices at 1325 Avenue of the Americas, New York, New York 10019. Warner Bros. is engaged in the business of, among other things, creating, producing, distributing and marketing motion pictures and goods related to the *Harry Potter* Books, including merchandise relating to these properties. Warner Bros. owns rights in the trademarks associated with the *Harry Potter* Films, pursuant to contractual agreement with Ms. Rowling.

9. Upon information and belief, defendant RDR Books is a publishing company with its principal place of business at 1487 Glen Avenue, Muskegon, Michigan 49441. RDR Books' books are available for sale to customers located in this judicial district through its website (www.rdrbooks.com), online vendors and retail stores located within this judicial district.

10. Plaintiffs are ignorant of the true names and capacities of the defendants used herein under the fictitious names DOES 1 through 10 inclusive. Plaintiffs will seek leave of court to amend this complaint to allege such names and capacities when they are ascertained. Plaintiffs are informed and believe, and based thereon allege, that each of the fictitiously named DOE defendants is responsible in some manner for the wrongful conduct alleged herein, specifically distribution and sale of the Infringing Book in the United States and abroad. Plaintiffs further allege that each defendant acted in concert with, as agent or representative for, or at the request or on the behalf of Defendant. Each charging allegation contained herein is, therefore, also hereby alleged against each fictitiously named DOE defendant.

JURISDICTION AND VENUE

11. This action asserts claims arising under the Copyright Act of 1976, as amended, 17 U.S.C. § 101 et seq., the Lanham Act, 15 U.S.C. §§ 1114(1) and 1125(a) and the Declaratory Judgment Act, 28 U.S.C. § 2201 (a). This Court has federal question jurisdiction over these claims pursuant to 15 U.S.C. § 1121, and 28 U.S.C. §§ 1331, 1338(a) and 1338(b). This Court also has subject matter jurisdiction over Plaintiffs' state law claims pursuant to the principles of pendant jurisdiction.

12. This Court has personal jurisdiction over RDR Books pursuant to C.P.L.R. §§ 302(a)(2) and 302(a)(3) because RDR Books has committed a tortious act both within and without the State of New York through the sale of the Infringing Book, which will be available nationally and within the State of New York through traditional and online retailers, causing injury to Plaintiffs within the State of New York, and RDR Books has regularly conducted or solicited business within the State of New York.

13. Venue is proper in this district pursuant to 28 U.S.C. §§ 1391(b) and 1400(a).

PLAINTIFFS' VALUABLE INTELLECTUAL PROPERTY

The *Harry Potter* Books

14. The *Harry Potter* Books are a modem day publishing phenomenon and success story. As has been widely publicized, author Ms. Rowling, who graduated from Exeter University, was divorced and living on public assistance in Edinburgh when she started writing the *Harry Potter* Books in the local coffee shop, drafting the manuscript in longhand while her infant daughter slept. In these unlikely circumstances, Ms. Rowling created a highly

detailed imaginary world, one that has come to be loved by millions of children and adults around the world.

15. The *Harry Potter* Books tell the story of an orphaned boy named Harry Potter. Harry lives a normal enough life, sleeping in a tiny room under the stairs in the home of his hated Aunt Petunia, Uncle Vernon, and cousin Dudley, all of whom are "Muggles" (humans without any magical abilities), until his eleventh birthday, when he begins to receive letters from the Hogwarts School of Witchcraft and Wizardry ("Hogwarts"), which he is invited to attend. Harry learns that his parents did not die in a car crash, but in fact were wizards who were killed by Voldemort, the Lord of Darkness, and that he himself is famous in the world of wizardry. Together with his magical snowy owl, Hedwig, Harry leaves his home and begins a new life at Hogwarts.

16. Each of the seven books cover one of Harry's seven years at Hogwarts. Over the course of these seven books, Harry learns many new things, makes new friends, travels, and has many adventures. He learns to hone his wizarding skills, cast spells, make potions and play new games, including "Quidditch" (a game Ms. Rowling invented in which two teams flying on broomsticks try to score points by getting balls through goals that are suspended in mid-air), which he plays as part of the Gryffindor House Quidditch team at Hogwarts. He learns of the Sorcerer's Stone and the three-headed dog that guards it, and battles Lord Voldemort. He travels in a magic flying car, meets Cornelius Fudge, the Minister of Magic, and visits the Leaky Cauldron pub. He attends the International Quidditch Cup and competes in the Triwizard Tournament. He organizes Defense Against the Dark Arts classes when the students are forbidden from practicing magic, attempts to rescue his godfather Sirius Black from danger and, along with his friends, battles supporters of Lord Voldemort. All of these adventures culminate in a final, climactic battle with the evil Lord Voldemort. Along the way, Harry faces the transition into adulthood, falls in love, and experiences personal tragedy with the loss of people close to him.

17. The first book in the series, *Harry Potter and the Philosopher's Stone,* was published in the United Kingdom in June 1997 with a substantially identical version of the book published in the United States in September 1998 under the title *Harry Potter and the Sorcerer's Stone* (the title of the United States version is used herein to refer to both the original United Kingdom version and the United States version). The six succeeding books in the series are titled: *Harry Potter and the Chamber of Secrets* (1999), *Harry Potter and the Prisoner of Azkaban* (1999), *Harry Potter and the Goblet of Fire* (2000), *Harry Potter and the Order of the Phoenix* (2003), *Harry Potter and the Half-Blood Prince* (2005), and, finally, *Harry Potter and the Deathly Hallows (2007).*

18. Since the release of the first book in the United Kingdom in 1997, the *Harry Potter* Books have been a tremendous popular and critical success. It has been reported that, collectively, the *Harry Potter* Books, which have been translated into more than 65 languages, have sold well over 325 million copies worldwide and have taken their place among the best loved children's classics, including *Winnie the Pooh, The Wizard of Oz, Little House on the Prairie* and *The Hobbit*. The *Harry Potter* Books have won numerous prizes and awards and received critical praise from such prestigious reviewers as *The New York Times, The Chicago Sun-Times,* and *The Wall Street Journal*.

19. In addition to the many prizes and accolades, the *Harry Potter* Books have spent many weeks on *The New York Times* bestseller list and other prestigious bestseller lists, demonstrating their enduring popular and critical acclaim. Adults and children have eagerly awaited each new book in the series and bookstores around the country have stayed open late to accommodate the eager customers who rush to buy the latest *Harry Potter* book at the stroke of midnight. The final book, *Harry Potter and the Deathly Hallows* sold 8.3 million copies in the first 24 hours of its release.

20. In addition to the *Harry Potter* Books themselves, Ms. Rowling has authored and published the two Companion Books so far -- *Quidditch Through the Ages* and *Fantastic Beasts and Where to Find Them*. Ms. Rowling generously donates royalties from the Companion Books to the charitable organization Comic Relief. To date these two Companion Guides have raised more than $30 million for charity. In creating the two Companion Books, Ms. Rowling succeeded in transforming a typically pedestrian book genre into highly imaginative and entertaining works. Ms. Rowling's present intention is to create additional companion books and to donate royalties to charitable organizations.

The Harry Potter Films

21. As a result of the popularity of the *Harry Potter* Books, Warner Bros. sought and obtained the film rights from Ms. Rowling to the series. To date, Warner Bros. has released five of the seven films including *Harry Potter and the Sorcerer's Stone* (2001), *Harry Potter and the Chamber of Secrets* (2002), *Harry Potter and the Prisoner of Azkaban* (2003), *Harry Potter and the Goblet of Fire* (2005), and *Harry Potter and the Order of the Phoenix* (2007). The sixth film, *Harry Potter and the Half-Blood Prince* is scheduled for a worldwide release in November 2008 and production of the seventh, *Harry Potter and the Deathly Hallows* is confirmed, but a release date has not yet been set. The five *Harry Potter* Films released to date represent the highest grossing film series of all time with over $4 billion in worldwide receipts.

Ms. Rowling's Intellectual Property Rights

22. The people, places, terms, and images in the *Harry Potter* Books and the Companion Books are Ms. Rowling's original creative work. The seven *Harry Potter* Books and two Companion Books published to date have been registered with the United States Copyright Office. The registration for *Harry Potter and the Sorcerer's Stone* is Serial No. TX 4-465-397. The registration for *Harry Potter and the Chamber of Secrets* is Serial No. TX 4-465-398. The registration for *Harry Potter and the Prisoner of Azkaban* is Serial No. TX 4-465-399. The registration for *Harry Potter and the Goblet of Fire* is Serial No. TX 5-122-771. The registration for *Harry Potter and the Order of the Phoenix* is Serial No. TX-5-705-321. The registration for *Harry Potter and the Half-Blood Prince* is Serial No. TX-6-179-388. The registration for *Harry Potter and the Deathly Hallows* is Serial No. TX-6-578-062. The registration for *Quidditch through the Ages* is TX-5-374-649, and the registration for *Fantastic Beasts and Where to Find Them* is TX-5-374-653. In addition, because of the goodwill and celebrity now associated with her own name, Ms. Rowling owns trademark registrations for J.K. ROWLING, Reg. No. 2,757,849 and J.K. ROWLING (Stylized), Reg. No. 2,818,636.

Warner Bros.' Intellectual Property Rights

23. Pursuant to its agreement with Ms. Rowling, Warner Bros. owns trademark rights in *Harry Potter* and *Harry Potter*-related designations in connection with its film rights and ancillary merchandising projects (collectively, the *"Harry Potter* Marks"). Warner Bros. has received registrations for numerous *Harry Potter* Marks around the world, including in the United States. For example, Warner Bros. has over 15 federal trademark registrations for HARRY POTTER, including, but not limited to, Registration Nos. 2,457,302, 2,685,932, 2,506,166 and 2,506,165.

24. In addition to these trademark registrations, each of the *Harry Potter* Films has been registered with the United States Copyright Office including: *Harry Potter and the Sorcerer's Stone*; *Harry Potter and the Chamber of Secrets*; *Harry Potter and the Prisoner of Azkaban*; *Harry Potter and the Goblet of Fire*; and *Harry Potter and the Order of the Phoenix*.

Ms. Rowling's Licensing Strategy and Plans for the Series

25. The tremendous success of the *Harry Potter* Books and Movies has led to tremendous interest in *Harry Potter*-related merchandise and books. Ms. Rowling has been selective in granting licenses in order to protect the integrity of the *Harry Potter* Books. Limiting the number of licenses that are

granted; the number of products that are made, and exercising stringent quality control are central to Ms. Rowling's licensing strategy.

26. In particular, Ms. Rowling has been careful not to license certain types of tiein" or "companion" books based on the *Harry Potter* Books, which merely regurgitate her creative expression without adding valuable analysis or scholarly commentary. Ms. Rowling has refused to license such books, in part, because as discussed above, she has authored and published her own Companion Books and intends to create additional companion books. As a result, Ms. Rowling has sought to reserve her exclusive right to do so by refraining from granting or licensing these rights to third-parties.

DEFENDANT'S INFRINGEMENT OF PLAINTIFFS' INTELLECTUAL PROPERTY RIGHTS

The *Lexicon* Website

27. Upon information and belief, Mr. Vander Ark runs the *Lexicon* Website which is an interactive site catering to fans of the *Harry Potter* Works. The site consists of over 700 web-pages of material including the definitional entries for the various characters, places and things associated with the *Harry Potter* Works at issue here, along with a variety of fan art, fan fiction, commentary about the series, and forums and discussion groups related thereto.

28. Mr. Vander Ark has long known of Ms. Rowling's plan to create a "reader's guide" style companion book to the *Harry Potter* Books. In July of 2007, in the midst of the rush surrounding the release of the final *Harry Potter* Book, Mr. Vander Ark contacted Ms. Rowling's representatives in order to obtain employment with Ms. Rowling on her long anticipated companion guide to the world of *Harry Potter*. After his services were declined, Mr. Vander Ark then set out to have materials from his own *Lexicon* Website turned into a book in competition with Ms. Rowling's planned book and in contravention of her rights. Knowing full well that Ms. Rowling would not even be finished with her book tour following the July release of the final *Harry Potter* book -- much less able to start on her next companion guide -- Mr. Vander Ark sought to finalize and release his Infringing Book almost immediately following that July release.

29. At the time Plaintiffs initiated suit, on October 31, 2007, Defendant was mere weeks away from publishing the Infringing Book in the United States and in the United Kingdom. Moreover, according to RDR Books' own statements in an advertisement it posted on the Publishers Marketplace website www.PublishersMarketplace.com, it had at that point

already sold the rights to the Infringing Book in France, Canada and
Australia.

Plaintiffs Learn that Defendant Intends to Publish the Infringing Book

30. Ms. Rowling's literary agent first learned of the Infringing Book
when he saw the advertisement on the Publishers Marketplace website
announcing that RDR Books would be publishing the *Harry Potter Lexicon,*
purportedly scheduled, at that time, for release in late October 2007. The ad
listed the author as Steve Vander Ark, the editor of the free *Lexicon* Website,
and made clear that the book was intended to be the definitive *Harry Potter*
encyclopedia of the entire series totaling approximately 400 pages long. The
advertisement also stated that RDR Books already had sold the rights to the
Infringing Book in England, France, Canada and Australia and that it was
offering for sale the worldwide rights to the Infringing Book with the
exception of those countries.

31. Based on the description in the Publishers Marketplace
advertisement and being familiar with the content of the *Lexicon* Website, Ms.
Rowling and her agent became concerned that the Infringing Book was
designed to unilaterally misappropriate Ms. Rowling's intellectual property
rights for Defendant's own financial gain. In addition, Ms. Rowling and her
representative were concerned that the title of the Infringing Book, devoid of
any disclaimer, gave the misleading and false impression that Ms. Rowling or
Warner Bros. had sponsored, licensed or were otherwise associated with the
infringing Book.

32. As a result, on September 12, 2007, Ms. Rowling's agent emailed
the book's author, Mr. Vander Ark, copying RDR Books, reminding them
that Ms. Rowling has publicly stated that she intended to write her own
companion guides to the *Harry Potter* Books in the future and donate
proceeds to charity. Ms. Rowling's agent also stated that Ms. Rowling did
not wish to grant rights to any third party to publish a companion book to
the *Harry Potter* series. Appealing to Mr. Vander Ark as a friend and
supporter of Ms. Rowling and the *Harry Potter* Books, Ms. Rowling's agent
asked Mr. Vander Ark to forgo publication of the infringing Book. Neither
Mr. Vander Ark nor Defendant RDR Books responded to this email for six
days.

33. Not having heard a response, on September 18, 2007, counsel for
Ms. Rowling and Warner Bros. forwarded a letter to RDR Books and Mr.
Vander Ark by email, notifying them that the Infringing Book would infringe
Ms. Rowling's copyrights and mislead consumers to believe that it had been
authorized by Ms. Rowling and Warner Bros. The letter cited two cases in

this Circuit on point: (1) a Second Circuit decision, affirming judgment that a book which contained detailed plot summaries of *Twin Peaks* episodes constituted copyright infringement, *Twin Peaks Productions, Inc.* v. *Publications Int 'l, Ltd.*, 996 F.2d 1366 (2d Cir. 1993) and (2) a decision from the Southern District of New York, holding that a book containing trivia questions about the *Seinfeld* television series constituted copyright infringement, *Castle Rock Entertainment* v. *Carol Publishing Group*, 955 F. Supp. 260 (S.D.N.Y. 1997). Counsel requested that Defendant (a) cease its efforts to publish the Infringing Book; (b) forward the letter to parties that have purchased rights to the Infringing Book in England, France, Canada and Australia; and (c) identify these parties so that counsel for Ms. Rowling and Warner Bros. could contact them directly.

34. Perhaps not coincidentally, that same day, September 18, 2007, Mr. Vander Ark informed Ms. Rowling's agent by email that he "[had] been asked to leave all correspondence on this matter to others." On September 19, 2007 RDR Books replied cursorily to Plaintiffs' counsel on behalf of the company and Mr. VanderArk, stating"[i]t is our intention to thoroughly study the various issues you have raised and discuss them with our legal advisers."

35. On October 3,2007, after waiting another two weeks and receiving no substantive response, counsel for Ms. Rowling and Warner Bros. wrote again to RDR Books, emphasizing their clients' concerns and the impending publication date and asking for a prompt substantive response. The president of RDR Books, Roger Rapoport, sent an email later that day, requesting more time to respond due to a death in his family. Sympathetic to Mr. Rapoport's situation, Plaintiffs' counsel replied that they understood Mr. Rapoport's circumstances and would honor his request for additional time to respond in good faith.

36. It was thus with great surprise and disappointment that Plaintiffs found that on October 11, 2007, after claiming he was not in a position to respond to Plaintiffs' letter, Mr. Rapoport sent a "cease and desist" letter of his own to Warner Bros. claiming that a timeline appearing on some of the *Harry Potter* DVDs infringed the *Lexicon* Website. Warner Bros. responded to Mr. Rapoport's letter indicating that it would look into the matter and respond more fully. In the meantime, Warner Bros. asked for a copy of the "print version" of the *Lexicon* Website referred to by RDR Books in order to aid in its evaluation of the claims. RDR Books summarily dismissed Warner Bros. reasonable request, stating rudely: "If you do not know how to print that material [from the *Lexicon* Website] please ask one of your people to show you how." RDR Books' unreasonable refusal of this simple request heightened Plaintiffs' fears that RDR Books was infringing Ms. Rowling's and Warner Bros.' rights.

37. Given the fact that RDR Books was asserting claims against Warner Bros., it was apparent that Mr. Rapoport was back to work despite having not yet responded to Plaintiffs' concerns about the Infringing Book. Thus, on October 19, 2007, Plaintiffs' counsel wrote a third letter to RDR Books, asking once again for a substantive response to their clients' concerns regarding the Infringing Book. As they had before, RDR Books responded only that "[w]e 'are looking in to your allegations and will get back to you with our response."

38. While patiently awaiting RDR Books' response, Plaintiffs became aware of yet more events that caused them intense concern. On or around October 23, 2007 Ms. Rowling's agent learned that RDR Books had recently offered the publishing rights for the Infringing Book in Germany to Random House and in Taiwan to Crown Publishing. Plaintiffs grew increasingly concerned during the course of these events because it appeared that RDR Books was duplicitously stalling its response to Plaintiffs' concerns in order to surreptitiously promote the Infringing Book in advance of the rapidly-approaching publication date.

39. Thus the following day, on October 24, 2007, in an effort to avoid the need to litigate the matter, counsel for Plaintiffs wrote for yet a fourth time to RDR Books, expressing their grave concerns about RDR Books' recent behavior and asking for confirmation that RDR Books would not publish the Infringing Book until it attempted to resolve this matter in good faith. In addition, Plaintiffs' counsel repeated Warner Bros.' earlier request for a copy of the Infringing Book (or the most recent draft) for review in order to facilitate the parties' discussions. Given RDR Books' previous course of conduct of delaying their response in order to get the Infringing Book closer to publication and having already refused to substantively respond to Plaintiffs' concerns for over a month, Plaintiffs' counsel set a deadline for a response of Monday, October 29, 2007.

40. RDR Books sent a brief email response on October 24,2007, stating that Plaintiffs "unwarranted" objections were not appreciated. RDR Books also stated that the Infringing Book was a "print version" of the *Lexicon* Website, which was allegedly permitted by Ms. Rowling, and that there were allegedly other *Harry Potter* guides similar to the Infringing Book on the market. While Ms. Rowling has permitted some fan sites certain latitude to make use of the material in her books, these sites are generally free to the public and exist to enable fans to communicate, rather than to create an unauthorized derivative work in order to turn a quick and easy profit based on her own creativity. Ms. Rowling never gave anyone permission to publish and offer for sale a 400-page *Harry Potter* "lexicon".

41. Ms. Rowling and Warner Bros. are concerned about the Infringing Book not only because of the infringing material it contains, as is discussed below, and not only because it will undermine the companion guide that Ms. Rowling herself intends to write, but also because RDR Books has confirmed -- through its refusal to be above-board about its intentions and engage in reasonable discussions about the Infringing Book -- that it cannot be trusted with one of the most beloved children's book series in history.

42. Not only does the Infringing Book violate Plaintiffs' intellectual property rights, it is also hypocritical. It should be noted that on his website, Mr. Vander Ark, the so-called "editor" of the Infringing Book states:

> I don't give permission for people to just copy my work for their own use. Not only is that illegal, since everything in the Lexicon is copyrighted, it's also just plain wrong. Hey, I did all the work, I put in all the time, it's my skill and talent in this area which allowed the Lexicon to come into being. No one else has the right to use my work.

Yet this is exactly what Defendant is attempting to do here in connection with Ms. Rowling's work.

43. Given RDR Books' continued unreasonable delay tactics, inexplicable refusal to postpone publication while the parties resolve these issues, and its unwillingness to even provide Plaintiffs with a review copy of the Infringing Book or a manuscript, it became apparent that RDR Books had no intention of working with Plaintiffs to resolve this matter amicably. Plaintiffs therefore had no choice but to file this lawsuit.

Defendant's Infringing Book - *The Harry Potter Lexicon*

44. While Defendant summarily and unreasonably refused to provide Plaintiffs with an evaluation copy of the Infringing Book, this Court ordered Defendant to produce the latest manuscript in accordance with Plaintiffs' motion for expedited discovery. Having now seen a copy of such manuscript, Plaintiffs are more concerned than ever about the possibility of its publication.

45. The Infringing Book is a self-described, 400-page "lexicon," comprising an alphabetical listing of hundreds of elements from all seven of the *Harry Potter* Books and the two Companion Books authored by Ms. Rowling. These entries include brief descriptions of each and every person, place or thing appearing in the Harry Potter Books without any analysis or

commentary. Sample entries from the Infringing Book, which include parenthetical citations to the chapters and pages of the *Potter* Books and Companion Books from which the protected material was copied, are as follows:

> **Abraxan** A breed of winged horse; the Abraxan is a gigantic, extremely powerful Palomino (FB). Madame Maxime, headmistress of Beaux batons, breeds them (OP20) and the winged horses that pull her carriage are Abraxans. They drink only single malt whisky and require "forceful handling" (GFI5).
>
> **"abstinence"** After over-indulging during the Christmas holidays, the Fat Lady decided that 'abstinence' would be the new password to get into the Gryffindor common room (HBP17).
>
> **Abyssinia** Another name for Ethiopia, and presumably the home of the Abyssinian Shrivelfig (PA7).
>
> **Abyssinian shrivelfig** Second-year herbology students work with these plants, learning to prune them (CS15). When peeled, shrivelfigs are used as an ingredient in Shrinking Solution (PA7).

46. Moreover, many of the entries in the Infringing Book contain lengthy plot summaries, spoilers and detailed descriptions of characters created by Ms. Rowling, recounting, for example, key features of each of the principal characters in each of the *Harry Potter* Books, such as Hermione Granger, Harry Potter, and Ron Weasley, and chronicling the events, physical space, and subjects associated with Hogwarts. In sum, the Infringing Book contains synopses of the major plots and story lines of the *Harry Potter* Books, descriptions of the history and personalities of nearly all of the *Harry Potter* characters, and detailed catalogues of the fictional creatures and magical elements that constitute the "heart" of the *Harry Potter* Books. These descriptions, character details and plot points comprise stories created and owned by Ms. Rowling, who has the sole right to control their distribution and who did not give permission to Defendant to publish a book that stands to make money off of the back of Ms. Rowling's creativity.

47. In addition to the infringing content, the Infringing Book cover is designed and will be marketed to mislead consumers into believing that it has been endorsed by Ms. Rowling. The original cover of the book was purposely designed to suggest a false association with Plaintiffs by using the terms *"Harry Potter Lexicon"* in large letters and in a font reminiscent of the one used in other *Harry Potter* Works, without any kind of disclaimer, and featuring numerous other indicia from the *Harry Potter* Works. On the back, a heading indicating that the *Lexicon* Website won a fan site award from Ms. Rowling, and a quote from Ms. Rowling made in connection therewith appear giving the false impression that Ms. Rowling gave the Infringing Book

an award or otherwise endorses the Infringing Book when she certainly does not. Although in response to the instant suit, Defendant has changed the proposed front cover of the Infringing Book to add inconspicuous disclaimers and the term "Unofficial" to the title, Defendant continues to prominently feature the heading, Ms. Rowling's trademarked name and the quote on the Infringing Book's back cover in an effort to confuse customers as to her approval or endorsement thereof.

48. In addition to the appearance of Ms. Rowling's name on the book itself, Defendant has utilized and, on information and belief, continues to utilize Ms. Rowling's name in advertising the Infringing Book. Ms. Rowling's name is prominently featured in marketing materials that Defendant apparently has used to market the Infringing Book to potential publishers and booksellers. Defendant neither sought, nor did Ms. Rowling grant, her written consent to use her name in connection with these materials or on the cover of the Infringing Book.

COUNT ONE - COPYRIGHT INFRINGEMENT
(17 U.S.C. §§ 101 et seq.)

49. Plaintiffs repeat and reallege each and every allegation set forth in Paragraphs 1 through 49, inclusive, and incorporate them herein by this reference.

50. By its actions alleged above, Defendant has infringed and will continue to infringe Ms. Rowling's copyrights in the *Harry Potter* Books and Companion Books and Warner Bros.' copyrights in the *Harry Potter* Films, by using their original copyrighted material as a basis for the Infringing Book, without permission.

51. Plaintiffs are entitled to an injunction restraining Defendant, its agents and employees, and all persons acting in concert or participation with them, from engaging in any further such acts in violation of the Copyright Act.

52. Plaintiffs are further entitled to recover from Defendant the damages, including attorneys' fees, they have sustained and will sustain, and any gains, profits and advantages obtained by Defendant as a result of their acts of infringement as alleged above. At present, the amount of such damages, gains, profits and advantages cannot be fully ascertained by Plaintiffs, but will be established according to proof at trial. Plaintiffs are also entitled to recover statutory damages for Defendant's willful infringement of their intellectual property in the *Harry Potter* Books and Films.

COUNT TWO -FEDERAL TRADEMARK INFRINGEMENT
(15 U.S.C. § 1114(1))

53. Plaintiffs repeat and reallege each and every allegation contained in paragraphs 1 through 53, inclusive, and incorporate them herein by reference.

54. Defendant's unauthorized and willful use of copies, variations, reproductions, simulations or colorable imitations of Plaintiffs' federally-registered trademarks in connection with the offering for sale and sale of the Infringing Book constitutes use in commerce. Such use infringes Plaintiffs' exclusive rights in their respective federally-registered trademarks, explicitly misleads as to the source or sponsorship of the Infringing Book, and has caused and is likely to cause confusion, mistake or deception as to the source of the Infringing Book written, published and sold by Defendant.

55. The aforesaid acts of Defendant, namely, the unauthorized and willful use of copies, variations, reproductions, simulations or colorable imitations of Plaintiffs' registered marks in connection with the sale of the Infringing Book, constitute trademark infringement in violation of Section 32(1) of the Lanham Act, 15 U.S.C. § 1114(1).

56. The aforesaid acts of Defendant have caused and, unless said acts are restrained by this Court, will continue to cause Plaintiffs to suffer irreparable injury.

COUNT THREE -UNFAIR COMPETITION, FALSE ENDORSEMENT
AND FALSE DESIGNATION OF ORIGIN
(15 U.S.C. § 1125(a)(1)(A))

57. Plaintiffs repeat and reallege each and every allegation contained in paragraphs 1 through 57, inclusive, and incorporate them herein by reference.

58. Through the use of the misleading cover and design of and marketing materials for the Infringing Book (including, *inter alia,* Plaintiffs' federally-registered trademarks, the heading referencing the fan site award, Ms. Rowling's name and Ms. Rowling's quote regarding the *Lexicon* Website), Defendant is knowingly and intentionally misrepresenting and falsely designating to the general public the affiliation, connection, association, origin, source, sponsorship, endorsement and approval of the Infringing Book, and intend to misrepresent and falsely designate to the general public the affiliation, connection, association, origin, source, approval, endorsement

or sponsorship of the Infringing Book, so as to create a likelihood of confusion by the public as to the affiliation, connection, association, origin, source, approval, endorsement and sponsorship of the Infringing Book.

59. The aforesaid acts of Defendant constitute false endorsement, false designation of origin and unfair competition in violation of 15 U.S.C. § 1125(a)(1)(A).

60. As a direct and proximate result of the foregoing acts of Defendant, Plaintiffs have been damaged and have suffered and will continue to suffer immediate and irreparable harm.

COUNT FOUR -FALSE ADVERTISING
(15 U.S.C § 1125(a)(1)(B))

61. Plaintiffs repeat and reallege each and every allegation contained in paragraphs 1 through 61, inclusive, and incorporate them herein by reference.

62. Through the use of the misleading cover and design of and marketing materials for the Infringing Book (including, *inter alia,* Warner Bros. federally-registered trademarks, the fan site award reference, Ms. Rowling's name and Ms. Rowling's quote regarding the *Lexicon* Website), Defendant is knowingly and intentionally misrepresenting the nature, characteristics, and qualities of the Infringing Book, and intends to misrepresent the nature, characteristics, and qualities the Infringing Book, so as to create a likelihood of confusion by the public as to the nature, characteristics, and qualities of the Infringing Book.

63. The aforesaid acts of Defendant constitute false advertising in violation of 15 U.S.C. § 1125(a)(l)(B).

64. As a direct and proximate result of the foregoing acts of Defendant, Plaintiffs have been damaged and has suffered and will continue to suffer immediate and irreparable harm.

65. Plaintiffs repeat and reallege each and every allegation contained in paragraphs 1 through 65, inclusive, and incorporate them herein by reference.

COUNT FIVE-RIGHT OF PRIVACY
(New York Civil Rights Law §§ 50-51)

66. The aforesaid acts of Defendant in using Ms. Rowling's name in connection with advertising without her written consent constitutes a violation of New York Civil Rights Law §§ 50-51.

67. As a direct and proximate result of the foregoing acts of Defendant, Ms. Rowling has been damaged and has suffered and will continue to suffer immediate and irreparable injury for which it has no adequate remedy at law.

COUNT SIX -UNFAIR COMPETITION
(New York Common Law)

68. Plaintiffs repeat and reallege each and every allegation contained in paragraphs 1 through 68, inclusive, and incorporate them herein by reference.

69. The aforesaid acts of Defendant's unauthorized use of Warner Bros.' trademarks in connection with the Infringing Book and use of the misleading cover and design of and marketing materials for the Infringing Book (including, *inter alia,* Warner Bros.' federally-registered trademarks, the fan site award reference, Ms. Rowling's name and Ms. Rowling's quote regarding the *Lexicon* Website) constitute unfair competition under the common law of New York in that Defendant has misappropriated, and unfairly competed with, Plaintiffs' commercial business and will continue to do so.

70. As a direct and proximate result of the foregoing acts, Defendant unlawfully derived and will continue to derive, income, profits and ever-increasing goodwill from its activities and Plaintiffs have been damaged and have suffered and will continue to suffer immediate and irreparable injury for which Plaintiffs have no adequate remedy at law.

COUNT SEVEN - DECLARATORY JUDGMENT
REGARDING COPYRIGHT INFRINGEMENT
(17 U.S.C. §§ 101 et seq.)

71. Plaintiffs repeat and reallege each and every allegation contained in paragraphs 1 through 66, inclusive, and incorporate them herein by reference.

72. Defendant contends that Warner Bros.' inclusion of the "Hogwarts Time Line" in the DVD versions of several *Harry Potter* Films

infringes Defendant's rights in another time line of *Harry Potter*-related fictional events. By virtue of Defendant's contentions, Warner Bros. has a real and reasonable apprehension of litigation and has been brought into adversarial conflict with Defendant.

73. The "Hogwarts Time Line" in Warner Bros.' DVDs is original to Warner Bros. and is based on the *Harry Potter* Books. The "Hogwarts Time Line" does not infringe on any rights of Defendant or anyone else.

74. By engaging in threatening conduct, Defendant threatens to place a cloud over Warner Bros.' right to exploit the *Harry Potter* DVDs.

75. By reason of the foregoing, there now exists between the parties an actual and justiciable controversy concerning Warner Bros.' and Defendant's respective rights and obligations with respect to the use of the "Hogwarts Timeline" in the DVD versions of several *Potter* Movies, requiring declaratory relief.

76. The aforesaid declaration is necessary and appropriate at this time so that Warner Bros.' right to continue its conduct can be affirmed.

77. Warner Bros. has no adequate remedy at law.

78. Accordingly, Warner Bros. seeks, pursuant to 28 U.S.C. § 2201, a judgment from this Court that its DVD versions of the *Harry Potter* Films do not violate any of Defendant's copyrights.

PRAYER FOR RELIEF

WHEREFORE, the Plaintiffs, Warner Bros. Entertainment Inc. and J.K. Rowling, respectfully demand:

1. That the Court find that Defendant has infringed Plaintiffs' copyrights in the *Harry Potter* Books, the Companion Books and the *Harry Potter* Films;

2. That the Court find that Defendant has infringed Warner Bros.' trademarks;

3. That the Court find that Defendant has used Plaintiffs' trademarks, a misleading book cover and design, and misleading advertising materials to falsely suggest Plaintiffs' endorsement of the Infringing Book, falsely designate the origin of the Infringing Book, falsely advertise the Infringing Book, and unfairly compete with Plaintiffs;

4. That the Court find that Defendant has engaged in deceptive trade practices and unfair competition, and violated Ms. Rowling's right of privacy;

5. That the Court find that the "Hogwarts Time Line" in the DVD versions of certain *Harry Potter* Films does not infringed Defendant's copyrights;

6. That the Court find a substantial likelihood that Defendant will continue to infringe Plaintiffs' intellectual property unless permanently enjoined from doing so;

7. A permanent injunction restraining Defendant, and its agents, servants, employees, attorneys, successors and assigns, and all persons, firms and corporations acting in concert with them, from directly or indirectly infringing Plaintiffs' copyrights and Warner Bros.' trademarks, including but not limited to continuing to manufacture, distribute, market, advertise, promote, solicit or accept orders for, sell or offer for sale the Infringing Book or any works derived or copied from Plaintiffs' copyrighted works and from participating or assisting in any such activity whether occurring within the United States of America;

8. An order instructing Defendant, its agents, servants, employees, attorneys, successors and assigns, and all persons, firms and corporations acting in concert with them, to recall from all distributors, wholesalers, jobbers, dealers, retailers and all others known to it the Infringing Book and any other works shown to infringe any of Plaintiffs' intellectual property;

9. That the Court enter judgment for Plaintiffs and against Defendant for Plaintiffs' actual damages according to proof, and for any profits attributable to infringements of Plaintiffs' intellectual property and unfair trade practices and unfair competition, in accordance with proof;

10. That the Court enter judgment for Ms. Rowling and against Defendant for statutory damages based upon their acts of infringement pursuant to the Copyright Act of 1976, 17 U.S.C. §§ 101, et seq.;

11. An award of three times the greater of:

    a. Warner Bros' damages for the wrongful acts of Defendant in an amount the Court deems appropriate, together with appropriate interest on such damages; or

    b. Defendant's profits in accordance with the accounting demanded in the preceding paragraph, pursuant to 15 U.S.C. § 1117; and ·

12. An award of Plaintiffs' costs and disbursements of this action, including reasonable attorneys' fees, pursuant to 17 U.S.C. § 505 and 15 U.S.C. § 1117; and

13. That the Court grant such other, further, and different relief as the Court deems just and proper.

Dated: January 15, 2008

Respectfully Submitted:

Dale M. Cendali
Melanie Bradley
O'MELVENY & MYERS LLP
Times Square Tower
7 Times Square New York, NY 10036
(212) 326-2000

DECLARATION OF J.K. ROWLING IN SUPPORT OF PLAINTIFFS' MOTION FOR PRELIMINARY INJUNCTION

WARNER BROS. ENTERTAINMENT INC. AND
J.K. ROWLING,

Plaintiffs,

-against-

RDR BOOKS and DOES 1-10

Defendants.

Case No. 07-09667 (RPP)   Filed: January 15, 2008

I, J.K. Rowling, declare and state as follows:

1. I am the author of the *Potter* book series (the *"Harry Potter* Books" or "Books"). Except for the facts stated on information and belief, all of the facts set forth herein are known to me personally, and if called as a witness, I could and would testify competently thereto.

2. The idea for the *Potter* series first came to me while riding a train to London nearly eighteen years ago. Since then, I have written seven books chronicling the lives and adventures of Harry Potter, Hermione Granger, Ron Weasley and their friends as they grew into adulthood at Hogwarts School of Witchcraft and Wizardry and fought the evil Lord Voldemort.

3. I wrote the first *Harry Potter* manuscript during a difficult time in my life. Between caring for my daughter single-handedly and preparing to resume my teaching career, I wrote furiously with every opportunity I had. As a result in part of the effort and sacrifice it took to write the first *Harry Potter* book, I grew very close to characters and the fictional world I created.

4. To this day, I care deeply about how the characters and story lines are presented and what type of derivative works I license based on the *Potter* Books. I require that all licensed materials, such as the films based on the Books, be of the highest quality. I also limit *Harry Potter* merchandising in an effort to maintain quality controls. In other words, I am careful about the way the *Harry Potter* Books are presented to the world. I believe I owe that much to the millions of *Harry Potter* fans who have grown to love the Books and to trust in the quality of the products associated with them.

5. I am extremely appreciative of the support both I and the *Harry Potter* Books have received the fan community. I enjoy and encourage the free flow of ideas, creativity, commentary and discussion of the *Harry Potter* Books, including on free-of-charge fan websites, even if it has meant allowing these fan sites to reference copyrighted *Harry Potter* materials or to create derivative works such as fan fiction or art. I express my appreciation for fan sites and the fan community by, among other things, bestowing a "fan site award" on one or more of the *Harry Potter* fan sites each year. In June of 2004, I granted just such a fan site award to the *Harry Potter* Lexicon fan site partly because of the free and open nature of the site. That being said, I never intended this award or my encouragement and support of the fan community to be taken by anyone as an authorization for them to create and sell an infringing *Harry Potter* book (or any other materials) for their own financial gain.

6. I have chosen not to license a *Harry Potter* companion book similar to RDR Books' proposed "lexicon" because I intend to write my own. In addition to the two companion books I have already written -- *Fantastic Beasts and Where to Find Them* and *Quidditch Through the Ages* (the "Companion Books") -- I have stated on my website, in numerous interviews in the press and elsewhere that I intend to publish a definitive guide to all of the creatures, characters, places, and other elements that comprise the *Harry Potter* world. Just as I did with the first two companion books, I will donate royalties from such a companion book to charity.

7. Moreover, I have made and kept notes in connection with each of the *Harry Potter* books, which I have recently begun to augment with additional materials that I intend to include in my own companion guide. In addition, I am aware that both my British and American publishers, Bloomsbury and Scholastic respectively, have each compiled and indexed the material from the previous *Harry Potter* books and that these materials would be made available to me if I chose to use them.

8. The seventh and final book in the *Harry Potter* series was only released less than six months ago on July 21,2007. I was touring in support of the book, most recently in the United States and Canada, until December, 2007, after which I took a much needed break.

9. I was thus sad and disappointed to learn while in the midst of touring in support of the last *Potter* book that RDR Books and Mr. Vander Ark planned to release a *Potter* "lexicon" directly contrary to my wishes. I understand that the proposed book is neither commentary nor criticism of the *Harry Potter* series – either of which would be entirely legitimate -- but instead lists in alphabetical order the various fictional characters and things in

the *Harry Potter* universe. It is as if I have been "scooped' before I even had the chance to wind up the book tour for the final *Harry Potter* installment, much less to write and publish my own *Harry Potter* guide.

10. Even worse, RDR Books and Mr. Vander Ark apparently are attempting to justify publication of the "lexicon" based on the past praise I had given to the *Harry Potter* Lexicon fan site. As I have already explained, I have always supported *Harry Potter* fans, even if it has meant allowing fan websites to reference copyrighted *Harry Potter* materials, but have drawn the line at selling such materials for commercial gain. By threatening to publish and sell the unauthorized "lexicon," RDR Books and Mr. Vander Ark have crossed that line.

11. It is incomprehensible to me that this "lexicon" should be allowed to be published simply because I encourage and support fan websites or because Mr. Vander Ark was able to finish his "lexicon" while I was still touring in support of the last *Harry Potter* Book. My fear is that if the "lexicon" is published, authors like myself will be forced to restrict the use of their materials on fan websites or risk losing their right to restrict other unauthorized uses of those materials. Such a result benefits no one and hurts the fan community most of all.

12. Contrary to assertions made by RDR Books and Mr. Vander Ark, there is an enormous difference between enjoying the free *Harry Potter* Lexicon fan site and allowing a book to be sold that directly competes with future *Harry Potter* works that I intend to author. Moreover, the website differs significantly from RDR Books' proposed book. The website, to which I gave a fan site award, features exciting graphics, user forums, and critical essays, whereas the proposed book simply repackages story lines and characters from the *Harry Potter* series in an alphabetical A-Z listing. Also, as I mentioned, the website is free whereas RDR Books plans to sell the book for $24.95. Lastly, the "lexicon" does not measure up to the standards that I have set for licensing derivative works. In short, I would never have approved of this "lexicon."

13. To add insult to injury, I have learned that RDR Books intends to market the "lexicon" in a way that suggests that I have endorsed it when, in fact, the opposite is true. The back cover of the proposed book contains a large and prominent quote by me that makes it look like I am endorsing the book. In fact, the quote was taken without my permission from a fan award I gave the *Harry Potter* Lexicon fan site in 2004, which as I explained above, is different in style, purpose and commercialism from the proposed book. Given the similarity between the names of both the website and the "lexicon," the book gives the false impression that I have approved of it and

suggests to my fans that I am encouraging them to buy the book, when I am not.

14. I feel as though my name and my works have been hijacked, against my wishes, for the personal gain and profit of others and diverted from the charities that I intended to benefit. Accordingly, I respectfully ask this Court to stop publication of RDR's Books' "lexicon" and send a message to other would-be infringers that they may not capitalize on the fame and success of the *Harry Potter* franchise in the future.

I declare under penalty of perjury under the laws of the United States of America that the foregoing is true and correct. Executed on January 15 2008, at London, England.

Respectfully submitted,

By:
J.K. Rowling

PLAINTIFFS' MEMORANDUM IN SUPPORT OF PRELIMINARY INJUNCTION

WARNER BROS. ENTERTAINMENT INC. AND
J.K. ROWLING,

                       Plaintiffs,

     -against-

RDR BOOKS and DOES 1-10

                      Defendants.

Case No. 07-09667 (RPP)   Filed: January 16, 2008

J.K. Rowling and Warner Bros. Inc. ("WB") (collectively, "Plaintiffs") respectfully submit this Memorandum of Law in support of their motion to preliminarily enjoin RDR Books ("RDR") from marketing or selling its planned book "The Harry Potter Lexicon" (the "Book").

PRELIMINARY STATEMENT

The *Harry Potter* series of books (the "Series") is a unique cultural phenomenon that has cast a worldwide spell. Although Ms. Rowling has allowed fans and scholars wide latitude to comment on, critique, and even create "fan fiction" and art based on her stories, the Book clearly crosses the line. Seeking to cash in and free ride on the Series' success, the Book copies from it wholesale, presenting snippets in alphabetical order while adding no creativity or inventiveness and contributing nothing original to the reader's understanding of the Series. RDR's use of Plaintiffs' works for its own commercial benefit stands in direct conflict with Ms. Rowling's long-stated plans to create her own comprehensive guide for the Series and donate the proceeds to charity, as she has done with the more than $30 million generated by the two more narrowly focused companion books that she has published (collectively, the "Companion Books").

RDR's attempt to justify its infringement as "scholarship" is a sham. It is not a reference book or scholarly critique, merely a mass-market work that lifts whole chunks of Ms. Rowling's text and orders them alphabetically, in effect "rearranging the furniture" that Ms. Rowling created while lacking any originality or invention. As discussed below, the Second Circuit has expressly stated that such works are copyright infringements warranting injunctive relief and not fair use. *See, e.g., Castle Rock Ent., Inc. v. Carol Publ'g,Group, Inc.,* 150 F.3d 132, 138-39 (2d Cir. 1998). The availability of the Book's content on "The Harry Potter Lexicon" website at <hp-lexicon.org> (the "Website") does not change the result; there is a world of difference between permitting a free fan site to operate and allowing RDR to commercialize those efforts in derogation of Plaintiffs' rights. Moreover, unlike the Book, an intangible website that takes several days to print is not a market substitute for Ms. Rowling's planned book. A contrary rule would also harm the fan community by necessitating more monitoring and restriction of an activity by copyright owners afraid of compromising their rights against infringers.

Injunctive relief is particularly appropriate here given the striking evidence of RDR's bad faith in proceeding with the Book despite knowing that its conduct was unlawful. Steven Vander Ark, owner of the Website and the Book's "author," has long been aware of Ms. Rowling's plan to write a comprehensive companion book. He even stated in a "smoking gun" e-mail that it would be "illegal" to sell such a work without Ms. Rowling's permission and that she had reserved her rights in the Series. Yet, after unsuccessfully seeking employment as a co-author of Ms. Rowling's planned encyclopedia, Vander Ark contracted with RDR, obtaining an express indemnity against any claims by Ms. Rowling based on the Book. RDR has also demonstrated its understanding that the Book is unlawful, instructing foreign publishing agents "shopping" the book to avoid foreign publishers of the Series and stalling Ms. Rowling's representatives who were attempting to discuss the Book with RDR, while continuing to hawk the Book overseas. Adding insult to injury, RDR has falsely advertised the Book, brazenly quoting Ms. Rowling prominently on the Book's back cover and in marketing materials so as to suggest she has endorsed the Book when she in fact vehemently opposes it.

Allowing RDR to proceed with the Book would irreparably injure Plaintiffs. In addition to the presumption of irreparable harm resulting from RDR's violation of Plaintiffs' intellectual property rights, Ms. Rowling would effectively be "scooped" by her own work and deprived of the exclusive right to be the first to create a definitive encyclopedia of the Series, as well as the right to exercise quality control over derivative works based on the Series. Moreover, when Ms. Rowling publishes her own guide she might find herself in the absurd position of defending a claim that she infringed RDR's copyright in its unauthorized derivative work based on *her* creation. Nor is this possibility remote: RDR has *already* written to WB claiming infringement of a timeline based on the Series and posted on the Website. There would also be a societal cost as permitting sale of the Book would open the door to similar unauthorized works, increasing transaction costs by making it unclear to prospective licensees who could grant all of the rights needed, confusing consumers as to what goods are authorized, and diluting the goodwill Plaintiffs have built up in the Series through their policing and quality control. For all of these reasons, this Court should bar RDR from publishing the Book in the United States and abroad.

FACTUAL BACKGROUND

The World of Harry Potter

The *Harry Potter* phenomenon began nearly 18 years ago when Ms. Rowling first put pen to paper during a train ride to London. Facing financial difficulties, the demands of single parenthood and the stress of preparing to resume a teaching career, she created a fictional world that has captured the imaginations of millions around the world. After publishing the first *Harry Potter* book in the United Kingdom in 1997 (1998 in the United States), Ms. Rowling chronicled the lives of Harry Potter and his friends in six subsequent books over the past 10 years. Ms. Rowling has been able to harness the Series' popularity for social good, including authoring the short Companion Books and donating all her royalties, now totaling over $30 million, to charity. Ms. Rowling has also repeatedly stated, since at least 2001, that she plans to publish a *Harry Potter* encyclopedia once the Series was finished and similarly donate the proceeds to charity. Ms. Rowling has created notes for that work and is also free to draw on the detailed alphabetical indices and other materials already prepared by her publishers in the United States and United Kingdom, which are similar in content to the Book. The final *Harry Potter* book was released in July 2007; Ms. Rowling toured in support of it until December 2007. Ms. Rowling owns valid U.S. copyright registrations to the Series and the Companion Books.

Plaintiffs' Licensing and Enforcement Strategy

Ms. Rowling has carefully selected the licensees with whom to work on projects based on the Series, including working with WB on the planned seven-film series based on the Series (the "Films"). Each film made to date is the subject of a copyright registration. Pursuant to its agreement with Ms. Rowling, WB also owns trademark rights in *Harry Potter*-related designations in connection with its film rights and ancillary merchandising projects (collectively, the "Marks"). To maintain the quality and integrity of the Series and Films (Collectively, the *"Harry Potter* Works") Ms. Rowling and WB carefully consider licensing requests. They deny many, making every effort to ensure that licensed materials are of the highest quality, and use licensee style guides and quality controls to ensure that their high standards are upheld.

Plaintiffs also carefully guard against individuals who seek to diminish the value of the Series and Films or free-ride on their success to the detriment of Plaintiffs' licensing programs. They have numerous cease and desist letters and filed several actions to protect their intellectual property rights. WB has spent hundreds of thousands of dollars in the past year alone protecting its rights and working with outside counsel, law enforcement agencies and customs officials to enforce its trademarks and copyrights around the world. As a result, Plaintiffs have safeguarded the goodwill and integrity associated with the Series, Films and Marks. Plaintiffs' efforts have involved policing their rights against infringement by unauthorized *Harry Potter-related* books, including unauthorized "companion" type books. Plaintiffs do not object to books that analyze or comment on the series -- even if they may not agree with the points made. They *do* object to books that simply repackage the world of *Harry Potter* in an unoriginal way to turn a profit, and to books that are marketed to falsely suggest that Plaintiffs have endorsed or approved them.

Ms. Rowling deeply appreciates the Series' fans and the enthusiasm and energy they bring to the *Harry Potter* fan community. Plaintiffs give fans wide latitude to comment on the *Harry Potter* Works, reference them on fan sites and create and post derivative works such as fan fiction/art. Ms. Rowling has even recognized the fans' hard work and dedication on her own website by giving "Fan Site Awards." However, these activities cross the line when they are offered for sale instead of fun. At that point they undermine the latitude given to true noncommercial fan activities and interfere with Plaintiffs' carefully monitored licensing program.

RDR's and Vander Ark's Infringing Activities

In July 2007, during the rush to release the final *Harry Potter* book, Vander Ark, the Website's owner and well-aware of Ms. Rowling's plans for a *Harry Potter* encyclopedia, emailed her agent seeking employment as co-author of that book. His request was declined. Less than two months later, RDR announced it would be publishing the Book. Ms. Rowling was concerned that the Book was designed to trade off the success of the Series and Films in violation of her rights and goals for the Series and Companion Books. For over six weeks, Ms. Rowling's agent and Plaintiffs' counsel tried to reach RDR, asking it to drop or at least postpone its plans for the Book and provide Plaintiffs with a copy so that they could assess it and potentially resolve any issues. These efforts were utterly rebuffed. Instead, RDR apparently sought to string Plaintiffs along while continuing surreptitiously to market the book. Plaintiffs filed this suit on October 31, 2007, after futilely offering RDR a last chance to cease publication, or at least provide a copy of the manuscript.

On November 6, 2007, after this Court granted Plaintiffs limited expedited discovery, RDR finally provided Plaintiffs a copy of the manuscript and proposed cover, which confirmed that the Book merely repackages the fictional facts created by Ms. Rowling in an unoriginal fashion. Despite indicating previously that the Book was a "print version" of the Website, the manuscript showed otherwise. Unlike other *Harry Potter*-related books that contain analysis, commentary, criticism or other original material, the Book simply lists, in alphabetical order, all of the characters, creatures, spells and other fictional elements from the Series and defines them as Ms. Rowling does in her works -- even going so far as to repeatedly quote verbatim and closely paraphrase significant passages from the Series. Short entries typically have direct quotations or paraphrases; large entries retell Ms. Rowling's story in an abridged fashion. As Professor Johnson of Oxford explains, the Book is not scholarly -- it merely "rearranges the furniture" of Ms. Rowling's masterpiece by chopping it into pieces.

Beyond its infringing content, RDR deliberately markets the Book so as to mislead consumers into believing that it has been endorsed by Plaintiffs. On the back cover, prominent, bold type reads "Winner of J.K. Rowling's Fan Site Award," with a misleading quotation from Ms. Rowling taken out of context from comments she made regarding the free Website in 2004. RDR's use of this quote falsely suggests to consumers that Ms. Rowling has given the Book an award and endorsement. RDR also has deliberately misused this quotation in its marketing materials and in direct solicitations to foreign publishers and domestic retailers to capitalize on Ms. Rowling's reputation and boost its own sales. The revised cover that RDR subsequently prepared included disclaimers, but they are not as prominent as is standard publishing practice or clear enough to dispel the confusion caused by the misleading use of Ms. Rowling's name and quotation --which tellingly remain on the revised cover despite RDR's knowledge that Ms. Rowling vehemently opposes the Book. Only a very careful reader would notice the disclaimers tucked away on the back cover. As detailed below, Plaintiffs' survey shows *at least* 38%, and possibly as high as 55%, of respondents think Ms. Rowling has endorsed the book as a result of that calculatedly misleading cover.

Even as RDR and Vander Ark infringe Ms. Rowling's work claiming fair use, Vander Ark aggressively protects what he believes to be his own copyrights by prohibiting any copying of his Website. This double standard is emblematic of Vander Ark's disingenuous claims to be a fan and RDR's position in this case. Vander Ark and RDR have proceeded with the Book despite knowing that it infringes Plaintiffs' rights. For example, in May 2005, two fans contacted Vander Ark to discuss the possibility of collaborating on a "Fan-Made Harry Potter Encyclopedia." In his reply, Vander Ark admitted that such a work would be unlawful: "Basically, it is illegal to sell a book like that. Jo [J.K. Rowing] has reserved all publishing rights to her intellectual property, which means that she's the only one who may publish any book that is a guide or encyclopedia to her world."

RDR and Vander Ark's contract supports this conclusion. Although normally an author warrants that a book does not infringe any third party rights and indemnifies the publisher, here *RDR indemnified Vander Ark* against any copyright infringement claims by *Ms. Rowling* (but not by others). It also tried to hide its infringement by insisting that foreign publishing agents not show or discuss the Book with publishers of the Series. Not even repeated letters from Plaintiffs' representatives could convince RDR to cease or even temporarily suspend its efforts to publish.

ARGUMENT

I. PLAINTIFFS HAVE MET THE STANDARD FOR INJUNCTIVE RELIEF

Injunctive relief is warranted when a plaintiff shows (1) irreparable harm; and (2) either (a) a likelihood of success on the merits or (b) sufficiently serious questions going to the merits of the case to make them a fair ground for litigation, and a balance of hardships tipping decidedly in Plaintiffs' favor. *See ABKCO Music v. Stellar Records,* 96 F.3d 60, 64 (2d Cir. 1996). Plaintiffs easily meet this test as to their copyright and misleading marketing claims.

II. PLAINTIFFS ARE LIKELY TO SUCCEED ON THE MERITS

A. The Book Infringes Plaintiffs' Copyrights

Plaintiffs can easily establish *prima facie* copyright infringement based on (1) ownership of a valid, existing copyright; and (2) RDR's unauthorized copying of their copyrighted material. *See Novelty Textile Mills v. Joan Fabrics Corp.,* 558 F.2d 1090, 1092 (2d Cir. 1977).

1. RDR Has Copied Plaintiffs' Copyrighted Works

Plaintiffs own United States copyright registrations for the Series, the two Companion Books and the Films. These registrations are *prima facie* evidence of the copyrightability of the *Harry Potter* Works and the validity of Plaintiffs' copyrights. *See* 17 U.S.C. § 410(c); *see also Novelty Textile Mills,* 558 F.2d at 1092 n.l.

Ms. Rowling also owns copyrights in the fictional characters, events, places, and things that she has created and developed. *See Castle Rock,* 150 F.3d at 139 (fictional characters and facts created by *Seinfeld* writers were protectab1e expression); *Paramount Pictures Corp. v. Carol Publ'g Group,* 11 F. Supp. 2d 329 (S.D.N.Y. 1998); *see also New Line Cinema Corp. v. Bertlesman Music Group, Inc.,* 693 F. Supp. 1517, 1521 n.5 (S.D.N.Y. 1988); *Burroughs v. Metro-Goldwyn-Mayer, Inc.,* 519 F. Supp. 388, 391 (S.D.N.Y. 1981). There can be no doubt that Plaintiffs own valid, existing copyrights.

Copying can be proven by direct evidence of copying or by showing access to the underlying work and similarities between the works that are probative of actionable copying. *Castle Rock,* 150 F.3d at 137; *Twin Peaks Productions, Inc. v. Publications Int 'I, Ltd.,* 996 F.2d 1366, 1372 (2d Cir. 1993); *Paramount,* 11 F. Supp. 2d at 332-33; *Castle Rock Entm 't v. Carol Publ'g Group,* 955 F. Supp. 260, 264 (S.D.N.Y. 1997), *aff'd* 150 F.3d 132 (2d Cir. 1998). Here, the Book indisputably copies the *Harry Potter* Works; Vander Ark freely admits that the Website's encyclopedia section is based on his detailed notes on the Series. *See Paramount,* 11 F. Supp. 2d at 332 (copying inquiry unnecessary where book took quotations from *Star Trek* television series and told its fictional "history"); *Castle Rock,* 955 F. Supp. at 264 (trivia book copied material from *Seinfeld* television series). Because the Book admittedly copies the *Harry Potter* Works, the only inquiry is whether such copying is actionable. *Castle Rock,* 150 F.3d at 138; *Paramount,* 11 F. Supp. 2d at 333.

In *Castle Rock,* which is directly analogous, the Second Circuit said that "substantial similarity depends on whether the copying is quantitatively and qualitatively sufficient to support a finding of actionable copying." *Castle Rock,* 150 F.3d at 138. Because the Book, in the aggregate, has appropriated 400 pages of material directly from the Series, just like the *Seinfeld Aptitude Test* in *Castle Rock* it clearly "has crossed the *de minimis* threshold." *Castle Rock,* 150 F.3d at 138 (copying 643 fragments from an 84-episode tv series was actionable); *see also Twin Peaks,* 996 F.2d at 1372 (2d Cir. 1993) (taking 89 lines of dialogue for companion book was actionable). As for the qualitative prong, the entire Book is based on Ms. Rowling's fictional facts and world. Even those few entries identifying real places or things are defined solely as Ms. Rowling defined them in the Series. Such wholesale copying of protected expression is clearly qualitatively significant. *Castle Rock,* 150 F.3d at 138; *see also Twin Peaks,* 996 F.2d at 1372-1373; *Paramount,* 11 F. Supp. 2d at 332-33. RDR's extensive copying, both quantitatively and qualitatively, plainly violates Plaintiffs' copyrights in the *Harry Potter* Works.

2. Defendant's Use Is Not "Fair"

Although RDR will presumably argue that its wholesale copying is a "fair use," the law is clear that repackaging "fictional facts" from another's creative work is *not* a fair use. *Castle Rock,* 150 F.3d at 142-43, 144 *(Seinfeld* trivia book containing numerous fictional facts and references not fair use); *Paramount,* 11 F. Supp. 2d at 335 (book that merely recounted television series' fictional history and characters not fair use); *Twin Peaks,* 996 F.2d at 1375, 1376-77 (companion book retelling fictional "plot details" from *Twin Peaks* was not fair use).

Authors have the exclusive right to control and authorize derivative works, 17 U.S.C. § 106, giving them an incentive to create. The fair use doctrine is a narrow exception that permits limited unauthorized use for purposes such as criticism, comment, news, reporting, teaching, scholarship, or research of a copyrighted work. 17 U.S.C. §107. The fair use doctrine should be cautiously applied, and is not applicable here because it would harm economic efficiency thereby contravening the policies that underlie the Copyright Act. In determining whether a use is "fair," courts analyze: (1) the purpose and character of the use; (2) the nature of the copyrighted work; (3) the amount and substantiality of the portion used in relation to the copyrighted work as a whole; and (4) the effect of the use upon the potential market for or value of the copyrighted work. *Campbell v. Acuff-Rose Music, Inc.,* 510 U.S. 569, 576-77 (1994); 17 U.S.C. §107. None of these factors favor RDR.

a. The Book is Not Transformative

To determine the purpose and character of a use, courts consider (1) whether the infringing work is commercial in nature; and (2) whether it transforms the original to create new, protected expression. *Campbell,* 510 U.S. at 578-579. The Book, a $24.95 mass-market book, undoubtedly is commercial. Profit is its only possible purpose as nearly all of its content is already freely available on the Website. Nor is it transformative, as it adds no value to the copyrighted work by using it as raw material "in the creation of new information, new aesthetics, new insights and understandings" and is merely meant to "repackage [the original work] to entertain [the original work's] viewers." *Castle Rock,* 150 F.3d at 142 (finding trivia book non-transformative).

The Book simply takes elements from the *Harry Potter* Works, using direct quotations, close paraphrasing or detailed plot summaries, and puts them in alphabetical order. "[C]ritically restructuring" elements of an original work into another "system of presentation" does not constitute a transformative purpose. *Castle* Rock, 150 F.3d at 142. In *Castle Rock,* for example, defendants created a quiz book based on *Seinfeld* that included "hundreds of spectacular questions of minute details from TV's greatest show about absolutely nothing." *Id.* at 136. The Second Circuit rejected defendants' argument that their book was transformative because it "decoded the...mystique that surrounds" the show and "articulate[d the sitcom's] true motive forces and its social and moral dimensions." *Id.* at 142. Here, as further evidence of the Book's lack of transformative purpose, it barely alters the original expression of the Series. *Id.* at 143. Vander Ark's diligence in listing the creative elements of Ms. Rowling's books does not make his alphabetical index a transformative fair use.

Further, where a detailed retelling of a plot merely "elaborates in detail far beyond what is required to serve any legitimate purpose," the first factor weighs in favor of the plaintiff. *Twin Peaks,* 996 F.2d at 1376. Because RDR's use of Ms. Rowling's protected expression "consists primarily of summarizing in great detail" the plots, characters and elements of the *Harry Potter* series and "goes far beyond merely identifying their basic outline for the transformative purposes of comment or criticism," the first factor favors Plaintiffs. *Id.* at 1375.

Finally, even where "the structure of the book differs from the dramatic linear format of the [underlying] Properties" RDR cannot show a transformative purpose. *Paramount,* 11 F. Supp. 2d at 332, 335 (book about *Star Trek* phenomenon consisted primarily of material taken from the various *Star Trek* properties and was insufficiently transformative despite humorous comments interspersed within plot summaries). Courts of other circuits agree. *See, e.g., Ty, Inc. v. Publications Int'l Ltd.,* 292 F.3d 512, 520 (7th Cir. 2002) (collector's guide for Beanie Baby dolls that contained only minimal accompanying commentary did not appear to constitute fair use), *on remand,* 333 F. Supp. 2d 705, 719 (N.D. Ill. 2004) (guide book was not transformative and not fair use); *Toho Co., Ltd. v. William Morrow and Co., Inc.,* 33 F. Supp. 2d 1206 (C.D. Cal. 1998) (rejecting fair use claim for a 227-page compendium containing detailed plot summaries in addition to commentary, critique, trivia and pictures from the *Godzilla* films and finding use non-transformative). Here, although the Book does not track the chronological format of the Series, it nonetheless contains all of the elements with which to reconstruct the "heart" (not to mention the minutia) of Ms. Rowling's story.

Moreover, RDR's portrayal of the Book as "scholarship" or "research" is a ruse, as it does not present "new information, new aesthetics, new insights and understandings." *Castle Rock,* 150 F.3d at 142. Just as it is not a "transformative use," the Book cannot reasonably be classified as a work of scholarship or research as understood in the field of scholarly publishing. The requirements for a "transformative" use are closely analogous to those for "scholarship" or "research," namely, that it have "some degree of originality or invention, constitute an original investigation, or invent or generate ... ideas leading to new or substantially improved insights." For a dictionary or "lexicon," in particular, the work must contribute in an original way to the creation, development or maintenance of the intellectual infrastructure -- that is, the language or discipline of "Harry Potter." The Book does none of these things, but as Vander Ark himself admits, merely catalogues information wholly and exclusively derived from Ms. Rowling. Moreover, notwithstanding its feigned argument that the Book is for academics and scholars, RDR specifically targeted mass-market children's bookstores and children's book buyers in its domestic sales strategy.

The Court need not decide whether every possible alphabetical catalogue of a work is a fair use. Given the unique facts *here,* where an author has long intended to publish an encyclopedia, her publishers have prepared material for her to use for that work, she is known for writing quickly and voluminously, she has granted fans wide latitude to create non-commercial websites and for scholars and others to do truly transformative works analyzing her books, and the content of the book at issue is available in a non-commercial way, to deprive Ms. Rowling of her right to reserve for herself the ability to create an encyclopedia for the Series is unwarranted.

b. Plaintiffs' Creative Works Deserve Strong Protection

The second factor, nature of the copyrighted work, recognizes that "some works are closer to the core of intended copyright protection than others," and considers whether the copyrighted work is expressive or creative and whether the work is published. *Castle Rock, 150* F.3d at 143. Here, the *Harry Potter* Works are clearly creative fictional works entitled to the strongest protection, particularly where the secondary work is "at best minimally transformative." *Id.* at 144; *see also Twin Peaks,* 996 F.2d at 1376 (second factor "must favor a creative and fictional work, no matter how successful"); *Paramount,* 11 F. Supp. 2d at 336 (resolving the factor in a single sentence because the determination was "straight forward").

c. The Book Misappropriates Ms. Rowling's Creative Expression

The third factor, the amount and substantiality of the portion used, asks whether the amount copied exceeds that necessary to further the purpose and character of the new work. *Campbell,* 510 U.S. at 586; *Castle Rock,* 150 F.3d at 144 (extensive use of underlying work suggested entertainment purpose rather than commentary). Here, RDR's Book takes every element and character from the Series and puts them in alphabetical order without a shred of analysis, commentary or reference to any other work. Entries for key characters "consist of long, detailed prose summarizing extensive portions of the plot" of the Series, far exceeding what would be necessary to comment on or analyze the *Harry Potter* Works. Other entries extensively paraphrase and quote lengthy portions verbatim, far beyond that necessary to create a legitimately transformative work. *See Castle Rock,* 150 F.3d at 144; *Twin Peaks Prods.,* 996 F.2d at 1376-77 (third factor favored plaintiffs where companion book "provides synopses for several episodes, lifting many parts verbatim from the script"); *see also Toho,* 33 F. Supp. 2d at 1217 (unauthorized *Godzilla* compendium not fair use; even some commentary on films did not justify pages and pages of plot summary). RDR's substantial taking from the Series weighs this factor in favor of Plaintiffs.

d. The Market For Ms. Rowling's Work Will Be Harmed

Under the fourth factor, courts must consider "the current and potential market" for derivative works in addition to the primary market for the original work itself, as well as whether "unrestricted and widespread conduct of the sort engaged in by the defendant...would result in a substantially adverse impact on the potential market for the original." *Campbell,* 510 U.S. at 590 (citations omitted). Unlike *Twin Peaks,* where the fourth factor favored defendant because its "work filled a market niche that the plaintiff simply had no interest in occupying," Ms. Rowling has made clear that she affirmatively intends to fill the market niche for a *Harry Potter* encyclopedia. *Twin* Peaks, 996 F.2d at 1377; *see also Toho,* 33 F. Supp. 2d at 1217 ("Because [defendant's] book and [plaintiffs licensee's] book are attempting to capitalize on this market, there would be an adverse effect on the potential market for [plaintiff]"); *Roy Export Co. Estab.* v. *Columbia Broad. Sys. Inc.,* 503 F. Supp. 1137, 1146 (S.D.N.Y. 1980) (value of author's exclusive right to make derivative work "would certainly seem to be diminished by the ability of another to use the copyrighted work in order to compete at will with the derivative work"). Not only is Ms. Rowling entitled to exclusivity in her derivative works under the Act, but from a marketing perspective RDR could usurp the benefits of first publication by using Ms. Rowling's own creative works.

Moreover, RDR has deliberately timed the release of the Book to follow close on the publication of the final installment of the Series, capitalizing on the excitement surrounding its release and cornering the market before Ms. Rowling has a chance to draft her companion guide and obtaining an undeserved market advantage while lessening the distinctiveness of Ms. Rowling's subsequent book. In addition, the Book's publication would rob Plaintiffs of licensing opportunities and undermine their licensing program because they would be unable to guarantee exclusivity to potential derivative works licensees or to properly enforce quality control.

In *Twin Peaks,* the Second Circuit held that a companion book to the *Twin Peaks* program would "almost certainly interfere with legitimate markets for derivative works," in part because the copyright owner had already licensed two companion books and stated its intention to license more. *Twin Peaks,* 996 F.2d at 1377. A copyright owner's claim is stronger where, as here, the infringing book merely reports on the content of the original in extraordinary detail. RDR seeks to occupy a market for derivative works that Ms. Rowling is exclusively entitled to exploit either herself or through the grant of exclusive licenses. This harm is not merely hypothetical: Ms. Rowling already has an extensive licensing program in place and plans to exercise certain of her exclusive rights *herself,* donating the proceeds to charity as she did with the $30 million generated by the Companion Books. Plaintiffs also carefully maintain their licensing programs to ensure the quality associated with the *Harry Potter* Works. RDR's attempt to destroy this exclusivity not only harms the market for currently licensed works by tarnishing the reputation of the *Harry Potter* Works by failing to meet Plaintiffs' exacting standards, but harms the potential market for future licenses by introducing additional transactions costs and uncertainty. If RDR is permitted to continue its infringement, the specter of many more unauthorized infringers would chill the license market that Plaintiffs have carefully cultivated. Thus, the fourth factor also favors Plaintiffs.

e. RDR's Bad Faith Precludes a Finding of Fair Use

Finally, in addition to the four statutory factors, courts consider whether a defendant has run afoul of principles of equity, "presuppos[ing] good faith and fair dealing." *Roy,* 503 F. Supp. at 1146-47. Here, RDR and Vander Ark conducted their entire enterprise in clandestine fashion. They knew Ms. Rowling intended to write her own encyclopedia. Mr. Vander Ark even told other fans that writing an encyclopedia without permission would be a violation of her rights. Yet he proceeded to do so anyway, after being indemnified by RDR, when he was rejected as a co-author by Ms. Rowling's agent. RDR then began its plan to market the book under the radar to publishers who do not publish the *Harry Potter* books, and, after Plaintiffs got wind of RDR's plans, to stall Plaintiffs while continuing to market the book and to refuse to produce a copy of the manuscript.

Because RDR intentionally sought to capitalize on the fame and success of the *Harry Potter* Works through unauthorized wholesale copying of those works, Plaintiffs are likely to succeed on their claim for copyright infringement. The record clearly supports injunctive relief.

B. RDR Has Engaged in False Endorsement and False Advertising

RDR's false and misleading promotion and marketing of the Book also warrant injunctive relief. Adding two artfully-placed disclaimers and the term "unofficial" to the revised cover still leaves the most pernicious element of the original, a 2004 quote by Ms. Rowling about the *Website*. RDR's use of this quote to suggest falsely that Ms. Rowling has endorsed the Book, which she vehemently opposes, constitutes false endorsement and false advertising under the Lanham Act. *See* 15 U.S.C. § 1125(a)(1)(A); § 1125(a)(1)(B).

1.   Use Of Ms. Rowling's Name Is An Actionable False Endorsement

A false endorsement claim requires a showing that: (1) goods or services were involved; (2) interstate commerce was affected; and (3) there was a false designation of origin or false description of the goods or services. *Allen v. Nat 'I Video, Inc.,* 610 F. Supp. 612, 625-26 (S.D.N.Y. 1985) (use of celebrity's picture falsely implied endorsement); *see also Dallas Cowboys Cheerleaders, Inc. v. Pussycat Cinema, Ltd.,* 604 F.2d 200, 204-05 (2d Cir. 1979).

The Book, a product sold in interstate commerce, satisfies the first two prongs. The third turns on whether RDR's use of Ms. Rowling's name and quote falsely suggests that she endorses the Book. *See Allen,* 610 F. Supp. at 627. In analyzing false endorsement, courts consider: (1) the strength of plaintiffs' marks and name; (2) the similarity of the marks; (3) the proximity of the products; (4) evidence of actual confusion as to source or sponsorship; (5) sophistication of defendant's audience; and (6) defendant's good or bad faith. *Tin Pan Apple, Inc.* v. *Miller Brewing Co.,* 737 F. Supp. 826, 834 (S.D.N.Y. 1990); *Allen,* 610 F. Supp. at 627.

The first factor, strength of the mark, measures the extent to which Ms. Rowling's name has developed a favorable association in the mind of consumers. *Allen,* 610 F. Supp. at 627. As the author of a true literary phenomenon, Ms. Rowling's name could hardly be more famous. She also owns a registered trademark in her name. Thus, that factor favors Plaintiffs, as does the second factor, similarity of the marks, because the marks are identical -- the Book's back cover uses "J.K. Rowling" twice. *See Virgin Enters. Ltd.* v. *Nawab,* 335 F.3d 141, 149-50 (2d Cir. 2003). The third factor, proximity of the goods, also favors Plaintiffs because the goods are both books about the fictional world of *Harry Potter. See Fun-Damental Too, Ltd.* v. *Gemmy Indus. Corp.,* 111 F.3d 993, 1003 (2d Cir. 1997).

As to the fourth factor, the Book is unreleased so there has not yet been an opportunity for consumer confusion. Nevertheless, it is well settled in this Circuit that a properly conducted survey is admissible to prove confusion. *Consumers Union of the U.S., Inc.* v. *The New Regina Corp.*, 664 F. Supp. 753, 768 (S.D.N.Y. 1987). Plaintiffs' expert, Dr. Helfgott, conducted such a survey in keeping with the guidelines set out by the *Manual for Complex Litigation. See Manual for Complex Litigation*, 116 (5th ed. 1981).

The survey showed that 55% of respondents believed the quote indicated that Ms. Rowling had endorsed the Book. Even discounting individuals who displayed other types of confusion, such as thinking that Ms. Rowling owned the Website or wrote the Book (arguably evidence of actual confusion), the survey still identified a 38% confusion rate, well above the level of actionable confusion. *See RJR Foods, Inc.* v. *White Rock Corp.*, 603 F.2d 1058, 1061 (2d Cir. 1979) (15-20% rate of confusion supported finding of trademark infringement); *Miramax Films Corp.* v. *Columbia Pictures Entm 't, Inc.*, 996 F. Supp. 294, 299-300 (S.D.N.Y. 1998); (17% and 20% confusion rates supported a §43(a)(1)(A) claim); *McNeil-PPC, Inc.* v. *Pfizer Inc.*, 351 F. Supp. 2d 226, 249 (S.D.N.Y. 2005) (20% confusion rate was considered significant).

Plaintiffs' survey produced these strong results despite RDR's recent addition of disclaimers. RDR has failed to meet its heavy burden of showing that its disclaimers are effective in reducing consumer confusion. *See Home Box Office, Inc.* v. *Showtime/Movie Channel, Inc.*, 832 F.2d 1311, 1315 (2d Cir. 1987); *Clinique Labs., Inc.* v. *Dep Corp.*, 945 F. Supp. 547, 556 (S.D.N.Y. 1996). When evaluating the effectiveness of a disclaimer, courts consider several factors, including the font size and text of the disclaimer. *Yurman Design, Inc. v. Diamonds and Time, Halton's Jeweler's, Inc.*, 169 F. Supp. 2d 181, 186 (SD.N.Y. 2001) ("miniscule" disclaimer did not effectively eliminate the confusion created by the ad). Here, both disclaimers are tiny and difficult to see, and are plainly ineffective.

As to the fifth factor (sophistication of defendant' s audience), RDR clearly seeks to mass-market the Book, targeting the children's book section of large retail chains. Given how the quote is used, even the savviest fans would believe that Ms. Rowling has endorsed the Book. *Allen*, 610 F. Supp. at 628 ("at a cursory glance, many consumers, even sophisticated ones, are likely to be confused."). Under the sixth factor, RDR unquestionably acted in bad faith by purposely including Ms. Rowling's name and quote on its proposed cover and marketing materials without her permission. Nor did RDR ever advise Ms. Rowling or her representatives of its plans to turn material from the Website into a book. In fact, RDR instructed foreign agents not to pitch the Book to any of Ms. Rowling's ublishers. Even now

RDR continues to use Ms. Rowling's name and quote to promote the Book by falsely suggesting she has endorsed it. *See Tin Pan Apple,* 737 F. Supp. at 835 ("That is bad faith raised to a higher power."). Because each of the factors weighs heavily in Plaintiffs' favor, this Court should find that Plaintiffs are likely to succeed on their false endorsement claim.

2. RDR's Conduct Constitutes False Advertising

RDR's use of Ms. Rowling's quote on the cover of the Book also constitutes false advertising under the Lanham Act. Plaintiffs can establish this claim by demonstrating that RDR (1) uses a false or misleading description of fact or representation of fact (2) in interstate commerce in connection with goods or services in commercial advertising or promotion and (3) it is likely that some harm will result from the misrepresentation. 15 U.S.C. § 1125(a)(1)(B); *see Coca-Cola Co. v. Tropicana Products, Inc.,* 690 F.2d 312, 314 (2d Cir. 1982).

As to the first element, Plaintiffs' survey shows that RDR's use of Ms. Rowling's quote tends to mislead a significant number of consumers into thinking that she endorsed the Book. Plaintiffs must also show that the misrepresentation is material and would influence consumers' purchasing decisions. *Vidal Sassoon Inc. v. Bristol-Myers Co.,* 661 F.2d 272, 278 (2d Cir. 1981). Clearly RDR feels that the quote is material in that it will cause fans to buy the Book otherwise it would not have included it on the Book's cover and kept it there even after this suit began. *See Mylan Pharms., Inc. v. Procter & Gamble Co.,* 443 F. Supp. 2d 453, 463 (S.D.N.Y. 2006) (ad falsely implying that products were the same was material). Plaintiffs can also satisfy the second prong, as RDR has marketed the Book using the misleading quote and made use of similar marketing materials in the course of its dealings with book buyers and stores across the country.

To establish the third prong, that the false advertising would give rise to harm, Plaintiffs need only show that they have a "reasonable interest" in being protected against the false advertising and a "reasonable basis" for believing that interest is likely to be damaged. *See Johnson & Johnson v. Carter-Wallace, Inc.,* 631 F.2d 186, 190 (2d Cir. 1980). Here, Plaintiffs have worked hard to maintain a licensing strategy and ensure that Ms. Rowling's name is used only in connection with high quality, authorized products. Plaintiffs also have a significant interest in protecting against misleading statements that could lead fans to mistakenly purchase the Book instead of Ms. Rowling's own future authorized encyclopedia. Thus, the Court should find that Plaintiffs are likely to succeed on their false advertising claim.

III. **PLAINTIFFS WILL SUFFER IRREPARABLE INJURY ABSENT RELIEF**

Courts routinely hold that trademark or copyright infringement gives rise to a presumption of irreparable injury. *See, e.g., ABKCO Music,* 96 F.3d at 66 (a *prima facie* case of copyright infringement supports a presumption of irreparable harm); *Hasbro Inc. v. Lanard Toys, Ltd.,* 858 F.2d 70, 73 (2d Cir. 1988) ("[i]n a Lanham Act case a showing of likelihood of confusion establishes both a likelihood of success on the merits and irreparable harm..."). As Plaintiffs have clearly demonstrated a likelihood of success on the merits of their copyright and trademark infringement claims, irreparable injury may be presumed.

Even beyond the presumption of injury in intellectual property cases, however, it is clear that Plaintiffs will suffer irreparable harm absent an injunction. Were RDR permitted to proceed, Ms. Rowling -- the copyright owner and creator of Harry Potter -- would be "scooped" from doing a companion guide based on her own original works. Ms. Rowling has clearly stated her intent to publish such a work, and has been preparing materials to do just that, but RDR's Book would make any subsequent work by Ms. Rowling less distinctive and therefore less successful. Moreover, allowing RDR to proceed would open the flood gates to other similar works, undermining Plaintiffs' long-term licensing and policing strategy -- to which they have devoted tremendous time and resources -- to protect and ensure the high quality of their book franchise and the strength of their intellectual property rights.

Additionally, as Prof. Landes, a noted economist focusing on intellectual property issues, has made clear, Ms. Rowling's right to control derivative works must be preserved not only to avoid the public harm, confusion and high transactions costs that would result from the myriad of individuals who could claim copyright protection in their unauthorized derivative works, but also to avoid the nonsensical result of Ms. Rowling facing liability for copyright infringement based on her encyclopedia of her own works. This is a real risk as RDR has already accused Warner Bros. of violating its copyright in a timeline based on the events of the Series. Moreover, in a striking case of double standards, the Website is replete with various copyright warnings to prevent individuals from copying material on the site. To avoid harm to Plaintiffs and the public, this Court should enjoin RDR. To find otherwise would narrow the scope of rights available to all copyright holders wishing to make use of their own creations in contravention to the constitutional grant intended to encourage creation.

IV. THE BALANCE OF HARDSHIPS FAVORS PLAINTIFFS, AND THERE ARE FAIR GROUNDS FOR LITIGATION

Because Plaintiffs have shown that they are likely to succeed on the merits, the Court need not consider whether the balance of hardships tips decidedly in favor of Plaintiffs and whether there are fair grounds for litigation. *See ABKCO Music,* 96 F.3d at 64. Nevertheless, Plaintiffs can satisfy the alternate test as well. As set forth above, if the Court allows RDR to release the Book, it would cause not just harm, but irreparable injury to Plaintiffs. *See New Line Cinema,* 693 F. Supp. at 1531 (balance of hardships favored copyright owner who offered evidence that the low-quality music video could dissuade an unspecified number of individuals from seeing its upcoming film). Nor would every person who purchases the Book necessarily purchase a second encyclopedia, even if it is written by Ms. Rowling.

In contrast, the only harm RDR would suffer if an injunction issued would be lost sales. RDR has not yet finished setting the type on the Book, much less expended much money on printing or marketing it. RDR's contract with Mr. Vander Ark does not even require payment of an advance. This Book is not the only work that RDR sells, as demonstrated by the listings on its website, but even if RDR had invested millions and the Book constituted its entire business, as Judge Hand made clear, injunctive relief would still be appropriate in light of RDR's deliberately infringing conduct. *See My-T Fine Corp. v. Samuels,* 69 F.2d 76, 78 (2d Cir. 1934) (Hand, J.) ("advantages built upon a deliberately plagiarized makeup do not seem to us to give the borrower any standing to complain that his vested interests will be disturbed"); *see also Concrete Mach. Co. v. Classic Lawn Ornaments,* 843 F.2d 600, 612 (1st Cir. 1988) (internal quotations and citations omitted) ("[w]here the only hardship that the defendant will suffer is lost profits from an activity which has been shown likely to be infringing, such an argument in defense merits little equitable consideration.... Such considerations apply even to a business which is exclusively based on an infringing activity and which would be virtually destroyed by a preliminary injunction."); *Apple Computer Inc.* v. *Franklin Computer Corp.,* 714 F.2d 1240, 1255 (3d Cir. 1983), cert. dismissed, 464 U.S. 1033 (1984) (internal citations omitted) (if defendant's reliance on infringing activity for survival barred issuance of injunction, "a knowing infringer would be permitted to construct its business around its infringement, a result we cannot condone.").

The Court should also take into account that RDR should not be allowed to wrongfully benefit from the promotional campaigns associated with the recently released final *Harry Potter* Book and the upcoming DVD Release of the fifth *Harry Potter* Film. *See New Line Cinema,* 693 F. Supp. at 1531 (defendants were not entitled to "obtain the benefits of [plaintiffs) massive promotional campaign"). Simply put, injunctive relief is a matter of equity and equity favors Plaintiffs in this case.

CONCLUSION

For all of the foregoing reasons, Plaintiffs respectfully request that the motion for preliminary injunction be granted.

Dated: January 15, 2008

O'MELVENY & MYERS LLP, Times Square Tower, 7 Times Square New York, New York 10036, Tel: (212) 326-2000 Fax: (212) 326-2061.

Attorneys for Plaintiffs

Respectfully Submitted:

Dale M. Cendali
Melanie Bradley

DEFENDANT'S MEMORANDUM IN OPPOSITION TO PLAINTIFFS' MOTION FOR PRELIMINARY INJUNCTION

WARNER BROS. ENTERTAINMENT INC. AND
J.K. ROWLING,

Plaintiffs,

-against-

RDR BOOKS and DOES 1-10

Defendants.

Case No. 07-09667 (RPP)   Filed: February 8, 2008

PRELIMINARY STATEMENT

In this action, a distinguished and tremendously successful novelist demands the suppression of a reference guide to her works. J.K. Rowling, author of the Harry Potter books, asserts that this reference guide infringes both her copyright in the seven Potter novels and her right to publish, at some unidentified point in the future, a reference guide of her own. In support of her position she appears to claim a monopoly on the right to publish literary reference guides, and other non-academic research, relating to her own fiction.

This is a right no court has ever recognized. It has little to recommend it. If accepted, it would dramatically extend the reach of copyright protection, and eliminate an entire genre of literary supplements: third party reference guides to fiction, which for centuries have helped readers better access, understand and enjoy literary works. By extension, it would threaten not just reference guides, but encyclopedias, glossaries, indexes, and other tools that provide useful information about copyrighted works. Ms. Rowling's intellectual property rights simply do not extend so far and, even if they did, she has not shown that the publication of *this* reference guide poses a sufficient threat of irreparable harm to justify an injunction. Her preliminary injunction motion should be denied.

FACTUAL BACKGROUND

The reference guide that Ms. Rowling seeks to suppress is the Lexicon. Its author, Steven Vander Ark, is a former grade school teacher who has spent much of the last eight years' running a web site devoted to the Harry Potter novels (variously, the "Lexicon Website," the "website and the "site"). The website, which has a volunteer staff of ten, has developed an enormous volume of material on the Potter books, material that analyzes and describes all the characters, places, spells, creatures and physical objects found in the seven novels. Vander Ark has organized this material in "A to Z" fashion, with concise entries presented in alphabetical order; he has called this material a "lexicon" and, since its first appearance on his website, this lexicon has been a favorite research tool of Harry Potter fans. In fact, it has long been a favorite of Ms. Rowling, who has called the materials on the website "great," given the site her "J.K. Rowling Fan Site Award" and recommended it to all Potter fans.

Last summer, shortly after the seventh and final Potter novel was released, the founder of Defendant RDR Books, Roger Rapoport, suggested to Vander Ark that RDR publish the A to Z listing in book form. Vander Ark agreed, and provided RDR with a manuscript, containing a condensed version of the website lexicon. Like the Lexicon Website, the Lexicon book was designed to provide a single source in which readers could find description, definitions, analyses and information about the world described in the Potter books.

Shortly after RDR Books announced its intention to publish the Lexicon, Plaintiffs commenced this action, alleging among other things that the Lexicon infringes Ms. Rowling's copyrights, and the Lexicon's cover and marketing plan are likely to confuse consumers and infringe plaintiff Warner's trademarks. Plaintiffs ask this Court to preliminarily enjoin publication and distribution of the Lexicon in order to protect Ms. Rowling's right to be the "first to publish" a companion book to the Potter series.

It is far too late, however, for Ms. Rowling to publish the first Potter companion book, or even the first Harry Potter lexicon. Nearly 200 Harry Potter companion guides already have been published, many of which incorporate A to Z listings in a manner that closely resembles the Lexicon's. Defendant RDR provides with its supporting papers six Harry Potter companion books that incorporate extensive lexicons; each was published since 2004, and is available in New York City. No injunction can undo that.

Unique or not, the Lexicon is a serious book – a reference guide that is the product of eight years work by Vander Ark and his staff. As Professor

Janet Sorensen explains in her declaration, lexicons like this one have an important and distinguished place in the literary world. Indeed, the value and importance of this lexicon is evident from its contents. It organizes a tremendous amount of information into a concise and readable form with citations to the scores of original sources it draws upon. At the same time, it provides a significant amount of original analysis and commentary concerning everything from insights into the personality of key characters, relationships among them, the meaning of various historical and literary allusions, as well as internal inconsistencies and mistakes in the novels. Finally, the Lexicon collects a wide array of additional information gleaned from painstaking collection and analysis of Ms. Rowling's interviews and public statements, which reveal additional details about not only the Harry Potter Works, but the creative inspirations behind them. In sum, the Lexicon "help[s] readers to construct the universe of the Potter books in their minds, to understand its rich connections to the wide world in which we live, and to encourage the impulse to imagine a universe beyond the one depicted in the books." It is the type of highly "transformative" work that has always been held to constitute fair use of copyrighted materials. It presents neither a Copyright nor Lanham Act violation, and Plaintiffs' motion for a preliminary injunction should be denied.

ARGUMENT

A preliminary injunction is an "extraordinary remedy." *Twentieth Century Fox Film Corp. v. Marvel Enterprises, Inc.*, 277 F.3d 253, 258 (2d Cir. 2002). A party seeking one must demonstrate (1) irreparable harm in the absence of an injunction, and (2) either (a) a likelihood of success on the merits or (b) sufficiently serious questions going to the merits and a balance of hardships tipping decidedly in the movant's favor. *See MyWebGrocer, L.L.C. v. Hometown Info, Inc.*, 375 F.3d 190, 192 (2d Cir. 2004). Plaintiffs have not made that showing. They fail to show likely success on any of their claims, or any irreparable harm in the absence of an injunction.

I. Plaintiffs Cannot Show Likelihood Of Success On Their Copyright Claim

A. Plaintiffs Fail To Show A Prima Facie Case Of Infringement
While the Copyright Act reserves certain exclusive rights to Ms. Rowling, it does not give her complete control over all things Harry Potter. In order to show a *prima facie* case of infringement, Ms. Rowling must first show that RDR exercised one of the exclusive rights reserved to her by the Copyright Act. *See* 17 U.S.C. § 106. But the Lexicon does not "reproduce" the Harry Potter Works (or any one of them) in any meaningful sense of the word. *See* 17 U.S.C § 106(1). Nor is it a derivative work. *See* 17 U.S.C. §

106(2). Examples of derivative works include "a translation, musical arrangement, dramatization, fictionalization, motion picture version, sound recording, art reproduction, abridgment, condensation, or any other form in which a work may be recast, transformed, or adapted." 17 U.S.C. § 101; *see also Twin Peaks Prods., Inc. v. Publ'ns Int'l, Ltd.*, 996 F.2d 1366 (2d Cir. 1993) (derivative work transforms original from one medium to another). A reference guide to copyrighted works is not among the examples listed, and does not recast, transform or adapt copyrighted works in comparable ways. *See Ty, Inc. v. Publ'ns Int'l Ltd.*, 292 F.3d 512, 520-21 (7th Cir. 2002) (Posner, J.) (collector's guide to Beanie Babies not a derivative work). If anything, the Lexicon is a "supplementary" work the purpose of which is "explaining . . . commenting upon [and] assisting in the use of" the Harry Potter Works. *See* Benjamin Kaplan, *An Unhurried View of Copyright* at 100, n.61 (1967). Congress has specifically considered and rejected the suggestion that "supplementary works" be added to the exclusive rights secured by section 106. *See id.* That decision should not be undone here.

Even if the Lexicon were a "reproduction" or a "derivative work," Ms. Rowling would still have to show substantial similarity between the Lexicon and the Harry Potter Works. *See e.g., Repp v. Weber*, 132 F.3d 882, 889 (2d Cir. 1997) (upon showing actual copying, plaintiff must still show substantial similarity between the works at issue). Ms. Rowling cannot do that under the traditional "ordinary observer" or "total concept and feel" tests, or under the quantitative / qualitative test applied in *Castle Rock Entertainment, Inc. v. Carol Publishing Group, Inc.*, 150 F.3d 132, 138-41 (2d Cir. 1998). On the contrary, *Castle Rock* itself acknowledged that a secondary work may cease to be substantially similar if it transforms the original sufficiently. *See id.* at 143 n.9. As explained below, that is precisely the case here.

B. The Lexicon Is Protected By Fair Use
The fair use doctrine protects the right to use copyrighted material for new and transformative purposes. *See Campbell v. Acuff-Rose Music, Inc.*, 510 U.S. 569 (1994). Here, it protects RDR's right to publish the Lexicon, a valuable reference tool that helps readers to better access, understand and enjoy the Harry Potter works.

Anticipating RDR's fair use rights, Plaintiffs assert that fair use is a "narrow exception" that should be "cautiously applied" only where it enhances "economic efficiency." But Plaintiffs have it backwards. Far from a "narrow exception," fair use is an integral part of the Copyright Act designed to further its most basic purposes by balancing the need to both protect copyrighted material and "to allow others to build upon it." *Campbell*, 510 U.S. at 575 (fair use is "necessary to fulfill copyright's purpose"); *see also*

Pierre N. Leval, *Toward a Fair Use Standard*, 103 Harv. L. Rev. 1105, 1107, 1110 (1990); 17 U.S.C. §§ 106, 107. The purpose fair use serves is not simply economic. It is a critical "First Amendment safeguard" designed to prevent copyright law from unduly burdening free speech. *Eldred v. Ashcroft*, 537 U.S. 186, 221 (2003); *Suntrust Bank v. Houghton Mifflin Co.*, 268 F.3d 1257, 1263-65 (11th Cir. 2001). Insofar as any "caution" is appropriate here, it should be exercised *against* injunctive relief in light of the free speech and First Amendment interests that fair use protects. *See Campbell*, 510 U.S. at 578, n.10 (urging caution against injunctive relief over "reasonable contentions of fair use") (internal citations omitted); *Suntrust*, 268 F.3d at 1265 (reversing preliminary injunction; courts must be cautious in granting injunctions over a "colorable fair-use defense"); Mark A. Lemley and Eugene Volokh, *Freedom of Speech and Injunctions in Copyright Cases*, 48 Duke L. J. 147 (1998) (preliminary injunctions in copyright and trademark cases should be subject to traditional First Amendment analysis as prior restraints on speech).

In assessing fair use, the Court is guided by four statutory factors. *See Campbell*, 510 U.S. at 577; 17 U.S.C § 107. They are non-exclusive and must be weighed together in light of the underlying purposes of copyright. *See Campbell*, 510 U.S. at 577-78. While they inform the fair use analysis, "the ultimate test of fair use" is whether copyright's goal of "'promot[ing] the Progress of Science and useful Arts' . . . would be better served by allowing the use than by preventing it." *Castle Rock*, 150 F.3d at 132 (quoting U.S. Const. art. I, § 8, cl. 8; *Arica Institute, Inc. v. Palmer*, 970 F.2d 1067, 1077 (2d Cir. 1992)). Here, there is no doubt RDR meets that test.

1.   Purpose And Character Of The Use

The "heart of the fair use inquiry" lies in the first factor – the purpose and character of the use. *Blanch v. Koons*, 467 F.3d 244, 251 (2d Cir. 2006); *see also* 17 U.S.C. § 107(1). The focus of this analysis is the "transformative" nature of the accused work. *See Campbell*, 510 U.S. at 579; *Bill Graham Archives v. Dorling Kindersley Ltd.*, 448 F.3d 605, 608 (2d Cir. 2006). A work is transformative when it does not "merely supersede the objects of the original creation," but rather "adds something new, with a further purpose or different character, altering the first with new expression, meaning, or message." *Campbell*, 510 U.S. at 579. This may involve combining copyrighted expression with original expression to produce a new creative work. *See, e.g., Blanch*, 467 F.3d at 251-52. Or it may involve incorporating copyrighted expression into a reference tool that organizes information and renders it more accessible. *See, e.g., Perfect 10, Inc, v. Amazon.com, Inc.*, 508 F.3d 1146, 1165 (9th Cir. 2007) (reversing preliminary injunction; search engine is "highly transformative" because it incorporates original work into reference tool); *Castle Rock*, 150 F.3d at 143 ("secondary work need not necessarily transform the original work's expression to have a transformative purpose"); *New York Times Co. v. Roxbury Data Interface, Inc.*, 434 F.Supp. 217, 221 (D. N.J. 1977) (denying preliminary injunction; index of names appearing in *New York Times* served public interest because it enables users to locate information more quickly).

Plaintiffs contend the Lexicon is not transformative because it merely "repackages" the Harry Potter Works and contains no original analysis. But a thoughtful review of the Lexicon reveals significant, transformative functions that add extensive value, understanding and insights to the original works.

Organizational Value. The Harry Potter universe is spread over seven novels totaling over a million words, five feature films, and other media, including video games and trading cards. Thousands of characters, places and things populate these works. Still more information about them is available from other sources, such as scores of interviews that J.K. Rowling has given over the years, and newsletters she prepared for fan club members. The Lexicon organizes, synthesizes and discusses this mass of information in the form of a reference volume that makes it easier for readers to locate, access, and understand the information that is spread across so many disparate sources. With its extensive citations to original sources, the Lexicon also permits readers to locate information in the original sources, much like an index would. This organizational function, and the utility that follows from it, is alone sufficient to show the Lexicon is transformative. *See Perfect 10*, 508 F.3d at 1165; *Roxbury Data*, 434 F.Supp. at 221.

The value of reference tools like the Lexicon is especially well-established in regard to literary works. Reference guides like the Lexicon that index the characters, spaces, and times of literary works "have been part and parcel of the literary culture for at least as long as such works have been circulated commercially." They help readers analyze, approach, and make sense of printed texts, and often spur further research and discussion. They are particularly valuable in regard to literary works that contain large and complex universes of characters and places, including not only Ms. Rowling's work, but also that of other authors like Charles Dickens, Thomas Hardy, Thomas Pynchon, J.R.R. Tolkien and C.S. Lewis. Rather than serving as a substitute for reading the original novels, these reference works help readers better understand, appreciate and enjoy the original literature.

Original Commentary and Analysis. The Lexicon also contains a significant amount of original commentary and analysis. It contains insightful discussions of key characters that go far beyond simply "tak[ing] elements from the Harry Potter Works" while "summarizing" and rearranging them. The entry for Neville Longbottom, for example, contains extensive observations about the nature of his bravery and leadership. The entry for Luna Lovegood likewise includes analytical observations about her nature, each supported by references to actions and events from the Harry Potter Works. Similarly, the entry for Draco Malfoy offers hypotheses about his motivations and his nature, and again supports these hypotheses with textual references. In other entries, such as the one for Wingardium Leviosa, the Lexicon authors theorize and interpret nuanced meaning of events in the books. These entries, and many others like them, do not simply "repackage" material found in the Harry Potter Works, they offer critical interpretations of the characters as a book review or essay might.

Still other entries analyze the relationship among characters, noting where shared names have no familial significance, or hypothesize on relationships and family trees. The Lexicon also offers observations regarding factual events, and the connections among events and the logical consequences of certain truths. This analysis of connections among disparate elements within the Harry Potter Works likewise enhances the reading experience by adding new insights, perceptions and judgments not found in the original works.

In addition to this analysis, the Lexicon decodes the meaning of many geographical and historical references, folklore and literary allusions, and provides etymologies of invented terms and names, as well as translates cross-cultural references used in the Harry Potter series. The vast bulk of this information is drawn not from any of the Harry Potter Works, but independent sources such as "Brewer's Dictionary of Phrase and Fable," etymological dictionaries, "Bullfinch's Mythology," "The Field Guide to the Little People," and the "New Shorter Oxford English Dictionary." This original analysis adds dimensions and layers to the characters, places, objects and spells found in Harry Potter by describing the roots of the words used and mapping the fictional facts onto places, activities and events of the real world, which in turn fosters a more complex and sophisticated comprehension, interpretations and enjoyment of the original works.

Finally, the detailed research that went into the Lexicon revealed myriad errors and inconsistencies in the Harry Potter Works and subtle differences among the books published in various locations. For example, students are only supposed to attend Hogwarts for seven years, yet Ms. Rowling included Hogwarts student Marcus Flint in one too many books, making him an "eighth year" student.

Additional Research and New Information. In addition to the above, the Lexicon incorporates additional research and new information about the characters and things that appear in them. Lexicon authors pored over scores of interviews, newsletters, webcasts and speeches in which Ms. Rowling provides clues and further information not found in the Harry Potter Works themselves. One entry, for example, discusses the significance of Platform 9 ¾ – a hidden platform in King's Cross Station in London. The Lexicon explains that the platform is purposely filled with romantic imagery because Ms. Rowling's parents met there and it became so much a part of her "childhood folklore" that she wanted to include it in Harry Potter's life. Another entry describes a character from the novel *Harry Potter and the Goblet of Fire*, Natalie McDonald, whom Ms. Rowling named in honor of a Canadian child who died after writing Ms. Rowling a fan letter.

Any fair reading of the Lexicon reveals significant transformative value. It organizes information into a useful reference tool, adds original commentary and analysis, and includes the fruits of significant outside research concerning everything from etymology to connections between Ms. Rowling's personal life and her fictional creations. Plaintiffs' suggestion that the Lexicon does no more than "rearrange the furniture" is simply mistaken.

Plaintiffs' attempts to analogize this case to *Castle Rock* are likewise misguided. The accused work at issue in *Castle Rock* was the *Seinfeld Aptitude Test (SAT)*, "a 132-page book containing 643 trivia questions and answers about the events and characters depicted in [the] *Seinfeld* [television series]," asking, for example, "What candy does Kramer snack on while observing a surgical procedure from an operating-room balcony?" The court found the *SAT* served no transformative purpose because the *SAT* "simply poses trivia questions," could not be "used to research *Seinfeld*" and did not "contain [any] commentary or analysis about *Seinfeld*." The Lexicon, by contrast, is a valuable research tool, and contains significant commentary about the Harry Potter Works, as well as analysis of the nature and names of characters, places and things that appear in them, along with extensive citations to original sources. Moreover, its contents are drawn not simply from the Harry Potter Works, but scores of other sources, including other references books and many interviews with J.K. Rowling. The Lexicon, therefore, does much more than simply pose trivia questions. It is a "research tool" and does contain "commentary [and] analysis." *Castle Rock*, 150 F.3d at 143. In short, the Lexicon passes the test the *SAT* failed.

Plaintiffs' reliance on *Twin Peaks Productions, Inc. v. Publications Int'l, Ltd.*, 996 F.2d 1366 (2d Cir. 1993), *Paramount Pictures Corp. v. Carol Publishing Group*, 11 F. Supp. 2d 329 (S.D.N.Y. 1998), and *Toho Co. Ltd. v. William Morrow & Co. Ltd.*, 33 F. Supp. 2d 1206, 1217 (C.D. Cal. 1998), is likewise misplaced. None of the works at issue in those cases served a purpose comparable to the Lexicon's; each was essentially an abridgement that retold the original story in its original sequence, albeit in shortened form. *See Twin*

Peaks, 996 F.2d at 1372-73, 1375-76 (work at issue found to be an abridgement because it recounted "precisely the plot details" of television episodes "in the same sequence" as they appeared in the original series); *Paramount*, 11 F.Supp.2d at 335 (work at issue "simply retells the story of Star Trek in a condensed version"); *Toho*, 33 F.Supp.2d at 1217 (work at issue contained "extensive detailed plot summaries"). Each was therefore a plausible substitute for the original work.

The Lexicon is no such thing. It complements the Harry Potter Works (in the economic sense) by providing an informational resource, as well as original commentary, analysis and research, along with extensive citations to primary sources. If it is comparable to anything, it is the Beanie Baby collector's guide at issue in *Ty, Inc.* That work contained photographs of Beanie Babies, factual information about them, and occasional criticism. *See id.* at 519-20. The court concluded the collector's guide was like a book review, "which is a guide to a book." *Id.* at 520-21. Both, it explained, were "critical and evaluative as well as purely informational" and ownership of copyrights did not confer the right to control public discussion of the copyrighted works. *Id.* at 521. Ms. Rowling's copyrights do not extend to suppress a guide to her books, either.

In the end, no analogy or comparison is necessary here. The purpose of the Lexicon is unmistakable. Rather than serving as a substitute for reading the original Harry Potter Works, it helps readers better understand, appreciate and enjoy them. The Lexicon therefore serves a significantly different purpose than the Harry Potter Works, and is highly transformative. *See Campbell*, 510 U.S. at 579 (central focus of fair use is whether the new work supercedes the objects of the original creation).

2. Nature Of The Copyrighted Work

The second fair use factor focuses on "the nature of the copyrighted work." 17 U.S.C. § 107(2); *Bill Graham*, 448 F.3d at 612. While Plaintiffs suggest this factor favors them because the Harry Potter Works are creative, they ignore the fact that the second factor is of "limited usefulness" where a creative work is being used for a transformative purpose. *Bill Graham*, 448 F.3d at 612; *see also Blanch*, 467 F.3d at 257. Here, the Harry Potter Works have been used to create a valuable reference tool that helps readers to better access, understand and enjoy the Harry Potter works. (pp. 8-12, above.) Accordingly, the second factor has "limited weight" in this case. *See Bill Graham*, 448 F.3d at 612 (giving second factor "limited weight" where creative work was put to transformative use); *Blanch*, 467 F.3d at 257 (same).

3. Amount And Substantiality Of The Portion Used

The third fair use factor requires the Court to assess "the amount and substantiality of the portion used in relation to the copyrighted work as a whole." 17 U.S.C. § 107(3); *see also Blanch*, 467 F.3d at 257. While the Court must consider both the quality and quantity of the portion of the copyrighted work that was used, the central question is whether the extent of copying is reasonable in light of its purpose. *See Campbell*, 510 U.S. at 586; *Blanch*, 467 F.3d at 257; *Castle Rock*, 150 F.3d at 144. Depending on the purpose, using a substantial portion of a work – or even the whole thing – may be permissible. *See Bill Graham*, 448 F.3d at 613 (citing *Kelly v. Arriba Soft Corp.*, 336 F.3d 811, 821 (9th Cir. 2003); *Nuñez v. Caribbean Int'l News Corp.*, 235 F.3d 18, 24 (1st Cir. 2000)). This is particularly true where the accused work is a reference tool that presents factual information about copyrighted works. *See Perfect 10*, 508 F.3d at 1167-68 (search engine may copy entire photograph to facilitate search function); *Kelly*, 336 F.3d at 821 (same); *Ty, Inc.*, 292 F.3d at 521 (collector's guide may need to depict the entire line of Beanie Babies to provide a useful and comprehensive reference volume).

Plaintiffs contend the third factor favors them because the Lexicon draws a significant amount of information from the Harry Potter Works. But Plaintiffs ignore the purpose of the Lexicon, which is to create a reference guide by collecting, organizing and presenting factual information. While this information is drawn from myriad sources, creating a useful and comprehensive reference guide requires borrowing a significant amount of information from the Harry Potter Works. *See Ty*, 292 F.3d at 521 (reference guide "has to be comprehensive"). *Castle Rock* is inapposite because the trivia book at issue in that case was not a reference book and did not attempt to organize information in any useful way. *See Castle Rock*, 150 F.3d at 144. Its purpose was therefore distinctly different.

While the Lexicon draws a significant amount of *factual* information from the Harry Potter Works, it does not borrow the overarching plot sequence or story arc of the Harry Potter Works, or the pace, setting or dramatic structure of the story these works tell. That distinguishes this case from *Twin Peaks, Paramount*, and *Toho, supra*, all of which concerned works that retold the entire story of the copyrighted work in its original form and sequence. Nor, save for occasional short quotes, does the Lexicon borrow Ms. Rowling's actual prose.

The Lexicon takes no more than what is necessary to its purpose. It borrows the factual information necessary to create a valuable reference tool, but does not use the narrative, plot sequence or prose. The third factor therefore weighs distinctly in favor of RDR. *See Blanch*, 467 F.3d at 258 (third factor weighs "distinctly" in defendant's favor where artist used only the portion of copyrighted work necessary to his purpose).

4. Market Effect

The fourth factor is "the effect of the use upon the potential market for or value of the copyrighted work." 17 U.S.C. § 107(4). This factor "requires a balancing of the benefit the public will derive if the use is permitted" versus "the personal gain the copyright owner will receive if the use is denied." *Bill Graham*, 448 F.3d at 613 (quoting *MCA, Inc. v. Wilson*, 677 F.2d 180, 183 (2d Cir. 1981)); *Wright v. Warner Books, Inc.*, 953 F.2d 731, 739 (2d Cir. 1991).

Substantial Public Benefit. There can be no dispute the Lexicon creates substantial public value. As many previous lexicons and reference works have done for other works, the Lexicon helps readers to better access, understand and enjoy the Harry Potter works. Its utility is confirmed not only by the website's 50,000 page views per day, but by Plaintiffs themselves. Ms. Rowling herself has used the Lexicon website to check facts, and Warner Brothers used it for the same purpose in creating the Harry Potter movies. Plaintiffs' licensees use it too; the video game designers at Electronic Arts had print-outs of the Lexicon posted all over their walls during the development process of the Harry Potter video games.

No Cognizable Market Harm. In considering potential market harm, the Court must consider harm to the markets for both the original Harry Potter Works and derivative works, while recognizing that the "more transformative the secondary use" the less likely the secondary work is to substitute for the original. *Castle Rock*, 150 F.3d at 145 (citing *Campbell*, 510 U.S. at 591); *see Bill Graham*, 448 F.3d at 614-15.

Here, Plaintiffs cannot point to any cognizable market harm. Plaintiffs do not suggest that the Lexicon is a plausible substitute for any of the original Harry Potter Works; they do not suggest anyone would purchase the Lexicon instead of a Harry Potter novel, or instead of seeing a Harry Potter movie. Accordingly, the Lexicon does not present any potential harm to the markets for the original Harry Potter Works. *See Bill Graham*, 448 F.3d at 614; *Castle Rock*, 150 F.3d at 145; *see also Ty, Inc.*, 292 F.3d at 517-18 (secondary works that are economic complements present no cognizable market harm).

Instead, Plaintiffs complain the Lexicon "seeks to occupy a market for derivative works" that is Ms. Rowling's alone to license and exploit. But Plaintiffs are wrong for at least three independent reasons. First, the Lexicon is not a derivative work because it does not adapt or recast the story, so it does not "occupy" any derivative market.

Second, derivative markets are not Plaintiffs' alone to exploit. Derivative works are eligible for fair use protection too, so Plaintiffs cannot prevail simply by showing the Lexicon is a derivative work. *See* 17 U.S.C. §§ 106 and 107; *Campbell*, 510 U.S. at 592-93 (applying fair use analysis to parody rap derivative).

If the Lexicon were a derivative work, the question would become whether the Lexicon presents any cognizable harm. *See Bill Graham*, 448 F.3d at 614-15 (no cognizable market harm where defendant's use of concert posters falls into a "transformative market"). The more transformative the derivative work, the less likely it is to present cognizable market harm. *See Campbell*, 510 U.S. at 592-93. The derivative works at issue in *Castle Rock*, *Twin Peaks* and *Toho* were found to be non-transformative, so the Court reserved the derivative markets in those cases to the copyright owner. *See Castle Rock*, 150 F.3d at 141-43; *Twin Peaks*, 996 F.2d at 1375-76; *Toho*, 33 F. Supp. 2d at 1216-18. Subsequent Second Circuit cases, however, make it clear that where a work is transformative, *Castle Rock* compels a finding of *no* cognizable market harm. *See Bill Graham*, 448 F.3d at 615 (citing *Castle Rock*); *see also Blanch*, 467 F.3d at 258-59 (disregarding potential future licensing of photograph at issue). The Lexicon is highly transformative. (pp. 7-13, above.) That precludes cognizable harm to any derivative market Plaintiffs may wish to exploit, and Plaintiffs cannot as a matter of law claim such "transformative markets" for themselves. *See Bill Graham*, 448 F.3d at 614-615; *Castle Rock*, 150 F.3d at 146 n.11 (copyright owner cannot prevent "transformative uses" of its creative work by developing licensing market for what would otherwise be fair use).

Third, even if Plaintiffs' assertions of market harm were cognizable, they are in the end unsupported. Insofar as Ms. Rowling wants to rely on harm to supposed derivative markets, she has to show the Lexicon is a substitute for the companion guide she wishes to publish or license. *See Campbell*, 510 U.S. at 593 ("the only harm to derivatives that need concern us is the harm of market substitution"); *Castle Rock*, 150 F.3d at 145 (fourth factor weighs against fair use because *Seinfeld* trivia book "substitutes" for derivative market reserved to copyright holder); *Twin Peaks*, 996 F.2d at 1377 (detailed abridgement was "adequate substitute" for original television series). But in her declaration, Ms. Rowling does not suggest anyone would purchase the Lexicon instead of her companion guide, should she ever publish it. Nor does her publisher, Suzanne Murphy. Instead, Murphy worries that publication of the Lexicon might make Ms. Rowling's guide "less distinctive" and suggests that there is some advantage to publishing first. But copyright does not protect the right to be "distinctive," and Murphy ignores the fact similar books are already on the market. Thus, while Murphy worries about the supposedly "poor quality" of the Lexicon, she does not point to any likelihood that it will diminish sales of Ms. Rowling's companion guide. Neither does Ms. Rowling's expert economist, William Landes. He simply speculates that Ms. Rowling "could" lose income from the sale of her companion guide. And even that is based on the advantage of being first, which has long since passed.

Even if Plaintiffs' submissions in support of their preliminary injunction motion did support their assertions of market harm, nearly everything Plaintiffs have said and done prior to suit disproves any plausible market harm. The entire contents of the Lexicon have been available to the public for free, much of it for years, on the HP Lexicon website. Neither Ms. Rowling nor Warner Brothers objected to the website, despite the fact Ms. Rowling has intended to write a companion guide for at least six years. Ms. Rowling attempts to draw a distinction between content available on the Internet and in printed form. But Ms. Rowling herself shows that distinction to be immaterial. Numerous other companion guides very similar to the format and content of the Lexicon have already been published. Ms. Rowling has apparently lodged no objection to these, or to the dozens of other Harry Potter companion books and reference guides that have been published, either in print or on the Internet.

This should come as no surprise. If and when Ms. Rowling decides to publish a companion guide, it will undoubtedly be unique. Ms. Rowling's own statements indicate the companion guide she intends to write will contain large quantities of material available exclusively to her. In a December 2007 interview with the Leaky Cauldron website, Ms. Rowling described her vision for her companion guide. She explained she imagined a layout featuring "facing pages" on which the left-facing pages would have "back story" and "extra details on characters" including for example, "an entry on wands showing what every character's wand was." The right-facing pages, by contrast, would feature "extra information" only Ms. Rowling could provide, such as "discarded plots, characters that didn't make it, [and] problems in the plot." Ms. Rowling's interrogatory responses confirm this material will be drawn from her personal notes, which she will "turn . . . into the definitive encyclopedic Harry Potter companion guide" and augment with additional material of her creation. So while the Lexicon provides information mainly about what does appear in the Harry Potter Works, Ms. Rowling envisions a companion guide that focuses largely on what does *not* appear in the Harry Potter Works – the rest of the story no one knows but her. Whatever the content of Ms. Rowling's companion guide will be, it is a long way off. Ms. Rowling herself acknowledges she has had "plans" to write her companion guide since 2000, but acknowledges that she has not started on the manuscript and that the companion guide may be as much as ten years off.

5. No Bad Faith

Plaintiffs try to string together a story of supposed bad faith, based mainly on the so-called "smoking gun" email in which Steve Vander Ark (not a party here, or an agent of RDR) suggests it would be unlawful for him to publish a printed version of the Lexicon, and the fact that RDR refused to submit a pre-publication copy of the Lexicon to Ms. Rowling. But Vander Ark is a layperson, not a lawyer, and his speculation as to the legal status of the Lexicon (since corrected) is beside the point. As for Ms. Rowling's demands to receive and review a copy of the manuscript prior to publication, RDR's failure to seek her blessing and permission before publishing the Lexicon simply has no bearing on the fair use issue. *See Campbell*, 510 U.S. at 585 n.18 ("If the use is otherwise fair, then no permission need be sought or granted."); *Blanch*, 467 F.3d at 256 (failure to seek permission is not bad faith).

II. Plaintiffs' Lanham Act Claims Are Moot And They Could Not Show Likelihood Of Success In Any Event

Plaintiffs assert Lanham Act violations based entirely on a quote that appears on the back cover of the Lexicon relating to the Fansite Award that Rowling gave to the Lexicon website in 2004. Specifically, the back cover states that the Lexicon website won J.K. Rowling's Fansite Award and quotes Rowling's praise of the website:

J.K. Rowling on the Harry Potter Lexicon website –

"This is such a great site that I have been known to sneak into an Internet café while out writing and check a fact. . . . A website for the dangerously obsessive; my natural home." (emphasis in original)

Plaintiffs assert this quote constitutes both false advertising and false endorsement. But the quote has been removed from the cover and RDR has confirmed it will not be included anywhere in the printed Lexicon. Accordingly, there is nothing to enjoin and this issue is moot. *E.g., Consumers Union of U.S., Inc. v. General Signal Corp.*, 724 F.2d 1044, 1052, n.11 (2d Cir. 1983) (reversing district court's grant of preliminary injunction where defendant eliminated allegedly infringing material from commercial); *Am. Express Travel Related Servs. Co. v. MasterCard*, 776 F. Supp. 787, 790-91 (S.D.N.Y. 1991) (holding injunctive relief unnecessary where defendant changed allegedly infringing commercial and assured that it would never be used in the future).

Even if the quote remained, it would present no violation on either a false endorsement or false advertising theory. Plaintiffs do not contend anything on the cover was literally false. They do not deny the Lexicon website received the Fansite award, or that Rowling, in fact, said the quoted words about the website. Nor do Plaintiffs contend that consumers might believe the quote refers to the book instead of the website. Instead, Plaintiffs complain the quote might mislead consumers by implying Rowling endorses the book. But all of the false endorsement cases Plaintiffs cite concern cases where defendants employed models, who looked like a celebrity, to pretend that the actual celebrity endorsed their product. *See Dallas Cowboy Cheerleaders, Inc. v. Pussycat Cinema*, 604 F.2d 200 (2d Cir. 1979) (Dallas Cowboy cheerleader look-alikes); *Allen v. National Video, Inc.*, 610 F. Supp. 612 (S.D.N.Y. 1985) (Woody Allen look-alike); *Tin Pan Apple, Inc. v. Miller Brewing Co. Inc.*, 737 F. Supp. 826 (S.D.N.Y. 1990) (rap group look-alikes). No such thing happened here, and no false endorsement is implied by accurately reporting the award, or what Rowling said about the Lexicon Website. *See e.g., Playboy Enterprises, Inc. v. Wells*, 279 F.3d 796, 800 (9th Cir. 2002) (rejecting false endorsement claim premised on model's truthful identification of herself as a Playboy "Playmate of the Year").

Plaintiffs' false advertising claim is premised on the same false endorsement theory but Plaintiffs point to no case that suggests printing a true and accurate quote constitutes false advertising, or has the potential to mislead anyone. Instead, Plaintiffs rely on a survey to show supposed confusion. But the survey focuses entirely on the quote that has now been removed and therefore cannot support an injunction against the revised cover. Even if the cover had not been revised, the survey would remain fatally flawed. The original cover used in the survey contains a disclaimer immediately below the quote at issue explaining that neither Plaintiff is affiliated with the Lexicon. "Disclaimers are a favored way of alleviating consumer confusion as to source or sponsorship." *Consumers Union v. General Signal Corp.*, 724 F.2d 1044, 1052-53 (2d Cir. 1983) (preliminary injunction reversed where advertisement reported positive review in Consumers Reports magazine and disclaimed any endorsement). But Plaintiffs' survey instructed respondents to look only at the quote, inviting them to *ignore* the disclaimer, and is therefore unreliable as evidence of confusion. Plaintiffs assert it should be RDR's "heavy burden" to show its disclaimer is effective under *Home Box Office, Inc. v. Showtime/The Movie Channel, Inc.*, 832 F.2d 1311 (2d Cir. 1987), and *Clinique Labs, Inc. v. Dep Corp.*, 945 F. Supp. 547 (S.D.N.Y. 1996). But neither case involved an implied falsehood claim. Where, as here, a false advertisement claim is premised on a statement that is literally true, it is the *plaintiff's* burden to establish confusion through survey evidence. *See Johnson & Johnson * Merck Consumer Phar. Co. v. Smithkline Beecham Corp.*, 960 F.2d 294, 297-98 (2d Cir. 1992). Here, Plaintiffs' defective survey fails to do that. *See id.* ("success of a plaintiff's implied falsity claim usually turns on the persuasiveness of a consumer survey").

III. Plaintiffs Cannot Show Irreparable Harm

In order to obtain a preliminary injunction on any of their claims, Plaintiffs must show irreparable harm. *See, e.g., NVIXM Corp. v. Ross Inst.,* 364 F.3d 471 (2d Cir. 2004). Plaintiffs suggest irreparable harm may be presumed upon showing a likelihood of success on the merits of their Copyright or Lanham Act claims. But Plaintiffs have shown no such likelihood (parts I and II, above) and even if they had, they are entitled to no such presumption. In *eBay, Inc. v. MercExchange, L.L.C.,* 126 S. Ct. 1837 (2007), the Supreme Court held presumptions in favor of injunctive relief are improper. *See id.* at 1838-39. Instead, courts must apply traditional principles of equity in determining whether to issue injunctive relief, which requires an actual showing of irreparable injury absent an injunction. *See id.* Following *eBay,* Plaintiffs must show, not presume, irreparable harm.

While *eBay* concerned a permanent injunction on a patent claim, its holding applies equally to copyright and trademark claims. *EBay* itself suggests that copyright and patent injunctions should be treated similarly, *see eBay,* 126 S. Ct. at 1840, and lower courts have proceeded to apply its rule to copyright and trademark cases. *See Christopher Phelps & Assocs., L.L.C. v. Galloway,* 492 F.3d 532, 543 (4th Cir. 2007); *Metro-Goldwyn-Mayer Studios, Inc. v. Grokster, Ltd.,* 518 F. Supp. 2d 1197, 1212-14 (C.D. Cal. 2007).

Nor is the *eBay* holding limited to permanent injunctions. The Court's reasoning applies with even greater force at the preliminary injunction stage, where a plaintiff has at best shown a likelihood of success, not actual success on the merits. Indeed, *eBay* rested its holding on *Amoco Production Co. v. Gambell,* 480 U.S. 531, 542, 545 (1987), which itself involved a preliminary injunction and rejected a presumption of irreparable harm in favor of traditional equitable factors. *See eBay,* 126 S. Ct. at 1839 (citing *Amoco,* 480 U.S. at 542). The Supreme Court's *eBay* decision therefore solidified the rule set out in *Amoco* that presumptions "contrary to traditional equitable principles" are not permissible for any type of injunction. *Amoco,* 480 U.S. at 545. Accordingly, Plaintiffs face the same burden of showing irreparable harm as any other party in a civil action requesting a preliminary injunction. *See Canon Inc. v. GCC Int'l, Ltd.,* 450 F. Supp. 2d 243, 251-52 (S.D.N.Y. 2006) (applying traditional rules of equity to party's request for preliminary injunctive relief in light of *eBay*), *aff'd,* 2008 WL 213883 (2d Cir. Jan. 25, 2008).

Plaintiffs attempt to show irreparable harm by repeating their contentions that Ms. Rowling would be "scooped" by publication of the Lexicon and that it would make Ms. Rowling's companion guide "less distinctive and therefore less successful." But Plaintiffs' "first to publish" theory fails for the same reasons explained before: the opportunity to be first has long since passed, and Ms. Rowling has explained in detail how different and distinctive her companion guide will be. Stretching further, Plaintiffs suggest irreparable harm exists because Steve Vander Ark suggested that Warner Brothers infringed the copyrights on a timeline he made, and the HP Lexicon website has copyright notices. But neither the timeline nor the website copyright notices are part of the Lexicon, and enjoining the publication of the Lexicon would not have any effect on either issue. Plaintiffs simply present no plausible basis for a finding irreparable harm absent an injunction here.

CONCLUSION

Plaintiffs have not sustained any of their claims. The Lexicon does not infringe Plaintiffs' copyright and in any event represents a fair use of Ms. Rowling's novels. The current cover presents no possibility of consumer confusion, and infringes no trademark belonging to either Plaintiff. Plaintiffs' motion for a preliminary injunction should be denied.

Dated: February 8, 2008

David Saul Hammer
LAW OFFICE OF DAVID SAUL HAMMER
99 Park Avenue, Suite 1600 New York, NY 10016
(212)-941-8118

Anthony T. Falzone
Julie A. Ahrens
Lawrence Lessig
STANFORD LAW SCHOOL CENTER FOR INTERNET & SOCIETY
559 Nathan Abbott Way
Stanford, CA 94305-8610
(650) 736-9050

Lizbeth Hasse
CREATIVE INDUSTRY LAW GROUP
San Francisco, CA

Robert Handelsman
Chicago, IL 60602   Attorneys for Defendant, RDR Books

PLAINTIFFS' REPLY MEMORANDUM OF LAW IN SUPPORT OF THEIR MOTION FOR PRELIMINARY INJUNCTION

WARNER BROS. ENTERTAINMENT INC. AND
J.K. ROWLING,

Plaintiffs,

-against-

RDR BOOKS and DOES 1-10

Defendants.

Case No. 07-09667 (RPP)   Filed: February 27, 2008

PRELIMINARY STATEMENT

RDR Books ("RDR") seeks to publish the infringing *Harry Potter* Lexicon ("Book") at the expense of Ms. Rowling, from whose novels the Book is derived. Rather than refute Plaintiffs' *prima facie* case with evidence or sound legal analysis, RDR's intellectual property counsel, the Stanford Fair Use Project, mischaracterizes the nature of the Book to advance its political agenda of "extend[ing] the boundaries of fair use." But the facts and law show that the Book simply does not qualify for the fair use as it exists, and must be enjoined.

ARGUMENT

A. Plaintiffs Have Shown A Likelihood of Success on the Merits on its Copyright Claim

1. Plaintiffs Have Established a Prima Facie Case of Copyright Infringement. Plaintiffs have established prima facie copyright infringement based on ownership of valid copyrights in the *Harry Potter* books (the "Series") and copying of them. *Castle Rock Ent., Inc. v. Carol Publ'g Group, Inc.,* 150 F.3d 132, 137 (2d Cir. 1998). RDR does not dispute the validity of Plaintiffs' copyrights and admits that the Book is based on Vander Ark's notes of the Series. Although RDR claims its copying is lawful because the Book is not a "reproduction" of the Series or a "derivative work" and, failing that, that the Book is not "substantially similar" thereto, it does not contest that the Book closely paraphrases and copies verbatim an enormous amount of Plaintiffs' protected expression. This clearly is "reproduction" of the underlying work under the plain language of the statute. 17 U.S.C. §106 (1); see *Salinger v. Random House, Inc.,* 811 F.2d 90,98-99 (2d Cir. 1987). It is also squarely within the Copyright Act's definition of a derivative work as "a work based upon one or more pre-existing works" (which definition RDR ignores). 17 U.S.C. § 101. Companion guides are derivative works where, as here, they "contain a substantial amount of material from [the underlying work]." *Twin Peaks Prods., Inc. v. Publ'ns Int'l, Ltd.,* 996 F.2d 1366, 1373 (2d Cir. 1993*); see also Castle Rock,* 150 F.3d at 140. RDR's reliance on *Ty, Inc. v. Publications Int'l Ltd.,* where defendant's photographs of copyrighted dolls undisputedly were derivative works, is misplaced. 292 F.3d 512, 515 (7th Cir. 2002). The court there found that "textual portions of a collector's guide" *(e.g.,* release dates, retirement dates, prices) were critical and evaluative rather than a mere recasting of the underlying dolls. *Id.* at 520-521. In contrast, RDR's Book is nothing more than a recast of Ms. Rowling's original text.

RDR calls the Book a "supplementary work" supposedly outside the scope of Ms. Rowling's exclusive rights, relying solely on a 1966 academic lecture discussing possible extension of an author's exclusive rights under the 1909 Act to works such as forewards, prefaces, prologues, epilogues and bibliographies. Benjamin Kaplan, *An Unhurried View of Copyright* at 100, n.61. Leaving aside that the 1976 Act only mentions "supplementary works" in the "work made for hire" definition, the Book is not even a "supplementary work" as Professor Kaplan defines it. Nor has RDR pointed to any case law suggesting that works like it should be classified as "supplementary works" or are somehow immune from copyright claims. To the contrary, courts in this Circuit have consistently stated that this type of work is *not* immune. *See Castle Rock* 150 F.3d 132; *Twin Peaks,* 996 F.2d at 1383; *Paramount Pictures Corp.* v. *Carol Publ'g Group,* 11 F. Supp. 2d 329,338 (S.D.N.Y. 1998).

2. RDR's Book is Substantially Similar to the *Harry Potter* Series. Plaintiffs' opening brief applied the quantitative/qualitative prongs of the substantial similarity test to the Series. *See Castle Rock* at 139. The Book consists of 400 pages of material taken from the Series. Its 2,437 entries use the Series' fictional facts including verbatim quotations, long plot summaries and paraphrased character descriptions, all of which is actionable. *Castle Rock* at 138; *Twin Peaks* at 1372. Qualitatively, the copying consists not of "unprotected facts, but creative expression." *Castle Rock,* 150 F.3d at 138-39. RDR's only response is a conclusory statement that Plaintiffs have not demonstrated substantial similarity, relying on a footnote in *Castle Rock* to the effect that a secondary work may be sufficiently transformative such that the secondary work is no longer derivative. 150 F.3d at 143 n.9. But RDR makes no showing that this theory applies here, and in fact *Castle Rock* found substantial similarity on similar facts. 150 F.3d at 141.

B. <u>RDR Has Failed to Show a Valid Fair Use Defense</u>

On a preliminary injunction motion, the burdens of proof "track the burdens at trial." *Gonzales v. Centro Espirita Beneficente Uniao de Vegetal,* 546 U.S. 418, 429 (2006). RDR must prove it is likely to succeed on its fair use defense, which it cannot do. *See College Entrance Exam. Bd. v. Pataki,* 889 F. Supp. 554,564-65 (N.D.N.Y. 1995); *Perfect 10, Inc. v. Amazon.com, Inc.,* 508 F.3d 1146, 1158 (9th Cir. 2007).

1. **Factor One: Purpose and Character of the Use**. The Book's undisputed commercial nature weighs against a finding of fair use. *See Castle Rock,* 150 F. 3d at 141. RDR's argument that the Book is "transformative" is wrong because, as Plaintiffs established in their opening brief, the Book does not create "new information, new aesthetics, new insights and understandings." RDR's implausible claim that the Book is a "serious book" filled with scholarly commentary and analysis is merely an attempt to excuse blatant infringement.

a. **Alphabetizing is Not Transformative**. Arranging a work in alphabetical order is not even sufficiently creative to render it copyrightable. *Feist Publ'ns v. Rural Telephone Svc. Co.,* 449 U.S. 340,363 (1991). RDR's analogy to search engines also is misplaced as the Book does not provide the combination of "organizational" value, public benefit and lack of market harm that has supported a finding of transformative purpose in the search engine context. *Perfect 10,* 508 F.3d at 1177; *Kelly* v. *Arriba Soft Corp.,* 336 F.3d 811,822 (9th Cir. 2003). *Perfect 10* is distinguishable not only because of the significant public benefit of an Internet search engine as opposed to a book lifting the contents of a children's book series, but also because the court there found that potential harm to plaintiff was speculative as plaintiff claimed it *could* enter the market for downloadable "thumbnail" images, but showed no actual intent to do so. 508 F. 3d. 1166-68. Nor did it claim to compete in the search engine market. *Id.* Here, in contrast, Plaintiffs have established Ms. Rowling's intent to enter the same market as the Book and she has already published two companion books. The same distinctions apply with respect to *Kelly* and *New York Times* v. *Roxbury Data Interface, Inc.* and thus RDR's argument fails. *See Kelly,* 336 F.3d at 821; *New York Times,* 434 F. Supp. 217, 223-24 (D. N.J. 1977).

b. **No Original Commentary or Analysis**. Plaintiffs have shown that the Book is devoid of analysis, commentary, or anything else rising to the level of scholarship. RDR's expert apparently agrees, only venturing that the book *"moves into the territory* of literary analysis" and admitting that "interpretive moves" are *"not the chief point* of the Book." Of the Book's 2,437 entries, 2,034 simply lift information straight from the Series. The remainder do little more than that, merely adding adverbs such as "unfortunately," "sadly," or "possibly" to descriptions wholly derived from the Series, or simply restating the obvious. Other entries simply contain facetious comments ("Junk Shop": "A shop in Diagon Alley filled with, well junk"), none of which make the Book transformative. *See Paramount* at 335. RDR accuses Plaintiffs of selectively choosing material to support their claims, but itself relies on fewer than 25 entries to "prove" sufficient original content to show fair use. However, "no plagiarist can excuse the wrong by showing how much of his work he did not pirate." *Paramount,* 11 F. Supp. 2d at 335. RDR ignores the innumerable entries that simply lift Ms. Rowling's work. It also offers no cases support for the argument that the jocosity described above constitutes analysis or commentary.

c. **No Additional Research or New Information**. RDR's claims that the Book is annotated with "information" and "additional research" are equally wrong. RDR has not shown that any such material was in more than a *de minimis* number of entries. Although Vander Ark claims that he utilized "reference works," none are cited in the Book or mentioned in its bibliography. The few entries that provide an extra line of definition appear to be taken verbatim from sources such as *Merriam Webster's Online Dictionary* without attribution. RDR's claim that the Book contains "significant outside research" is merely wishful thinking.

2. **Factor Two: The Nature of the Work**. RDR does not dispute that Ms. Rowling's highly creative works are entitled to heightened protection, so this factor favors Plaintiffs. RDR's suggestion that this Court effectively ignore the remaining fair use factors if the book is found to have a transformative purpose overlooks the fact that the fair use factors must "all ...be explored, and the results weighed together, in light of the purposes of copyright." *Campbell,* 510 U.S. at 581.

3. **Factor Three: The Amount and Substantiality of the Portion Used**. RDR admits that it uses a "significant amount" of Ms. Rowling's work in the Book, but claims that it took no more than necessary for its purposes. The Book, however, clearly takes the heart of the *Harry Potter* works plus everything else, even if one focused solely on entries such as "Harry Potter" and "Voldemort" that basically retell the entire Series. *See Harper & Row Pub., Inc. v. Nation Enters.,* 471 U.S. 539, 565 (1985). The Book also quotes numerous passages, poems and songs verbatim. Even where it paraphrases, the Book's "description[s] conjure[ ] up vivid images that cannot be considered necessary for a critical commentary" or, similarly, for a reference guide. *Toho Co. Ltd. v. William Morrow & Co. Ltd.,* 33 F. Supp. 2d 1206, 1217 (C.D. Cal. 1998).

4. **Factor Four: Harm to the Market**. RDR must show the Book's effect upon "the potential market for or value of the copyrighted work." *See Campbell* at 590. RDR argues that the Book is not a derivative work, but as explained above, under the plain language of the Copyright Act the Book is a derivative work that occupies the market for companion guides, admittedly a natural outgrowth of a popular series. The exclusive right to create derivative works is subject to the sole exception of derivative works that qualify as a fair use, which the Book does not. 17 U.S.C. §§ *106-107; Pacific & Southern Co. v. Duncan*, 744 F.2d 1490,1496 (11th Cir. 1984). RDR again argues that because the Book is purportedly transformative, it "precludes cognizable harm to any derivative market Plaintiffs may wish to exploit." There is no support for such a circular argument. *Bill Graham v. Dorling Kindersley* and *Blanch v. Koons* are inapposite because there, either the copyright holders were deemed unlikely to compete with the defendants' works, or there was a question as to whether such a market even existed. *Koons,* 467 F. 3d 244, 258 (9th Cir. 2006); *Bill Graham,* 448 F.3d 605, 615. Here, there can be no doubt as to either consideration. RDR also argues that Plaintiffs' purported inaction against other allegedly infringing books shows that the Book will not damage Ms. Rowling's potential market. But Plaintiffs have extensively policed the marketplace to preserve Ms. Rowling's rights. While there are many non-infringing books about the Series, books such as the Book are few in number and have been pulled from distribution as a result of Plaintiffs' efforts.

As explained in Plaintiffs' opening brief, the Book is a significant market threat to Ms. Rowling's planned companion guide. It would divert sales of her own encyclopedia as many consumers who purchased the Book would find it unnecessary, or would not have the means, to also purchase Ms. Rowling's encyclopedia. *See Telebrands Corp. v. Wilton Industries, Inc.,* 983 F. Supp. 471, 476 (S.D.N.Y. 1997) ("once purchased, the consumer is unlikely to purchase a second can opener"). RDR admits as much. Nor does RDR refute that the Book would result in lost licensing revenue. *Campbell,* 510 U.S. at 593; *Bill Graham,* 448 F.3d at 614. It thus constitutes a potential market substitution for Ms. Rowling's encyclopedia, precisely the kind of harm that weighs against fair use. *Campbell* at 593. The Book also would usurp Plaintiffs' right to publish the first encyclopedia covering the whole Series. RDR does not dispute the advantage of being first, which it sought for itself. It argues that injury to Ms. Rowling has already occurred due to the publication of other similar books. But as RDR's own marketing materials show, it is positioning the Book as more comprehensive than existing books. The books RDR cites are different in scope, have been or are the subject of Plaintiffs' policing efforts, or had meager sales prior to being discontinued.

5. **Ms. Rowling may still be the first mover**. The market harm inquiry also extends to "whether unrestricted and widespread conduct of the

sort engaged in" by RDR "would result in a substantially adverse impact on the potential market" for the original and derivative works. *Campbell* at 590 (citation omitted). Publication of the Book would signal that others may also free ride off of Ms. Rowling's works, flooding the market with copycat works and likely diminishing her sales. Faced with these facts and controlling law, RDR repeatedly refers to the existence of the *Lexicon* Website (the "Website"), seemingly to obliquely suggest a waiver or implied license argument. The law is clear that these doctrines do not help RDR. Nor can RDR successfully argue that the Website already scoops Ms. Rowling's encyclopedia. The Website is not a substitute for the Book. The Website cannot be purchased and it certainly cannot be given as a gift. In fact, RDR recognized the Book as filling a different market than the Website. Fans of the Series have recognized this difference as well. That RDR chose to publish the Book in the first place proves that even RDR does not view the Website as a substitute for a real book.

C. Plaintiffs' Claims for False Endorsement and Advertising Warrant Injunctive Relief

RDR argues that its willingness to remove Ms. Rowling's quote from the Book's cover renders Plaintiffs' Lanham Act claims moot and bars injunctive relief. But an injunction may issue despite a defendant's voluntary cessation of illegal activity where there is a cognizable danger that its conduct will be repeated. *U.S. v. W.T. Grant,* 345 U.S. 629, 632-33 (1953). Such is the case here as RDR's "promise" to remove the quote came only in response to Plaintiffs' opening brief. *See R.C. Bigelow, Inc. v. Unilever N. V.,* 876 F.2d 102, 106-07 (2d Cir. 1989).

Moreover, a significant number of consumers believe from the quote that Ms. Rowling endorses the Book. RDR does not dispute that misuse of a celebrity's name is actionable false endorsement or advertising, instead arguing the quote is literally true and therefore not actionable. This misstates the law and ignores the fact that RDR has used an old quote about the Website to suggest falsely Ms. Rowling endorses a book she opposes. RDR's attempt to distinguish the cases cited by Plaintiffs is unavailing, as is RDR's reliance on *Playboy Enterprises, Inc. v. Wells,* 279 F.3d 796 (9th Cir. 2002).

D. Plaintiffs Have Established Irreparable Harm

Plaintiffs have shown that they will suffer irreparable injury absent injunctive relief. First publication of the Book would divert sales from Ms. Rowling's own encyclopedia. *See Wainwright Sec. Inc. v. Wall Street Transcript Corp.,* 558 F.2d 91, 94 (2d Cir. 1977). It would also usurp Plaintiffs' right to publish the first complete encyclopedia. *Herbert Rosenthal Jewelry Corp. v. Zale*

Corp., 323 F. Supp. 1234, 1238 (S.D.N.Y. 1971). Plaintiffs would also be unable to enforce their exclusive rights. *See Tom Doherty Assocs., Inc. v. Saban Entm 't.,* 60 F. 3d 27,38 (2d Cir. 1995). The Book's poor quality also causes irreparable harm. *Firma Melodiya v. ZYXMusic,* 882 F. Supp. 1306, 1315 (S.D.N.Y. 1995). And irreparable harm will result if RDR is not enjoined from making use of Ms. Rowling's name and quote to mislead consumers. *See Columbus Rose Ltd. v. New Millennium Press,* 2002 U.S. Dist. LEXIS 9130, *31 (S.D.N.Y. 2002).

E. <u>Plaintiffs Have Shown That The Balance of Hardships Favors Them</u>

As shown above, the irreparable harm to Plaintiffs strikingly outweighs any potential harm suffered by RDR. In fact, RDR concedes this point as it does not identify *any* potential hardships it would suffer if a preliminary injunction is issued.

Dated: February 27,2008

Respectfully Submitted:

Dale M. Cendali (DC 2676)
O'MELVENY & MYERS LLP
7 Times Square New York, New York 10036
(212) 326-2000

DECLARATION OF J.K. ROWLING IN SUPPORT OF PLAINTIFFS' MOTION FOR PRELIMINARY INJUNCTION

WARNER BROS. ENTERTAINMENT INC. AND
J.K. ROWLING,

Plaintiffs,

-against-

RDR BOOKS and DOES 1-10

Defendants.

Case No. 07-09667 (RPP)   Filed: February 27, 2008

I, J.K. Rowling, declare and state as follows:

1. I am the author of the *Harry Potter* book series (the "*Harry Potter* Books" or "Books"). Except for the facts stated on information and belief, all of the facts set forth herein are known to me personally, and if called as a witness, I could and would testify competently thereto.

2. I have read the papers submitted by RDR Books ("RDR") in opposition to Plaintiffs' Motion for Preliminary Injunction. I am deeply troubled by the portrayal of my efforts to protect and preserve the copyrights I have been granted in the *Harry Potter* Books and feel betrayed by Steven Vander Ark, as a person who calls himself a fan.

3. I am particularly concerned about RDR's continued insistence that my acceptance of free, fan-based websites somehow justifies its efforts to publish for profit an unauthorized *Harry Potter* "lexicon" directly contrary to my stated intention to publish my own definitive Harry Potter encyclopedia. Such a position penalizes copyright owners like me for encouraging and supporting the activities of their respective fan communities. If RDR's position is accepted, it will undoubtedly have a significant, negative impact on the freedoms enjoyed by genuine fans on the Internet. Authors everywhere will be forced to protect their creations much more rigorously, which could mean denying well-meaning fans permission to pursue legitimate creative activities.

4. In my opinion, 99% of *Harry Potter* fans are acting entirely in good faith, and I have excellent relations with many members of the fan

community. I find it devastating to contemplate the possibility of such a severe alteration of author-fan relations. I continue to believe that the online fandom has been a wonderful experience for thousands of people, myself included; that it has become, not only an enormous global book club, but engendered an explosion of creativity and communication rooted in a world we would all like to inhabit.

5. As indicated in my prior declaration, I have stated on my website, in numerous interviews in the press and elsewhere that I intend to publish a definitive guide to all of the creatures, characters, places, and other elements that comprise the *Harry Potter* world. Just as I did with the first two companion books, I intend to donate royalties from such a companion book to charity. The Bloomsbury and Scholastic lexicons will be available to me as I write my own encyclopedia. In fact, the Bloomsbury version already has been given to me at my request as I am in the process of assembling and organizing materials from which I will work. Naturally this means that my encyclopedia will contain all information in the published books. To suggest that I would omit from my encyclopedia the information already made available in the novels, can only spring from a willful misinterpretation of a selective quotation.

6. It has been well-known within the fan community for years that I intended to write my own Harry Potter encyclopedia. Mr. Vander Ark, as a member of that community, has also been long aware of my intentions as demonstrated in the exhibits annexed to the declarations of Neil Blair and Cheryl Klein (supplemental) submitted in this case. It is extremely disheartening to me that, despite his knowledge of my plans, Mr. Vander Ark intends to proceed with the publication of his Harry Potter "lexicon."

7. In spite of my repeated assertion that I intend to write this encyclopedia, and the preliminary work I have already undertaken, Mr. Vander Ark and RDR suggest that I ought to provide a timeline to demonstrate my sincerity. As I have already promised and then delivered seven *Harry Potter* books, plus two extra books for charity, I do not think that any reasonable person would question my good faith in this regard. I fully intend to write this encyclopedia, however, after ten years of deadlines, coupled with intense pressure from media and fans, plus the demands of a young family, I am not prepared to commit to another deadline a bare seven months after the publication of my last book. I do not believe I should be forced to make such a commitment or run the risk of losing the right to create my own encyclopedia on an exclusive basis. I thought that this was part of what my rights were as an author and copyright holder. I also feel strongly that RDR is attempting to interfere with my creative process by repeatedly arguing that a timeline for publication of my *Harry Potter*

encyclopedia is necessary in order to prove that I mean to publish one at all. I am not a person to make statements lightly, particularly when it comes to statements that ultimately will set expectations for my fans.

8. RDR's position that fans of the *Harry Potter* series can simply buy two encyclopedias is both presumptuous and insensitive. RDR's position is presumptuous because it assumes that everyone would want to have two *Harry Potter* encyclopedias and insensitive in thinking that everyone that would want to have both could afford to purchase both. Although *Harry Potter* is now a worldwide success, it had its roots in a time when I was very far from wealthy. While I am extremely fortunate now, having had periods in my life when I worried about having enough money to feed and clothe my daughter, it is obvious to me that many people do not have money to buy every book that appeals to them.

9. It is clear to me that RDR and Mr. Vander Ark have either misquoted me or presented many of my statements out of context. For example, in the declaration of Shawn Malholtra, he takes a statement I made jokingly in a taped interview for the PotterCast about taking "ten years" to do the *Harry Potter* encyclopedia and describes the statement as a public admission that I "did not expect to finish writing [the Harry Potter companion guide] for another ten years." My quote clearly was misrepresented and inappropriately cut off at a selective moment. Mr. Malholtra only later mentions in passing the rest of my statement which was that I absolutely intended to do the encyclopedia, had my notes and needed to get working on it.

10. In addition, Mr. Malholtra identifies certain comments I made about including scrapped material and character "back stories" in my version of the *Harry Potter* encyclopedia as evidence that I did not intend to include materials that appeared in the *Harry Potter* novels, without which, in my view, the *Harry Potter* encyclopedia would not be the complete reference guide I intend it to be. In fact, the very next thing I said in that interview is that I wanted to give people everything in the companion guide and do "the absolute definitive guide." As I stated above, my encyclopedia will include materials from the original *Harry Potter* novels.

11. Still another example is with respect to the Fan Site Award -- which I instituted in order to honor Harry Potter fan sites, many of whom were clearly manned by real enthusiasts, some of them very young, and who clearly had invested significant amounts of time and energy in their respective sites.

12. When I awarded the Fan Site Award to the Lexicon website, it never occurred to me for a moment that the Award might subsequently be used by Mr. Vander Ark in an attempt to legitimize an attempt to profit financially from my work. At that time I believed him to be, in common with the fans who ran the other sites I honored, a true enthusiast who simply wished to share his enjoyment of *Harry Potter* with others. In the 'citation' for the Award, I said that I had 'been known to sneak into an Internet Cafe while out writing and check a fact' rather than purchasing a copy of one of my own books from a bookshop 'which embarrassing'. As this statement makes quite clear, the Lexicon could not give me anything that my own books could not. Its only value to me was that it was occasionally more convenient to access, in a situation where I was likely to be recognized in public, than it would have been to walk into a bookstore and purchase one of my own novels.

13. Additionally, while I granted a fan site award to the *Harry Potter* website, the Lexicon website shared that distinction with three other fan sites that year. Since then, I have granted fan site awards to four additional websites wholly unrelated to the Lexicon website. At no point have I indicated, or would I indicate that anyone of these websites is a "favorite." They all have much to lend themselves to the fan community and it is in recognition of their endeavors for the fan community that they received a fan site award in the first place. Again, I never intended for this award or my encouragement and support of the fan community to be taken by anyone as an authorization for them to create and sell an infringing *Harry Potter* book for profit and certainly not to sell a book designed to compete with a book I intended to write myself for charity.

14. For seven years, *Harry Potter* was nothing but an ever-growing pile of paper and notebooks on which I worked very hard whenever I could make the time. By the time of the publication of the seventh novel I had been writing about *Harry Potter* for 17 years. As a result, I feel intensely protective, firstly, of the literary world I spent so long creating, and secondly, of the fans who bought my books in such huge numbers. I feel that I have a duty to these readers to ensure, as far as possible, that *Harry Potter* does not become associated with substandard versions, whether in the world of film, or in any other medium. I believe that RDR's book constitutes a Harry Potter 'rip-off' of the type I have spent years trying to prevent, and that both I, as the creator of this world, and fans of Harry Potter, would be exploited by its publication.

15. I am very frustrated that a former fan has tried to co-opt my work for financial gain. The *Harry Potter* books are full of moral choices and ethical dilemmas, and, ironically, Mr. Vander Ark's actions tend to

demonstrate that he is woefully unfit to represent himself as either a "fan of" or "expert on" books whose spirit he seems entirely to have missed. Despite RDR's lawyers' attempts to cloak the true nature of RDR's plans, I hope it is as obvious as it is to me that what they are trying to do is wrong and interferes with my rights as a creator and copyright holder. Accordingly, I respectfully reiterate my request that this Court stop publication of RDR's "lexicon."

I declare under penalty of perjury under the laws of the United States of America that the foregoing is true and correct. Executed on February 26, 2008, at London, England.

Respectfully submitted,

By: _____

J.K. Rowling

DEFENDANT'S ANSWER TO PLAINTIFFS' AMENDED COMPLAINT

WARNER BROS. ENTERTAINMENT INC. AND
J.K. ROWLING,

                           Plaintiffs,

        -against-

RDR BOOKS and DOES 1-10

                           Defendants.

Case No. 07-09667 (RPP)   Filed: March 11, 2008

NATURE OF ACTION AND RELIEF SOUGHT

1. With respect to the allegations in paragraph 1 of the Amended Complaint, Defendant admits that Plaintiffs allege claims under the Copyright Act, the Lanham Act, and New York state law (Civil Rights Law §§ 50-51 and unfair competition under New York Common Law). Defendant denies all other allegations in paragraph 1, and asserts that this case really is about Plaintiffs' effort to suppress Defendant's publication of an original literary reference guide. Defendant denies that its cover design, as revised, misleads consumers or purports to show an endorsement by or approval of Ms. Rowling, since its revised cover design makes no mention of Ms. Rowling. Moreover, although Plaintiffs repeatedly refer to the literary reference guide that Defendant sought to publish as the "Infringing Book", Defendant denies that the book it seeks to publish ("The Lexicon") has infringed any right belonging to either Plaintiff. In this regard, Defendant alleges that this suit has stopped the publication or distribution of The Lexicon, and that, even had the Lexicon been published, it would not infringe any right belonging to either Plaintiff.

2. Defendant is without knowledge or information sufficient to form a belief as to any of the allegations contained in paragraph 2 of the Amended Complaint.

3. Defendant is without knowledge or information sufficient to form a belief as to the truth of any of the allegations contained in paragraph 3 of the Amended Complaint, except denies that it was "well aware of Ms. Rowling's intentions", or believed that publishing The Lexicon would violate any right belonging to Ms. Rowling.

4. Defendant denies the allegations in paragraph 4 of the Amended Complaint that it "rebuffed" Plaintiffs or treated them rudely, and vigorously denies the allegation that it somehow misrepresented the existence of a "family tragedy" for some strategic advantage. Defendant admits that: (1) it negotiated during the period referred to in paragraph 4 with certain foreign publishers, and (2) that Plaintiffs contacted Defendant on several occasions demanding that it enter discussions to suppress The Lexicon. Defendant further admits that it accused Warner Bros. of violating the rights of Steven Jan Vander Ark, the Lexicon's author, in a timeline on the *Harry Potter* Books, but denies that this accusation was "audacious" or in any way a fabrication.

5. Paragraph 5 of the Amended Complaint consists of over-heated legal argument that does not require a response. However, Defendant admits in response to the final sentence in Paragraph 5 that certain materials present on the Lexicon Website have not been included in the manuscript of the Lexicon Book.

6. With respect to the allegations contained in paragraph 6 of the Amended Complaint, Defendant denies that Plaintiffs "had no choice but to file this lawsuit." Defendant admits that Plaintiffs have alleged claims under 17 U.S.C. §§ 101 et seq., 15 U.S.C. § 1114(1), §1125(a)(1)(A), 1125(a)(1)(B), Civil Rights Law of New York §§ 50-51 and unfair competition under the common law of New York. Defendant denies that Plaintiffs have alleged any claims under deceptive trade practices under § 349 of the General Business Law of New York as there is no count for § 349 of the General Business Law of New York in the Amended Complaint. Defendant is without knowledge or information sufficient to form a belief as to the truth of the remaining allegations in paragraph 6.

PARTIES

7. Defendant is without knowledge or information sufficient to form a belief as to the truth of the allegations contained in paragraph 7 of the Amended Complaint, except admits that Ms. Rowling is a highly respected world-famous author.

8. Defendant is without knowledge or information sufficient to form a belief as to the truth of the allegations contained in paragraph 8 of the Amended Complaint, except admits that Plaintiff Warner Bros. purports to hold rights in certain trademarks associated with the *Harry Potter* films, based on records of the U.S. Patent & Trademark Office.

9. With respect to the allegations contained in paragraph 9 of the Amended Complaint, Defendant admits that it is a publishing company

whose principal place of business is located at 1487 Glen Avenue, Muskegon, Michigan 49441, and denies all other allegations.

10. Defendant is without knowledge or information sufficient to form a belief as to the truth of the allegations in paragraph 10 of the Amended Complaint.

JURISDICTION AND VENUE

11. Paragraph 11 of the Amended Complaint consists of legal assertions that do not require a response.

12. Paragraph 12 of the Amended Complaint consists of legal assertions that do not require a response.

13. Paragraph 13 of the Amended Complaint consists of legal assertions that do not require a response.

14. Defendant admits the allegation contained in paragraph 14 of the Amended Complaint that the *Harry Potter* Books are a modern day publishing phenomenon. Defendant is without knowledge or information sufficient to form a belief as to the truth of the remaining allegations.

15. With respect to the allegations contained in paragraphs 15 of the Amended Complaint concerning the contents of the *Harry Potter* Books, Defendant asserts that the contents of those books speak for themselves.

16. With respect to the allegations contained in paragraph 16 of the Amended Complaint concerning the contents of the *Harry Potter* Books, Defendant asserts that the content of those books speak for themselves.

17. Defendant admits the allegations contained in paragraph 17 of the Amended Complaint concerning the publication history of the *Harry Potter* Books.

18. Defendant is without knowledge or information sufficient to form a belief as to the allegations contained in paragraph 18 of the Amended Complaint.

19. Defendant is without knowledge or information sufficient to form a belief as to the truth of the allegations contained in paragraph 19 of the Amended Complaint, except admits that the *Harry Potter* Books have been very popular and sold very well.

20. Defendant is without knowledge or information sufficient to form a belief as to the truth of the allegations contained in paragraph 20 of the Amended Complaint, except admits that Ms. Rowling has authored and published *Quidditch Through the Ages* and *Fantastic Beasts and Where to Find Them.*

21. Defendant is without knowledge or information sufficient to form a belief as to the allegations contained in paragraph 21 of the Amended Complaint, except that Defendant is aware that Plaintiff Warner Bros. has released films based on the *Harry Potter* Books.

22. Defendant asserts that the allegations contained in the first sentence of paragraph 22 of the Amended Complaint constitute legal contentions for which no response is necessary. Defendant is without knowledge or information sufficient to form a belief as to the truth of the remaining allegations contained in paragraph 22.

23. Defendant is without knowledge or information sufficient to form a belief as to the truth of the allegations contained in paragraph 23 of the Amended Complaint.

24. Defendant is without knowledge or information sufficient to form a belief as to the truth of the allegations contained in paragraph 24 of the Amended Complaint.

25. Defendant is without knowledge or information sufficient to form a belief as to the truth of the allegations contained in paragraph 25 of the Amended Complaint, except that Defendant is aware that the *Harry Potter* Books and movies have been successful.

26. Defendant is without knowledge or information sufficient to form a belief as to the truth of the allegations contained in paragraph 26 of the Amended Complaint.

27. Defendant is without knowledge or information sufficient to form a belief as to the truth of the allegations contained in paragraph 27 of the Amended Complaint, except that Defendant admits that it is aware that Steven Jan Vander Ark runs the Lexicon Website, and is further aware that the Lexicon Website contains materials related to the Harry Potter Works.

28. Defendant is without knowledge or information sufficient to form a belief as to the truth of the allegations in paragraph 28 of the Amended Complaint, which refer to the knowledge and activities of Steve Vander Ark.

29. Defendant admits the allegation contained in paragraph 29 of the Amended Complaint that it was planning to publish The Lexicon at the time the instant suit was commenced and further admits that it had sold the rights to The Lexicon in France and Canada. Defendant denies the allegation that it sold the rights to The Lexicon in Australia.

30. Defendant is without knowledge or information sufficient to form a belief as to the truth of the allegations contained in paragraph 30 of the Amended Complaint about the knowledge of Ms. Rowling's literary agent. Defendant denies the allegation that it sold the rights to The Lexicon in Australia and England. Defendant admits the remaining allegations contained in paragraph 30.

31. Defendant is without knowledge or information sufficient to form a belief as to the truth of the allegations contained in paragraph 31 of the Amended Complaint concerning the state of mind and actions of Ms. Rowling and her agents.

32. Defendant is without knowledge or information sufficient to form a belief as to the truth of any allegations contained in paragraph 32 of the Amended Complaint concerning the state of mind of Ms. Rowling's literary agent. With respect to the remaining allegations in paragraph 32, Defendant admits it received an email from Ms. Rowling's agent, and further admits that it did not immediately reply to that email, but asserts that it did not immediately reply because it had been told by Ms. Rowling's agent to expect a call from Ms. Rowling's attorney. Defendant denies all other allegations.

33. Defendant is without knowledge or information sufficient to form a belief as to the truth of any allegations contained in paragraph 33 of the Amended Complaint about the state of mind or behavior of Ms. Rowling's attorney. With respect to the remaining allegations in paragraph 33, Defendant admits that it did not contact Ms. Rowling's agent or her attorneys, but asserts that it did not do so because it had been told to expect a call from Ms. Rowling's attorneys. With respect to the letter that Plaintiffs' counsel sent Defendant on September 17, 2007, Defendant asserts that the contents of the letter speak for itself.

34. Defendant is without knowledge or information sufficient to form a belief as to the allegations contained in paragraph 34 of the Amended Complaint, but admits that it corresponded on September 19, 2007 with one of Plaintiffs' representatives.

35. Defendant admits the allegation contained in paragraph 35 of the Amended Complaint that on October 3, 2007 counsel for Plaintiffs sent him a letter, and further admits informing these representatives that there had been a death in his family. Defendant denies however that paragraph 35 correctly characterizes counsel's letter, which in fact demanded that "RDR Books cease its efforts to publish the Book", and that it identify any parties who had purchased rights to the Book. Defendant denies the remaining allegations in paragraph 35.

36. With respect to the allegations contained in paragraph 36 of the Amended Complaint, defendant admits that it sent a letter to Plaintiff Warner Bros. on or about October 11, 2007, in hopes of finding a solution favorable to the parties. This letter, however, was not a "cease and desist" letter, nor did it claim that Warner Bros. had violated any rights belonging to RDR Books. Rather, the letter stated that RDR Books was representing Mr. Vander Ark, that Warner Bros. had used Mr. Vander Ark's timeline, and that "you will surely agree it is only fair and just that he (Mr. Vander Ark) receive acknowledgment and tangible rewards for his contribution." Defendant denies other allegations in paragraph 36 of the Amended Complaint.

37. With respect to the allegations contained in paragraph 37 of the Amended Complaint, Defendant admits to corresponding with the representative of Plaintiffs, but denies the remaining allegations in the paragraph.

38. Defendant is without knowledge or information sufficient to form a belief as to the truth of the allegations contained in paragraph 38 of the Amended Complaint concerning the fears or concerns of Plaintiffs or Ms. Rowling's agent. With respect to the remaining allegations, Defendant admits that it sold the rights to The Lexicon in France and Canada in September 2007, and denies all other allegations. Defendant contends that it has the right to publish an original literary reference guide and Plaintiffs' attempt to suppress publication of The Lexicon violates Defendant's rights.

39. With respect to the allegations contained in paragraph 40 of the Amended Complaint, Defendant admits that counsel wrote RDR Books on or about October 24, 2007 asking for confirmation that RDR Books would not publish The Lexicon, but denies the remaining allegations in the paragraph. Defendant has the right to publish an original literary reference guide and Plaintiffs' attempt to suppress publication of The Lexicon violates Defendant's rights.

40. With respect to the allegations contained in paragraph 40 of the Amended Complaint, Defendant admits the allegations concerning its email

to counsel for Ms. Rowling on October 24, 2007, but denies the remaining allegations in the paragraph, and specifically denies that it has created a derivative work. Defendant has the right to publish an original literary reference guide and Plaintiffs' attempt to suppress publication of The Lexicon violates Defendant's rights.

41. Defendant is without knowledge or information sufficient to form a belief as to the truth of any allegations contained in paragraph 41 of the Amended Complaint about plaintiffs concerns, but vigorously denies the allegations that it has refused to be "above-board about its intentions and engage in reasonable discussions", or that "it cannot be trusted." Defendant has the right to publish an original literary reference guide and Plaintiffs' attempt to suppress publication of The Lexicon violates Defendant's rights.

42. Defendant denies the allegation in paragraph 42 of the Amended Complaint that it has been "hypocritical", and is without knowledge or information sufficient to form a belief as to the truth of the remaining allegations in the paragraph. Defendant asserts that it has the right to publish an original literary reference guide and Plaintiffs' attempt to suppress publication of The Lexicon violates Defendant's rights.

43. Defendant denies the allegations in paragraph 43 of the Amended Complaint.

44. Defendant denies the allegations contained in paragraph 44 of the Amended Complaint, except admits that it produced a manuscript for The Lexicon in response to the Court's order.

45. Defendant admits the allegations contained in the first sentence of paragraph 45 of the Amended Complaint, but denies the allegation contained in the second sentence that it has provided no "analysis or commentary". In fact, The Lexicon is replete with both analysis and commentary, as well as with etymology, reference material, and interpretation. Defendant admits that the examples listed in paragraph 45 are taken from the Harry Potter Lexicon.

46. Defendant denies the allegations in paragraph 46 of the Amended Complaint, and specifically denies that The Lexicon contains "lengthy plot summaries, spoilers . . . synopses of the major plots and story lines of the *Harry Potter* Books" and other materials that together "constitute the 'heart' of the Harry Potter Books. Defendant further denies the melodramatic contentions in paragraph 46 that it has infringed any right belonging to Plaintiff Rowling, or sought to "make money off of the back of Ms. Rowling's creativity."

47. With respect to the allegations contained in paragraph 47 of the Amended Complaint, Defendant denies that the description of The Lexicon Book is accurate. The current design of the cover of the proposed Lexicon book contains no quote of J.K. Rowling on either the front or the back, nor does it include her name except as part of a disclaimer. Moreover, the statement that the Lexicon Book previously had included from Plaintiff Rowling, endorsing the Lexicon Website, will not appear anywhere on the cover, or in the text of the Lexicon. With respect to the remaining allegations in paragraph 47, Defendant admits that The Lexicon contains disclaimers but denies that the disclaimers are inconspicuous.

48. With respect to the allegations contained in paragraph 48 of the Amended Complaint, Defendant denies that Ms. Rowling's name appears anywhere on the cover of The Lexicon, except in disclaimers. Defendant denies that Ms. Rowling's name is featured in marketing materials.

COUNT ONE – COPYRIGHT INFRINGEMENT
(17 U.S.C. §§ 101 et seq.)

49. Defendant hereby incorporates its responses to Paragraphs 1 through 48 above as if fully set forth herein.

50. Defendant denies the allegations in paragraph 50 of the Amended Complaint. The Lexicon does not infringe Ms. Rowling's copyrights. Any alleged use of copyrighted material is lawful based on the doctrine of fair use. Defendant has the right to publish an original reference guide and Plaintiffs' attempts to suppress publication of The Lexicon violate Defendant's rights.

51. Defendant denies the allegations in paragraph 51 of the Amended Complaint. Defendant's Lexicon does not infringe Ms. Rowling's copyrights. Any alleged use of copyrighted material is lawful use based on the doctrine of fair use as Defendant has the right to use such material for new and transformative purposes, and Defendant's Lexicon is new, original and transformative, presents factual information, and creates substantial public value. Defendant has the right to publish an original literary reference guide and Plaintiffs' attempts to suppress publication of The Lexicon therefore violate Defendant's rights.

52. The allegations contained in paragraph 52 represent legal conclusions to which no response is required, except that Defendant denies that Plaintiffs are entitled to any damages from any act Defendant has taken so far, or anticipates taking with respect to The Lexicon.

COUNT TWO – FEDERAL TRADEMARK INFRINGEMENT
(15 U.S.C. § 1114(1))

53. Defendant hereby incorporates its responses to Paragraphs 1 through 52 above as if fully set forth herein.

54. Defendant denies the allegations contained in paragraph 54 of the Amended Complaint. Defendant has the right to publish an original literary reference guide and Plaintiffs' attempts to suppress publication of The Lexicon violate Defendant's rights. Defendant further denies that it uses *Harry Potter* as a trademark. Defendant alleges that it only uses *Harry Potter* to the extent necessary to identify Defendant's Lexicon, and that any alleged use of the mark therefore is lawful based on the doctrine of fair use. Defendant uses disclaimers and the term "Unofficial" in the title of the Lexicon book, and as disclaimers are a favored way of alleviating any alleged consumer confusion as to source or sponsorship, there is no likelihood of confusion with Plaintiffs' trademarks. Defendant only uses J.K. Rowling's name on the cover of the Lexicon book in the context of its disclaimer and it creates no likelihood of confusion with Plaintiff J.K. Rowling's mark.

55. The assertions contained in paragraph 55 of the Amended Complaint represent legal conclusions and argument, to which no response is required.

56. Defendant denies the allegations in paragraph 56 of the Amended Complaint, and specifically denies that its acts have caused injury of any kind to Plaintiffs.

COUNT THREE – UNFAIR COMPETITION AND
FALSE DESIGNATION OF ORIGIN
(15 U.S.C. § 1125(a)(1)(A))

57. Defendant hereby incorporates its responses to Paragraphs 1 through 56 above as if fully set forth herein.

58. Defendant denies the allegations in paragraph 58 of the Amended Complaint. Defendant has the right to publish an original literary reference guide and Plaintiffs' attempts to suppress publication of The Lexicon therefore violate Defendant's protected rights. Defendant's proposed Lexicon cover has disclaimers and the term "Unofficial" in its title, and as disclaimers are a favored way of alleviating any alleged consumer confusion as to source or sponsorship, there is no likelihood of confusion with Plaintiffs' trademarks. Defendant does not use *Harry Potter* as a trademark, but rather only to the extent necessary to identify Defendant's Lexicon, and

therefore any alleged use of the mark is lawful based on the doctrine of fair use. Defendant only uses J.K. Rowling's name on the cover of the Lexicon book in the context of its disclaimer and it creates no likelihood of confusion with Plaintiff J.K. Rowling's mark.

59. The allegations contained in paragraph 59 of the Amended Complaint constitute legal conclusions to which no response is required.

60. Defendant denies the allegations in paragraph 60 of the Amended Complaint, and specifically denies that any of its actions has caused or threatens to cause any damage to Plaintiffs. Defendant has the right to publish an original literary reference guide, and Plaintiffs' attempts to suppress publication of The Lexicon therefore violate Defendant's protected rights.

COUNT FOUR – FALSE ADVERTISING
(15 U.S.C. § 1125(a)(1)(B))

61. Defendant hereby incorporates its responses to Paragraphs 1 through 60 above as if fully set forth herein.

62. Defendant denies the allegations contained in paragraph 62 of the Amended Complaint. Defendant has the right to publish an original literary reference guide and Plaintiffs' attempts to suppress publication of The Lexicon therefore violate Defendant's protected rights. Defendant's proposed cover has disclaimers and the term "Unofficial" in its title, and as disclaimers are a favored way of alleviating any alleged consumer confusion as to source or sponsorship, there is no likelihood of confusion with Plaintiffs' trademarks. Defendant does not use *Harry Potter* as a trademark, but rather only to the extent necessary to identify Defendant's Lexicon, and therefore any alleged use of the mark is lawful based on the doctrine of fair use. Defendant only uses J.K. Rowling's name on the cover of the Lexicon book in the context of its disclaimer and it creates no likelihood of confusion with Plaintiff J.K. Rowling's mark.

63. Defendant denies the allegations in paragraph 63 of the Amended Complaint. Defendant has the right to publish an original literary reference guide and Plaintiffs' attempts to suppress publication of The Lexicon violate Defendant's rights. Defendant's proposed Lexicon cover has disclaimers and the term "Unofficial" in its title, and as disclaimers are a favored way of alleviating any alleged consumer confusion as to source or sponsorship, there is no likelihood of confusion with Plaintiffs' trademarks. Defendant does not use *Harry Potter* as a trademark, but rather only to the extent necessary to identify Defendant's Lexicon, and therefore any alleged use of the mark is

lawful based on the doctrine of fair use. Defendant only uses J.K. Rowling's name on the cover of the Lexicon book in the context of its disclaimers and it creates no likelihood of confusion with Plaintiff J.K. Rowling's mark and these allegations in paragraph 63 of the Amended Complaint are moot.

64. Defendant denies the allegations contained in paragraph 64 of the Amended Complaint that it has damaged Plaintiffs, and further denies that anything it has done threatens Plaintiffs with "immediate and irreparable harm".

COUNT FIVE – RIGHT OF PRIVACY
(New York Civil Rights Law §§ 50-51)

65. Defendant hereby incorporates its responses to Paragraphs 1 through 64 above as if fully set forth herein.

66. The allegations contained in paragraph 66 of the Amended Complaint constitute legal argument and conclusion, and do not require a response.

67. Defendant denies the allegations contained in paragraph 67 of the Amended Complaint that it has damaged Plaintiffs, and further denies that anything it has done threatens Plaintiffs with "immediate and irreparable harm."

COUNT SEVEN – UNFAIR COMPETITION
(New York General Common Law)

68. Defendant hereby incorporates its responses to Paragraphs 1 through 67 above as if fully set forth herein.

69. Defendant denies the allegations in paragraph 69 of the Amended Complaint. Defendant specifically denies that the cover or marketing materials are deceptive. Defendant has the right to publish an original literary reference guide and Plaintiffs' attempts to suppression publication of The Lexicon therefore violate Defendant's protected rights. Defendant's proposed Lexicon cover has a disclaimer and the term "Unofficial" in its title, and as disclaimers are a favored way of alleviating any alleged consumer confusion as to source or sponsorship, there is no likelihood of confusion with Plaintiffs' trademarks. Defendant does not use *Harry Potter* as a trademark, but rather only to the extent necessary to identify Defendant's Lexicon, and therefore any alleged use of the mark is lawful based on the doctrine of fair use. Defendant only uses J.K. Rowling's name on the cover of the Lexicon book in the context of its disclaimer and it creates no

likelihood of confusion with Plaintiff J.K. Rowling's mark and these
allegations in paragraph 69 of the Amended Complaint are moot. The quote
of J.K. Rowling on the back cover of the Lexicon book has been removed
from the cover and Defendant has confirmed it will not be included
anywhere in the printed Lexicon, and therefore these allegations in paragraph
69 of the Amended Complaint are moot. Defendant specifically denies any
unfair competition in that Defendant never published The Lexicon nor
released it into any market.

70. Defendant denies the allegations in paragraph 70 of the Amended
Complaint, and contends that Plaintiffs lack any basis for alleging damages
since Defendant never released or published its Lexicon and no members of
the public ever purchased The Lexicon. With respect to actual damages,
Defendant asserts that no members of the public (consumers) have been
actually confused and no sales have been diverted from Plaintiffs, as The
Lexicon has never been published or sold. Defendant further alleges that The
Lexicon would not compete either with the Harry Potter Books or the Harry
Potter films, and notes that Plaintiffs have not even alleged otherwise.
Defendant denies that Plaintiffs have any basis for alleging actual damages
with respect to a lexicon or encyclopedia by Ms. Rowling, and note that Ms.
Rowling has not released any lexicon or encyclopedia concerning the Harry
Potter Books.

COUNT EIGHT – DECLARATORY JUDGMENT
REGARDING COPYRIGHT INFRINGEMENT
(17 U.S.C. §§ 101 et seq.)

71. Defendant hereby incorporates its responses to Paragraphs 1
through 70 above as if fully set forth herein.

72. Defendant denies the allegations in paragraph 72 of the Amended
Complaint and reasserts to this Court its withdrawal of any allegations that
Plaintiffs may have infringed any rights of Defendant in the timeline.

73. Defendant is without knowledge or information sufficient to
form a belief as to the truth of the allegations in paragraph 73 of the
Amended Complaint.

74. Defendant denies the allegations in paragraph 74 of the Amended
Complaint.

75. Defendant denies the allegations in paragraph 75 of the Amended
Complaint.

76. Defendant denies the allegations in paragraph 76 of the Amended Complaint.

77. Defendant denies the allegations in paragraph 77 of the Amended Complaint.

78. Defendant is without knowledge or information sufficient to form a belief as to the truth of the allegations in paragraph 78 of the Amended Complaint, and notes that it has withdrawn any possible allegations, express or implied, that Warner Bros. has violated Defendant's copyright in the timeline.

79. All allegations of the Amended Complaint not specifically admitted or denied above are hereby denied.

FIRST AFFIRMATIVE DEFENSE (Failure to State a Claim)
80. Plaintiffs have failed to state a claim against Defendant upon which relief may be granted.

SECOND AFFIRMATIVE DEFENSE (Estoppel/Laches/Waiver)
81. Plaintiffs' claims are barred in whole or part under principles of equity, including laches, waiver, and/or estoppel.

THIRD AFFIRMATIVE DEFENSE (Unclean Hands)
82. Plaintiffs' claims are barred by the doctrine of unclean hands.

FOURTH AFFIRMATIVE DEFENSE (Fair Use - Copyright)
83. Defendant's alleged use of the *Harry Potter* Works is lawful and constitutes fair use pursuant to 17 U.S.C. § 107.

FIFTH AFFIRMATIVE DEFENSE (Fair Use - Trademark)
84. Defendant's alleged use of *Harry Potter* is lawful based on the doctrine of fair use as Defendant does not use the mark as a trademark, but only as much as is reasonably necessary to identify Defendant's Lexicon.

SIXTH AFFIRMATIVE DEFENSE (First Amendment)
85. Plaintiffs' claims are barred by the First Amendment's guarantees of free speech.

86. Plaintiffs' claims are barred because Plaintiffs acquiesced, ratified or consented to Defendant's alleged actions alleged use of Plaintiffs' marks in its acquiescence to the *Harry Potter* Lexicon website.

EIGHTH AFFIRMATIVE DEFENSE (Copyright Misuse)

87. Plaintiffs' claims for copyright infringement are barred by the doctrine of copyright misuse.

NINTH AFFIRMATIVE DEFENSE (Standing)

88. Plaintiffs' claims for trademark infringement, false designation of origin, false advertising, unfair competition and alleged deceptive trade practices are barred because Plaintiffs lack standing to prosecute these claims against Defendant. Defendant and Plaintiffs were not in competition at the time of the alleged violation and Defendant did not release its book or sell a product.

TENTH AFFIRMATIVE DEFENSE (Disclaimer)

89. Plaintiffs' claims for trademark infringement, false designation of origin, false advertising, unfair competition and deceptive trade practices are barred because an injunction is improper where an explanation or disclaimer will suffice.

ELEVENTH AFFIRMATIVE DEFENSE (No Damages)

90. Plaintiffs' claims are barred because Plaintiffs suffered no legally cognizable damages as a result of any act or omission by Defendant.

94. Plaintiff has failed to mitigate its purported damages and recovery of any such damages, if any, must be reduced accordingly.

THIRTEENTH AFFIRMATIVE DEFENSE (Non-Willfulness)

95. Defendant's actions were innocent and non-willful.

FOURTEENTH AFFIRMATIVE DEFENSE (No Profits)

96. Defendant has not reaped any profits attributable to any alleged infringements.

FIFTEENTH AFFIRMATIVE DEFENSE (Further Affirmative Defenses)

97. Defendant reserves the right to plead additional defenses as they become known during investigation and/or course of this case.

Dated: March 11, 2008 New York, New York

Respectfully submitted,
David S. Hammer (DH 9957)
99 Park Avenue, Suite 1600
New York, New York 10016
Anthony Falzone, Esq.   Attorneys for Defendant RDR Books

TRANSCRIPT OF J.K. ROWLING
TRIAL TESTIMONY (EDITED)
April 14, 2008 and April 16, 2008

TESTIMONY GIVEN ON APRIL 14, 2008

THE COURT (Judge Patterson): All right. First witness.

MS. CENDALI: Thank you, your Honor. (Dale Cendali, attorney for Ms. Rowling)

MS. CENDALI: Plaintiffs call Joanne Rowling.

JOANNE ROWLING, called as a witness by the plaintiff, having been duly sworn, testified as follows:

DEPUTY COURT CLERK: Please state your name and spell your last name slowly for the record, please.

THE WITNESS: Joanne Rowling, R-O-W-L-I-N-G.

MS. CENDALI: May I proceed, your Honor?

THE COURT: Yes, you may.

DIRECT EXAMINATION BY MS. CENDALI

Q. Good morning, Ms. Rowling.

A. Good morning.

Q. Do you also have a pen name?

A. I do.

Q. What is it?

A. J.K. Rowling.

Q. Have you ever testified in any court proceeding?

A. No.

Q. Are you nervous?

A. I am.

Q. Are you the creator of the Harry Potter series?

A. Yes, I am.

Q. Do you own the copyrights to the seven Harry Potter books?

A. Yes, I do.

MS. CENDALI: Your Honor, may I approach and hand the witness an exhibit?

THE COURT: Surely.

MS. CENDALI: I would like to hand the witness what has been previously marked as Plaintiff's Exhibit 1, The Lexicon manuscript.

Q. Have you seen that manuscript before, Plaintiff's Exhibit 1?

A. Yes, I have.

Q. Is that the manuscript that's the subject of this lawsuit?

A. Yes, it is.

Q. Did you license any of your copyrights to RDR for use in connection that book?

A. No, I did not.

Q. Do you have a view as to whether that book should be published?

A. Yes, I have a very strong view.

Q. Could you please briefly tell the court what your view is?

A. I believe that this book constitutes wholesale theft of 17 years of my hard work. I believe that it adds little if anything in the way of commentary, that the quality of that commentary is derisory, and that it debases what I worked so hard to create.

Q. Now, Ms. Rowling, I'd like to talk to you a little bit about your background and how you came to create the world of Harry Potter. Let's start in the beginning, where were you born?

A. I was born in Yate, in England.

Q. Did you go to university in England?

A. I did, yes.

G. Where do you live now?

A. I live in Scotland, in Edinburgh.

Q. Are you married?

A. Yes.

Q. To who?

A. To Dr. Neil Murray.

Q. Does he work as a doctor?

A. He does, yes.

Q. Do you have children?

A. We have three children.

Q. What are their names and ages?

A. Jessica, 14; David, 5; and Kenzie, 3.

Q. Now, let's talk about how you came to write the Harry Potter books. When did you start writing the first Harry Potter book?

A. I started writing the first book in 1990.

Q. So that would have been 18 years ago?

A. Yes.

Q. How old were you at the time?

A. 25.

Q. How long did it take you to finish writing that first book?

A. It took -- between having the idea for the book and the book being published was seven years, but that sounds as though I'm a very slow worker, but I was holding down a day job for most of that time, and I was also planning what subsequently became a seven book series.

Q. How were you supporting yourself while you were writing the Harry Potter first book?

A. I worked for a time for Amnesty International. Then I was working as a teacher, but in the later stages of writing the book I was on what you call in America welfare.

Q. Why was that necessary?

A. My first marriage had broken down, and I was a full-time caretaker for my eldest daughter, who was a very small baby at the time.

Q. Was this a difficult period in your life?

A. It was an extremely difficult period, yes.

Q. At some point did you ever get a grant to help you support your writing?

A. Yes, I did. After the first book had been accepted for publication, the Scottish Arts Counsel made me a grant to enable me to provide child care for my daughter so that I could write a second book.

Q. Do you remember what that grant was for?

A. I believe it was for $8,000 pounds, which for me at the time was an absolute fortune.

Q. Now, was it an easy process to find an agent and publisher for the Harry Potter books?

A. I would say that it wasn't although I did manage to get an agent on my second attempt, but then he had some difficulty in finding a publisher.

Q. Is the Christopher Little agency your literary agency?

A. Yes.

Q. Did they immediately accept your manuscript?

A. No. I had submitted the first three chapters, so they asked could they see the balance of the book, so I then had to type it up, which was 95,000 words. I submitted that to them, and they said they liked it double spaced, so I had to type it yet again.

Q. And why didn't you get somebody to do it for you?

A. Because I literally did not -- well, there were weeks when the food ran out, you know, so to pay someone hundreds of pounds to type a manuscript, there was simply no money for that.

Q. Ms. Rowling, Harry Potter was eventually accepted by publishers, correct?

A. Yes, it was.

Q. Who is your publisher in the United Kingdom?

A. Bloomsbury.

Q. Who is your publisher in the United States?

A. Scholastic.

Q. Ms. Rowling, have you been surprised by the success of the Harry Potter books?

A. There isn't a word big enough. Flabbergasted, astonished.

Q. Have the books won any awards?

A. Yes, they have.

Q. What types of awards have they won?

A. The British Book Award, many children's literary awards.

Q. Now, Ms. Rowling, when was the last of the seven Harry Potter books published?

A. July 2007.

Q. What was its title?

A. Harry Potter and the Deathly Hallows.

Q. Overall, how long did it take you to write the Harry Potter series?

A. 17 years.

Q. And how much time did that take?

A. It was my life. Apart from my children, it was my life.

Q. Ms. Rowling, what does Harry Potter mean to you?

A. I really don't want to cry because I'm British, you know. It means setting aside my children, everything.

Q. Ms. Rowling, I noticed this morning you were wearing a bracelet. Can you tell the court about that bracelet?

A. It's a bracelet my UK publisher gave to me on publication of the seventh book.

Q. Is there anything unusual about it?

A. It's a charm bracelet representing things that I invented in Harry Potter books.

Q. Do you care, Ms. Rowling, about how your Harry Potter characters are presented?

A. Very, very deeply, yes.

Q. Does that affect any decision you make about licensing Harry Potter?

A. It's my prime concern, if not my only concern.

Q. Could you explain what you mean?

A. I mean that these characters meant so much to me, and continue to mean so much to me over such a long period of time. It's very difficult in fact for someone who is not a writer to understand what it means to the creator. I think the very closest you could come is to say to someone how do you feel about your child. You know, these books, they saved me not just in the very obvious material sense, although they did do that, they provided security for my daughter that I never thought I would be able to provide her, but I would have to say that there was a time when they saved my sanity. It was a place into which I liked to vanish, and it was a discipline that was very important in keeping me sane.

Q. And, Ms. Rowling, other than the seven Harry Potter novels, have you written any other books about Harry Potter?

A. Yes, I've wrote two companion books which were books within the novels, Fantastic Beasts and Where to Find Them and Quidditch Through the Ages.

Q. Do you own the copyright to those books?

A. Yes, I do.

Q. Why did you publish those books?

A. I was approached by Richard Curtis who is the screen writer and director, and who is the head of Comic Relief, which is a very big charity in the UK, and he asked me would I consider writing a Harry Potter short story for the charity. And I said to him, well, what I thought would be good and would raise more money would be to write these two short books. I thought that children particularly would find them entertaining.

Q. Have you been able to give any money to charity as a result of those books?

A. I think the last figure I heard for Fantastic Beasts and Quidditch Through the Ages was 18 million pounds had gone to charity.

Q. So with this current exchange rate would be over $30 million?

A. Yes, I think so.

Q. Now, to be clear, were you donating just a portion of the proceeds or were you donating all your proceeds?

A. All the royalties went to the charity.

Q. Have you ever written a Harry Potter-related story for auction?

A. Yes. Last year I hand wrote seven copies of the Tales of Beedle the Bard, which is another book within the Harry Potter novels.

Q. And why did you do that?

A. Six of the copies were to give to people who had been key in the Harry Potter series, people who had worked with me for ten years. And the seventh book I decided to auction, and the proceeds went to a charity I cofounded.

Q. Tell us about that charity.

A. It's a charity called the children's voice, and it campaigns for children's health and human rights, mostly in Eastern Europe.

Q. Ms. Rowling, have you ever licensed anyone to publish an A to Z encyclopedia of your work?

A. No.

Q. Why not?

A. Because it's been my long-stated intention that I wanted to do that myself.

Q. When did you first announce that you wanted to write your own encyclopedia?

A. It's very hard to be accurate about a date, but I know I've been saying it in interviews and in conversations with fans since I believe about '98. I know that I was being asked questions about further books after the series as early as that.

Q. How often have you repeated to the press your interest in writing a Harry Potter encyclopedia?

A. Many, many times.

Q. Were you on a book tour in relation to the release of Harry Potter book seven this summer and fall?

A. Yes, I was, yes.

Q. And in connection with the release of Deathly Hallows, the last -- the seventh, I hope not the last -- Harry Potter book, did you again tell the press in July 2000 that you intended to write a Harry Potter encyclopedia?

A. Yes, I did.

Q. Have you begun working on that encyclopedia?

A. Yes, I have.

Q. What stage are you at?

A. An early stage, but I'm assembling all my materials. I'm fleshing out the plan, and I have requested certain materials from my publishers that I hope to use to complete the book, so I'm hoping to move forward with that.

Q. I would like to put up the screen the first page of Plaintiff's Exhibit 23A. Do you recognize that document, Ms. Rowling?

A. Yes, I do.

Q. What is it?

A. It's what is called, without any intent at blaphesmy, it's what is known as the bible at my UK publisher.

Q. And how is it organized?

A. Largely A to Zed, I dare say. A to Z, story.

Q. Let's turn to the page of the Beasts and Beings section of Exhibit 23A. Can you tell us about that page?

A. This is simply an alphabetical list of animals that appear in the Harry Potter books.

Q. Did you ask Bloomsbury to provide you with a copy of this material?

A. Yes, I have.

Q. And do you intend to use it in working on your encyclopedia?

A. Yes, I do.

Q. You mentioned your publisher Scholastic as well. Let's look at Exhibit 18A, the first page of that. Do you recognize that document?

A. Yes, I do.

Q. What is it?

A. Scholastic also called that the bible. It's their bible, and that's also a list of major -- well, all characters, I believe, in the Harry Potter books.

Q. And are you planning to use the Scholastic material to help you write your encyclopedia?

A. Yes, I am.

Q. Are you planning on using an A to Z format for your encyclopedia?

A. Yes, I am.

Q. When do you expect to complete your encyclopedia, Ms. Rowling?

A. Well, until quite recently I would have said two to three years would be a reasonable estimate. I want to do it properly. I don't want to rush it.

Q. What happened recently?

A. I would say that about four weeks ago maybe the demands of this court case have been such that it's caused me to halt work on the novel I am writing. It's really decimated my creative work over the last month. Again, it's very hard to describe to someone who isn't engaged in creative writing, but you lose the threads, you worry if you will be able to pick them up again in exactly the same way. It's certainly caused harm to my writing process currently. And I must admit that at that time I began to contemplate the possibility of The Lexicon being published, and should it be published I firmly believe that carte blanche will be given to anyone who wants to make a quick bit of money, to divert some Harry Potter profits into their own pockets. They can do it very easily; they can simply lift my words verbatim wholesale, put it into an alphabetical rearrangement and call it a guide. And should that happen, should my fans be glutted with a surfeit of substandard so-called lexicons and guides, I'm not at all convinced that I would have the will or the heart to continue with my encyclopedia. I already have enormous negative connotations. Every time I think of my encyclopedia, all I think of frankly is The Lexicon, and RDR, and Mr. Vander Ark, and all the stress and heartache that has gone along with wanting to take a stand on this book. And I think it's important to explain that writing a novel is a labor of love, it's an exciting project for me, but an encyclopedia is very different, it's not something that I approach with passion. The encyclopedia I always saw as a kind of give-back to fans who had been amazing and loyal to me over ten years waiting for these books to come out, and I also saw it as another very magnificent opportunity to make money for charity, but I never approached it with the same lightness of heart that you would approach a novel.

Q. Ms. Rowling, if you do publish your encyclopedia, do you intend to make money from it?

A. It was always my intention, as I've been saying for years, that any royalties I made would be given probably to my charitable trust.

Q. Now, let's talk more about The Lexicon that's at issue in this case. When did you learn that defendant was planning on publishing this book?

A. October last year.

Q. And was this during your book tour for the Deathly Hallows?

A. It was, I was here in the States, yes.

Q. What was your reaction upon hearing the news?

A. I was extremely shocked. I had assumed all along that Mr. Vander Ark was operating in good faith. Indeed, I believed his pronouncements that this was something that he did as a hobby. There had never been any intimation to me that he intended to publish The Lexicon. And I did feel a degree of betrayal.

Q. Ms. Rowling, that big binder that I gave you, Exhibit 1, have you read it?

A. Yes, I have read it.

Q. Have you read every word?

A. I believe I have.

Q. Based upon your review of The Lexicon, what's your overall impression of the book?

A. I believe that it is sloppy, lazy, and that it takes my work wholesale verbatim. There is an absolutely minimal amount of paraphrasing. It abridges my plots. And what does it add? What benefit does the reader have? There are facetious asides, comments occasionally tacked on to the end of entries. There is a tiny amount of etymologies, always of the easiest kind. A child with a pocket Latin dictionary could decipher what Mr. Vander Ark has deciphered, and worryingly, given that the excuse apparently for this massive wholesale copying is that this is some kind of reference book. There are incorrect translations, there are incorrect etymologies, and there are places where Mr. Vander Ark quite literally has not understood the books. So, even in the loosest, most popular sense, I do not consider this a worthwhile guide. And to me the idea of my readership parting with their or their parents' hard earned cash for this, I think it's a travesty.

Q. You have heard the opening statement of RDR's counsel talking about how the Lexicon was useful in some way. As the author of the Harry Potter books, do you think it's useful?

A. No, I absolutely see no use for it. I don't see what the use is.

Q. Now, let's put on the screen Exhibit 501A, the proposed cover for the Lexicon. Do you see there is a monitor right there, Ms. Rowling?

A. Yes, I do.

Q. You can see his Honor has one at the bench as well. On the cover it says The Lexicon, an Unauthorized Guide to Harry Potter Fiction and Related Materials, by Steve Vander Ark. Having read the manuscript, does the Lexicon appear to you to contain Mr. Vander Ark's creative work?

A. In my view from what I've read, absolutely not.

Q. Whose creative work do you believe is in the Lexicon?

A. It is mine.

Q. And why do you say that?

A. Because every entry you will see my plots, my words often verbatim, rarely with quotation marks around them. As I say, what Mr. Vander Ark has added is not only of little use, it sometimes actually would mislead.

MS. CENDALI: May I approach, your Honor, to hand the witness an exhibit?

THE COURT: Yes, you may.

Q. I'd like to hand you Plaintiff's Exhibit 47.

A. Thank you very much.

Q. Ms. Rowling, I will put the first page of Exhibit 47 on the screen. Could you please tell the court what that document is.

A. Yes, it's a chart I made to show what I felt was the constant pilfering of my work.

MS. CENDALI: Mr. Hoy, would you please scroll down that chart, Exhibit 47, to publish it to the court.

Q. Ms. Rowling, did anyone assist you in drafting that document?

A. My 14-year-old daughter. She sat alongside the table, and I told her where to look for the parts I recognized from the Lexicon, and she would look them up and read them out to me, and I would type out what I had written, and next to it I would type out almost the identical passage that came from the Lexicon.

Q. So you typed this yourself?

A. I did, yes.

Q. Did anyone ask to you draft this document?

A. No.

Q. Why did you do it?

A. Because I feel extremely strongly about this case, and I wanted to show -- I felt the need to show what my problem with the book is in this very graphic form.

Q. Well, let's put up on the screen one of the entries from your chart which is Exhibit 47, which is in demonstrative form with regard to the brain room. Now, the brain room is something you created in the Harry Potter universe, is that right?

A. Yes.

Q. And what about this comparison interests or concerns you?

A. Well, to me at least, if to someone to no one else, but to me it's a memorable image. I worked hard to find a way of expressing this fact that this disembodied brain was leaking memories and thoughts as it flew through the air, and I decided that the image I wanted to use was that of strips of film untangling and unraveling behind it as it came. So, to find this precise image, one word changed, with no quotation marks around it, in Mr. Vander Ark's so-called book, I mean it's an assertion that he wrote this. There are no quotation marks around it. I feel if he put quotation marks around everything he has lifted from my book, there would pretty much be quotation marks around the whole substance of the book, with a few little sides omitted.

Q. Well, let's take a look at another example, to the Lexicon entry for "armor, goblin-made". And on the left is your writing from Deathly Hallows, is that correct?

A. Yes.

Q. And on the right is the Lexicon entry, correct?

A. Yes, that's right.

Q. Again, can you explain again what if anything concerns you about that entry in the Lexicon?

A. Well, again there is a very recognizable phrase of mine at the end of this passage, "imbibing only that which strengthens it ..." This was a key plot point about the goblin silver. And, again, the Lexicon, without quotation marks, has lifted "imbibing only that which strengthens it." So, Mr. Vander Ark without using quotation marks are claiming these words are his own invention.

Q. Did you struggle to coin that phrase?

A. I would say that one came quite easily. I can't pretend I bled over that one, but this happens in virtually every entry. Even my list is not exhaustive.

Q. Let's look at another entry, the one for clankers. Again on the left, is that text from Deathly Hallows, your novel?

A. Right.

Q. And on the right is The Lexicon entry?

A. Yes.

Q. And could you explain to the court your view about that example.

A. Well, again, this is just evidence, in my view, of the utter laziness of Mr. Vander Ark. He simply copies. He says that the dragon has apparently been taught to fear hot swords whenever it hears the clankers. Well, that is exactly what I wrote. These things have no existence except in my words, so he is taking my creation.

Q. Now, Ms. Rowling, to what extent do you think the Lexicon abridges your work?

A. At every possible opportunity.

Q. Well, can you give us some examples?

A. The approach of the Lexicon, I believe, is wherever it lists a character, Mr. Vander Ark generally gives the character's appearance verbatim in my words without quotation marks and then he abridges the plots of any book in which that character appears.

MS. CENDALI: Can you put up on the screen from Exhibit 1, The Lexicon, the first page of the entry for Voldemort. Forgive me for speaking the name. Mr. Hoy, could you please scroll down so that the entire entry can be published to the court.

Q. OK. Ms. Rowling, is the entry for the Voldemort character a lengthy one?

A. Very lengthy, yes, several pages.

Q. And again, Ms. Rowling, could you scroll down to publish that entry to the court. Ms. Rowling, what's your view of that entry?

A. I think it represents both wholesale lifting again of my plots -- that's plots 1 to 7 -- of books 1 to 7 -- and it also represents the most enormous missed opportunity. Other critics in genuine guides to Harry Potter that are already published have found a lot to say about Voldemort, about what he represents, his psychology, the archetype of a villain, of this particular kind of super natural villain. And we have none of that here at all, nothing. I think it's lazy, just very, very lazy.

Q. Now, so far we've mainly discussed your Harry Potter books themselves. Let's turn to your book Quidditch Through the Ages. Do you have a view of whether the Lexicon copies that book?

A. I would say Quidditch Through the Ages has been plundered by Mr. Vander Ark. There is absolutely no reason if this lexicon is published why anyone would want to buy that book that I created for charity.

Q. Well, let's put on the screen what has been marked as Exhibit 43A. Do you recognize that document?

A. Yes, I do.

Q. What is it?

A. That's a chart showing the copying from Quidditch through the ages by the Lexicon.

Q. And have you studied that chart?

A. I have. I have looked right through it, yes.

Q. Have you compared it to your work in the Lexicon?

A. Yes, I have.

Q. And could you please explain the chart to the court.

A. On the left-hand side you see examples of what I wrote within Quidditch Through the Ages. On the right-hand side we have the Lexicon's marginal paraphrasing of what I wrote. Mr. Vander Ark has gutted that book. That book -- there is nothing interpretive there, there is no commentary. He has simply copied it. He has just taken it and copied it.

MS. CENDALI: Mr. Hoy, would you please scroll down that exhibit to publish it to the court.

Q. Approximately how many pages is the exhibit, Ms. Rowling?

A. My goodness, is it 32 pages? That's very shocking.

Q. Now, let's take a look at one of the comparisons in the chart, the Lexicon entry for Chudley Cannons. Now, am I correct that on this what's been marked for identification as Plaintiff's Exhibit 168, on the left is what you wrote in Quidditch Through the Ages and on the right is what is in the Lexicon?

A. That's correct, yes.

Q. Could you explain your views about this lexicon entry to the court.

A. I mean again these fictional facts -- which evidently they have intrinsic entertainment value to anyone who likes Harry Potter and wants to read this book -- have simply been taken. There is nothing there that I haven't written. There is a tiny paraphrase. I think what particularly galls is the lack of quotation marks. As I say, if Mr. Vander Ark had put quotation marks around everything he has lifted, most of the Lexicon would be in quotation marks.

Q. Ms. Rowling, does the Lexicon add any commentary or analysis to your Quidditch Through the Ages book?

A. I don't believe it does.

Q. Now, let's talk about your book Fantastic Beasts and Where to Find Them. Do you have a view as to whether the Lexicon copies that work?

A. Again, a very strong view. I feel that as with Quidditch Through the Ages, Fantastic Beasts has been simply taken and taken wholesale. Again, I see no incentive whatsoever for anyone to give their money to Comic Relief if they had bought a copy of the Lexicon, because the whole book is repeated virtually word for word in the Lexicon.

Q. Let's look at Exhibit 44, the Fantastic Beast comparison chart. Have you studied that chart?

A. Yes, I have.

MS. CENDALI: Mr. Hoy, again could you scroll down so that that entire exhibit in its length can be presented to the court.

Q. Ms. Rowling, could you explain briefly that comparison chart to the court.

A. Once again on left-hand side you have what I wrote in Fantastic Beasts and Where to Find Them, and on the right-hand side you have The Lexicon's entries, which as you can see are virtually identical in all respects to my precise wording.

Q. Let's look at an example from Exhibit 44. Let's put up on the screen what's been marked for identification as Exhibit 169 which shows an entry from Exhibit

444 comparing the Lexicon entry for Chinese Fireball with the text from Fantastic Beasts. Again, could you explain to the court your view about this example.

A. I think this is far from exceptional. This is very typical of the kind of entries that concern me so much. But once again there is a dragon type or species that I have invented, and Mr. Vander Ark has simply copied my words. And in doing that, he has effectively taken -- he's taken my creation because, after all, it has no existence outside my words. He is simply taking what I recreated. If we were both describing a giraffe, then inevitably certain words would occur in both descriptions, but it's not as though we're both describing a creature that actually exists. The Chinese Fireball has no existence outside the words and phrases I have used to describe it, which he has taken.

Q. Does the Lexicon add any of its own commentary to the Chinese Fireball entry?

A. Nothing at all.

Q. Does it add any commentary at all in your reviewing the Lexicon to the Fantastic Beast entries?

A. I don't believe it does.

Q. Now, you touched on this a little bit earlier. I believe you talked about -- you mentioned analysis and commentary, but I want to be clear. As the author of the Harry Potter books, did you see any analysis or commentary of your books in the Lexicon?

A. There is a tiny amount of what purports to be commentary, but I think for those who haven't read the Lexicon it must be understood that what Mr. Vander Ark puts -- his so-called commentary is in italics at the bottom of an entry. Occasionally it's a facetious remark. Occasionally it's an etymology. The number of invented words and terms, names in my books, given the number of those things, he has done a tiny, tiny, tiny fraction of them has he attempted to give some kind of etymology for. And many of those are erroneous; he has mistranslated. As it is my belief, as I say, that most of the etymologies are cases where I give a spell that's recognizably from the Latin, and in that case he will simply translate the Latin word. Any seven-year-old with a pocket Latin dictionary could do that. And he doesn't even do that exhaustively, so it's not as though everything that came from the Latin is translated. I think it's a tiny and derisory quality of commentary.

Q. Now, earlier I believe you said something about missed opportunities. Are there examples of the Lexicon of missed opportunities that you believe highlight the lack of analysis in the Lexicon?

A. Where to begin? Where to begin? I mean the letter -- oh, where to begin? The letter A, if we literally go through the book alphabetically there are -- abraxan -- we just saw the word abraxan on the screen from Fantastic Beasts -- there is no attempt at an etymology.

MR. HAMMER (attorney for RDR Books): I'm sorry. I object. What the book does not contain really is not at issue in the case; it's what it does contain.

THE COURT: Objection overruled. I'm going to take the testimony.

Q. Ms. Rowling, let's put on the screen the ogre entry in the Lexicon. Could you read that to the court.

A. Ogre. Ron and Hermione think they see an Ogre at Three Broomsticks.

Q. What is your view of this entry, Ms. Rowling?

A. I think this goes to the heart of one of my largest objections about the Lexicon. If the child spread the word Ogre -- particularly a child, because I'm thinking largely for the value of companion books to younger readers who might not have the broad cultural understanding or the understanding of literature that an adult may -- if the child wondered what is an ogre, then what is the Lexicon telling them? It's telling them Ron and Hermione thought they saw an ogre. There is no explanation of what an ogre is. I mention ogres once in the whole seven book series, and I mention them when Ron and Hermione go into village Hogsmeade, to the Three

Broomsticks Pub, and Hermione comes back and says to Harry, Ron and I thought we saw an ogre in the Three Broomsticks. So, that's what the Lexicon gives the reader on ogre. And an ogre in folklore, European folklore, was a flesh-eating giant, which I think is of some interest if you have an interest in ogres. It would be interesting to know that, not to be told what you have already read in the Harry Potter book.

MS. CENDALI: Let's put on the screen the entry for death from the Lexicon, Plaintiff's Exhibit 1. What is your view of that entry, Ms. Rowling?

A. Well, here again I think it's truly laughable that even in -- as I say, even in the loosest, most popular sense, even if no one is asserting that this is a scholarly work -- many of the books that have been published on Harry Potter books, they're light hearted, they are not purporting to be works of deep scholarship, but they give the reader something. Any guide to the Harry Potter books should have a lengthy entry on death. It is probably the major theme of the whole seven book series, and it appears in so many different ways. You can discuss the attitude of the leading characters to death, which is enormously revealing about their psychology. You can talk about the fantastic objects that I created that either attempt to overcome death or are dangerous and may cause fatalities. And yet the Lexicon -- presumably because saying of that would involve some independent work and research -- simply says that death appears in a children's story within my novel. That's the entry on death.

MS. CENDALI: Let's put on the screen the entry for occamy. Am I pronouncing that correctly

A. Yes. You can pronounce it any way you like; it's not a real thing, you know.

Q. Again from Exhibit 1, The Lexicon. Which of your works did you write about occamy?

A. This is from Fantastic Beasts and Where to Find Them.

Q. And again do you have a view of this entry in yhe Lexicon?

A. Well, this one I found. When I read the Lexicon and I saw this one, this one made me smile to myself, because this should have been a sitting duck for Mr. Vander Ark.

Q. What do you mean?

A. I mean I read that he claims that one of the works he used to help him add value, as it were, to my work, one of his research tools was the Dictionary of Phrase and Fable. Now, I was pretty sure that he should have been able to work out my little joke if he had looked in the Dictionary of Phrase and Fable, and so I went and looked it up, and I was correct. Ockham was a philosopher, an English philosopher, most famous for what is known as Ockham's Razor, which is the statement nothing should be presumed to exist which is not absolutely necessary. So, this was my little joke, my little private joke to create an occamy in a book of things that were quite clearly not at all necessary. And there is nothing there. All the Lexicon has done is reprint what I wrote about the fictional creature the occamy.

Q. Let's look at some of your longer -- some of the longer entr ies in the Lexicon manuscript. Let's look at the one for Remus Lupin. That's again from Exhibit 1. Under L for Lupin, Remus. What's your view of that entry?

A. First it does what the Lexicon always does, which is to abridge the books in which this character appears. But I was surprised, very surprised, when I turned to Remus Lupin, because I thought this would be a very easy one to add some commentary to.

Q. Why is that?

A. Well, first Mr. Vander Ark does occasionally give the meaning of the names I've given to my characters. I would think this is a very, very obvious one to explain. Generally he does go to the obvious ones. This is a double allusion to the fact this character is a werewolf, so there is Remus, who is one of the brothers who was raised by wolves in Roman anthology, and Lupin, which comes from "lupine," wolf-like. But there was more on Lupin. And again, it

should have been easy to anyone writing a -- genuinely attempting to write a guide. I know that I've said publicly that Remus Lupin was supposed to be on the H.I.V. metaphor. It was someone who had been infected young, who suffered stigma, who had a fear of infecting others, who was terrified he would pass on his condition to his son. And it was a way of examining prejudice, unwarranted prejudice towards a group of people. And also, examining why people might become embittered when they're treated that unfairly. There is not one single attempt to examine that, which is a key factor in the creation of the character. There is not even a gesture towards explaining any of that on this entry. All we have are abridged plots of the books in which Lupin appears.

Q. Now, in addition to, in your view, taking material from your books, does the Lexicon take material from any of your other creations?

A. Yes, it does.

Q. Let's talk about the Daily Prophet. What is the Daily Prophet?

A. Back in -- very early on in my publishing career, when – I think in about 1998, I produced a small run of fictional newspapers, Daily Prophet Newspapers. Which were sent out free to thousands by my UK publisher. They were very time consuming to produce, and I think my publisher decided they'd rather I concentrated on writing novels. I think three went out to fans, and Mr. Vander Ark has again lifted wholesale from those publications.

Q. Where did you create the Daily Prophet?

A. In the UK.

Q. And was it was distributed there as well?

A. Yes, it was.

Q. Do you own the copyright to the Daily Prophet?

A. Yes.

Q. Let's put on the screen Exhibit 46. Can you describe to the Court what Exhibit 46 is.

A. Again this is a comparison. On the left-hand side you have the fictional stories I put in my Daily Prophet newspapers, and on the right-hand side you have what the Lexicon has decided to take and reprint.

Q. Do you have a view as to whether the Lexicon copies the Daily Prophet?

A. It definitely copies the Daily Prophet.

Q. Now, let's look at one of the examples from the chart. Let's put on the screen what's been marked for identification as Exhibit 170, the Lexicon entry Dagbert Pips. Is there really such a person as Dagbert Pips?

A. If there is, I'm sure we'll find out after this court case. But I do not believe there is a Dagbert Pips.

Q. Could you explain to the Court your view about that Lexicon entry.

A. Yet again, this was just a very lighthearted news story, sort of fictional news story.

Q. Ms. Rowling, is there any commentary or analysis provided about your Dagbert Pips character?

A. None at all.

Q. Do you have a view as to how much commentary or analysis is provided to any of your Daily Prophet material?

A. There is no analysis that I can see.

Q. What are wizard cards?

A. Within the world of Harry Potter, if you buy a chocolate frog, then you receive a famous wizard card inside the wrapping.

Q. Did you create wizard cards for use in an Electronic Arts video game?

A. Yes, I did.

Q. And do Warner Bros. and Electronic Arts own the copyright to those cards?

A. Yes, I believe so.

Q. Let's put on the screen Exhibit 34. Can you please tell the Court what Exhibit 34 is.

A. This is a list of the famous wizards, well, fictional famous wizards, and their achievements and dates of life and death -- of birth and death, that I provided to Electronic Arts.

Q. Did you make these wizards up?

A. I did. Occasionally there is someone who existed in reality. I've taken some liberties with their biography.

Q. Did you create this chart yourself?

A. No, I didn't create this chart.

Q. But this was something that was used for making the wizard cards?

A. Yes, that's right.

Q. Now, to what extent do you believe the Lexicon copies your wizard cards?

A. Wholesale. Simply copied.

Q. Let's put on the screen Exhibit 45, The Wizard Cards comparison chart. Ms. Rowling, could you explain to the Court the Exhibit 45.

A. Here you have artwork that was produced by Electronic Arts, matched with the legends that I provided to them from my notebooks and various creations.

Q. To what degree do you believe the Lexicon copies your material from your magic cards?

A. As you can see from this page, they simply copy.

Q. Let's look at one of the examples from this chart which was one of the examples on the list of 75 that we gave counsel on Friday. Let's look at the example of Andros the invincible. To make it easier to read we just blew that up as a demonstrative, Plaintiff's Exhibit 171, but it is taken from Exhibit 45. And Ms. Rowling, could you explain that comparison to the Court.

A. On the left-hand side you have a text that I provided to Electronic Arts. And on the right-hand side the entry under Andros the Invincible in the Lexicon, as you can see, they're virtually identical.

Q. Does the Lexicon add any commentary or analysis to your descriptions of these wizard cards?

A. No, it does not. No.

Q. Now, Ms. Rowling, are you aware of books other than the Lexicon that have been written about Harry Potter?

A. Yes, I'm aware of many.

Q. Now, do you yourself handle the day-to-day policing of the Harry Potter copyrights?

A. No.

Q. Are you aware that your lawyers have occasionally taken action to protect your copyrights in the Harry Potter series?

A. Yes, I am.

Q. What types of books have raised concerns for you?

A. Books that are very similar to the Lexicon that's the subject of this case. Books that I -- I feel are an attempt to jump on the bandwagon. They are profit-driven attempts to resell to the public what it already owns. In other words, to lift the facts that make up the -- well, fictional facts, because it doesn't exist and I have to keep reminding myself that. The facts that make up the Harry Potter universe as it were, and resell them.

Q. Now, are there books written about Harry Potter -- well, are all A-to-Z guides necessarily off limits?

A. No. Definitely not.

Q. Are there books written about Harry Potter that use an A-to-Z format that you think take less of your work and provide more commentary?

A. Yes. Many of them.

Q. Do you have a problem with those books?

A. No problem at all. I like many of them.

MS. CENDALI: Just so the record is clear, Plaintiff's Exhibit 75, The Magical World of Harry Potter, by David Colbert. Exhibit 74, Fact, Fiction and Folklore in Harry Potter's World by George Beahm. Exhibit 73, The Complete Idiot's Guide to the World of Harry Potter by Tere Stouffer. Exhibit 192, The Sorcerer's Companion: A Guide to the Magical World of Harry Potter.

Q. Ms. Rowling, are you familiar with these books?

A. "Familiar" may be overstating it, but I have seen them before.

Q. Well, have you read many of the entries?

A. I've skim read a couple of them.

Q. Let's look at Plaintiff's Exhibit 73. And let's put the cover on the screen so we know which one we're talking about. Does this book contain an alphabetized guide to the Harry Potter books?

A. Yes, it does.

Q. Does it raise copyright concerns for you?

A. No, not at all.

Q. Did you sue to enjoin that book?

A. No.

Q. Let's put on the screen an entry from the Lexicon Exhibit 1. The Lexicon entry for Parcelsus. Can you read that to the court?

A. Paracelsus. A secretive wizard about whom little is known. There is a bust of him in a Hogwarts corridor that Peeves have been known to drop on people's heads.

Q. Did you read the entire Lexicon entry?

A. Yes, I did.

Q. Let's put on the screen the Paracelsus entry from the Idiot's Guide on Exhibit 73. What is your view as to how the Lexicon entry compares to the Idiot's Guide entry?

A. Well, there is absolutely no comparison. The Lexicon does not even explain that Paracelsus existed. Several of the incidental wizards and witches that I mentioned within the world of -- within the novel, Harry Potter novels, were believed to be real. Or certainly were real as in the case of Paracelsus. And so what Ms. Stouffer has done is to provide a succinct but very informative paragraph about that real person.

Q. Does that make a difference to you in terms of whether you object to a book?

A. An enormous difference. Clearly the Lexicon is – I believe trying to sell people what they already own. If they already own the Harry Potter books, then this is a shameless attempt to resell them the same information. Whereas this book, this guide, which is a genuine guide, is giving them all sorts of background information and additional information.

Q. Now, let's turn to Exhibit 74. The Fact, Fiction and Folklore in Harry Potter's book. Let's put that cover on the screen so people know what we're talking about and it can be published to the Court. Does this book contain an alphabetized guide to the Harry Potter books?

A. Yes, it does.

Q. Does it raise copyright concerns with you?

A. No.

Q. Did you sue to enjoin the book?

A. No.

Q. Why not?

A. I like this book. I haven't read it cover to cover, but it looks good to me.

Q. Well, let's look -- let's put on the screen the entry in the Lexicon Exhibit 1 for Florean Fortescue's ice crime parlor. Could you read that entry to the Court.

A. Florean Fortescue's ice cream parlor, a shop Harry has frequented in Diagon Alley where the owner gave him free sundaes and advice about his homework.

Q. Now let's put on the screen the first page of the entry for Florean Fortescue's ice cream parlor in Fact, Fiction and Folklore. Ms. Rowling, approximately how long is that entry?

A. About a page in total.

Q. What is your view as to how that entry compares with the entry in the Lexicon?

A. Well, once again, after stating briefly where ice cream appears, what happened at Florean Fortescue's, you then have some information, certainly which I didn't know, about ice cream. So you're certainly buying extra information if you get this book.

Q. Let's turn to Plaintiff's Exhibit 75, the Magical Worlds of Harry Potter by David Colbert. Ms. Rowling, does this book contain an alphabetized guide to the Harry Potter books?

A. Yes, it does.

Q. Does it raise copyright concerns for you?

A. No.

Q. Did you sue to enjoin that book?

A. No.

Q. Why not?

A. I really like this book. They can put that on the blurb if they like. This is my favorite one.

Q. Ms. Rowling, I need to discuss this with them after that. But let's put on the screen the entry in the Lexicon, Exhibit 1, for Fawkes. And can you in general, Ms. Rowling, describe that entry.

A. The Lexicon entry?

Q. Yes.

A. This is a far from exhaustive list of times that the pet phoenix of the headmaster appears in the books. And it repeats information that I give within the novels.

Q. Now, let's put on the screen the entry for Fawkes in the Magical Worlds of Harry Potter.

A. About approximately three and a half pages.

Q. And what is your view as to how that entry compares to the Lexicon entry for Fawkes?

A. I think this is a wonderful entry. It makes reference to works such as the Egyptian book of the dead. It sets the idea of the phoenix in the context, in the mythological context. And it also of course explains Fawkes' name, because Fawkes was named for Guy Fawkes who attempted to blow up the Houses of Parliament.

Q. Why was that a suitable name for this character?

Well, Fawkes periodically explodes and then is reborn from the ashes. So that was my joke.

Q. Let's turn to Plaintiff's Exhibit 193. The Sorcerer's Companion: A Guide to the Magical World of Harry Potter by Allen Cronzck and Elizabeth Cronzck. Does this book contain an alphabetized guide to the Harry Potter books?

A. Yes, it does.

Q. Does it raise copyright concerns for you?

A. No, it doesn't.

Q. Did you sue to enjoin that book?

A. No.

Q. Why not?

A. Again because I consider this is a genuine guide or a reference book to the Harry Potter books. This provides a lot of additional information.

Q. Let's put on the screen the entry in the Lexicon, Exhibit 1, for flying carpet. And could you explain to the Court your view of that particular Lexicon entry.

A. Again, there is -- Mr. Vander Ark has copied what I've written about flying carpets. He does not go beyond that. He doesn't explain the history of the flying carpet in other eastern fairy tales and so on. He's copied certain phrases without adding any commentary.

Q. Let's look at page 86. The flying carpet entry in the Sorcerer's Companion book. And how long is that entry, Ms. Rowling?

A. Nearly two pages.

Q. And what is your view as to how that entry compares to the Lexicon entry?

A. It is infinitely superior. The references to the Koran and to other fairy tales and a broader culture of magical myths. It is a very -- it is an interesting entry.

Q. And does that make a difference to you in deciding whether to enforce your copyright rights?

A. Well, it makes a difference because I consider that this genuinely is -- this is an original work. This is – the   author of this book took as much of my work as they needed to illustrate their own points. Their own attempt to analyze certain elements that go into making the Harry Potter novels.

Q. Let's look at the Lexicon entry for rune stones. Could you read that entire entry to the Court.

A. Rune stones. A method of divination which Umbridge forces Trelawney to demonstrate when she's on probation.

Q. Ms. Rowling, what page of the Sorcerer's Companion has the entry for runes?

A. 232.

Q. How long is that entry, Ms. Rowling?

A. Nearly three pages.

Q. And what is your view as to how that entry compares with the Lexicon entry for rune?

A. Well, again in this -- in compared to the Lexicon, you're getting an almost an incomparable amount of information, including examples of runes, of ancient runes, discussion of where they came from, which peoples used them. So it is extremely informative.

Q. And let's, since I brought up the subject of The Idiot's Guide, Exhibit 74, I believe, can you turn to page 183 of The Idiot's Guide book.

A. Ah, yes.

Q. Is there in fact an entry that deals with runes in The Idiot's Guide book on page 183?

A. Yes, there is, yes.

Q. And does it -- how does the information provided there compare with that of the Lexicon?

A. Again, they have given examples of the runes, they've given entire runic alphabet.

Q. Does that make a difference to you from the copyright point of view?

A. It certainly does. Because I think that there is value in this book. Independent value. It is an original work, and some research has gone into the creation of that book.

Q. Now, switching gears a bit, you can put the books aside for the moment, Ms. Rowling. Before this lawsuit, had you ever visited the Harry Potter Lexicon Web site?

A. Yes, I have.

Q. Did, in 2004, did you give a fan site award to that Web site?

A. Yes, I did.

Q. Is that the only Web site you've given fan site awards to?

A. No. I believe I've given the fan site award to about eight -- about eight Web sites now.

Q. Why did you give the award to the Lexicon?

A. I believed then that Mr. Vander Ark was showing quite obsessive interest in the Harry Potter books. But in a positive way. I didn't think that what he created was of immense use, but I thought that it demonstrated a real passion for my work. And I -- I gave the award, I would have to say, as a kind of A for effort. I could see that time had gone into his creation.

Q. Did you give the award because you thought the site was of great quality?

A. No.

Q. Now, have you ever tried, even after this case was filed, have you ever tried to stop the Harry Potter Lexicon Web site from posting online its alphabetical listings?

A. No, I haven't.

Q. Why not?

A. I never saw any harm in the Lexicon. I didn't consider that anyone was being exploited by it. No child was being made to view it, and I didn't feel certainly at the time when I gave the fan site award, that any great claims were being made for it. It simply seemed to be a fan who had decided to rearrange my work alphabetically.

Q. When you are saying the Lexicon, you meant the Lexicon Web site?

A. Yes, yes, of course, yes.

Q. Now, do you see the Lexicon Web site as competing with your planned Harry Potter encyclopedia book?

A. No, not at all.

Q. Why not?

A. It is not a book.

Q. Now, we've talked a lot about the content of the Lexicon manuscript. Now let's talk about the consequences if any that you feel you would face if the Lexicon book were published. Ms. Rowling, do you believe the publication of the Lexicon would cause you harm as a writer?

A. Yes, definitely, I believe not only that it would cause me harm, but that the publication of the Lexicon would represent a change to copyright law that would harm any creative writer. Anyone who struggled to create something out of nothing. I worked exceptionally hard, and I made sacrifices for my work. And if, when I had been literally choosing between food and a typewriter ribbon, I had been told I did not own these words, these words were not mine, they could be taken, lifted by anyone and resold under a different author's name, so-called author's name, I would have found that quite devastating. And I believe that publication of the Lexicon would mean a shift that would protect not creators and certainly not legitimate critics or reviewers or scholars, but I believe it would protect -- such a change would be to the advantage of plagiarizers, people who are seeking to make a fast buck off the back of other people's hard work.

Q. Ms. Rowling, you had talked a lit bit about this earlier. But would publication of the Lexicon in any way disincentivize you in your own writing?

A. Well, I certainly don't think it would disincentivize me from writing something entirely different. It would be very pleasant to escape to a world that no one else could invade. But as far as anything related to Harry Potter is concerned, as I've already stated, the encyclopedia does not hold the same allure for me as an author as a novel. I always saw it as slightly more drudgery. But something that I was very happy to do because I saw its worth to fans, whose loyalty I value immensely, and to whom I'm enormously grateful. And also because I saw its potential in making money for charity. But, I mean, the associations as I've already said, every time think of the encyclopedia lately, I, far from wanting to settle down blithely to work, I would rather lock it away. I don't want to think about it. It is associated with stress and legal documents and long legal discussions, and, no offense, but it is time consuming and it is not really what I know. I'm a writer.

Q. Do you feel any timing pressure because of the Lexicon?

A. Certainly I -- Mr. Vander Ark's counsel have been vocal in their attempts to make me say that I'm producing the book within a certain period of time. And I did feel that I didn't owe anyone a promise. I said I would do it, and I've never yet failed to do what I promised to do in my work. I set out to write seven Harry Potter novels, I did that. I promised Richard Curtis two companion volumes, I did that. And yes, I intend to write the encyclopedia, but of course it adds pressure. Anything like that adds pressure.

Q. Do you have any concerns about quality due to timing issues?

A. Well, I will resist very strongly being forced to rush – I would rather not write it at all, in truth, than be forced to rush it on to the market before the avalanche starts. I wanted to do it properly. There was no other reason to do it than to do it properly. And that will take time.

Q. Do you feel -- you said this avalanche starts. What do you mean?

A. I mean that I sincerely believe if the Lexicon is published, that the law will have changed, and it will be considered fair use to copy wholesale with virtually no commentary the most token gesture toward commentary, essentially anyone would be able to repackage a popular author's work and sell it as their own. And I think that's -- this is the reason I flew here. This is the reason I wanted to testify. This is very personal to me. This is not -- this is not something that I felt at all comfortable happening arm's length or with my representatives speaking on my behalf. I am an author. 17 years of my work are being exploited here. And this is not about money. There is a massive principle at stake here. And I am determined to have my say, if nothing else, as the author.

Q. Ms. Rowling, do you have any other creative fears about the publication of the Lexicon?

A. Well, I have one I think very justifiable fear, which is that if the Lexicon is published, and I then produce my encyclopedia, on the assumption that I do still have the will to go on after all of this, I do wonder, and I think with good cause, whether Mr. Vander Ark will not seek to sue me because my paraphrase ran a little too close to his paraphrasing if he has copied my work. In restating any of my work, will I then be accused of plagiarizing Mr. Vander Ark. And he has formed, as we say, he has been very open in his desire to receive spectacularly large amounts of money, way more money that I received for my first three novels, Mr. Vander Ark has been asking for, for writing a timeline based on my fictional characters' lives.

Q. What do you mean by that, Ms. Rowling?

A. I mean that Mr. Vander Ark took the dates within the Harry Potter books and he wrote a timeline on his online Lexicon. And he has since claimed that he's owed money for doing that.

Q. And why -- and has he presented any claims to Warner Bros. as a result of that?

A. Absolutely. He has asked for an absolutely extortionate amount of money for a timeline that, that I mean -- he's copied down some dates.

Q. Ms. Rowling, let's put 14-H on the screen. Ms. Rowling, could you please read to the Court the first line of that exhibit.

A. "Dear Mr. Meyer, as publishers of the print version of Steven Vander Ark's popular international Web site the Harry Potter Lexicon, we represent Mr. Vander Ark in matters of subsidiary rights to the content of the Lexicon."

Q. Would you also read to the Court at the bottom it says "regarding the countless millions of copies the Harry Potter DVDs that have been and will be sold around the world," would you read that to the Court.

A. "Regarding the countless millions of copies the Harry Potter DVDs that have been and will be sold all over the world, you will surely agree that it is only fair and just that he receive acknowledgment and tangible rewards for his contribution."

Q. Does it concern you at all, Ms. Rowling?

A. Very much so.

Q. Why?

A. Mr. Vander Ark is seeking to be paid for writing a timeline based on my fictional facts. Now, anyone could do that. Any -- absolutely any fool, forgive me, but any fool can write a timeline based on a number of dates given in a book. I – I cannot -- I literally do not understand what he thinks he's done of value and why he deserves money for that.

Q. Are you concerned that if you were to write your encyclopedia, Mr. Vander Ark might sue you?

A. I am very concerned. I have to say there came a day when I nearly choked on my coffee as I looked at, having been told that this was the case, and I went and looked at the Lexicon and suddenly found --

Q. The Lexicon?

A. Online. I'm sorry. The online version of the Lexicon. And I found that

Mr. Vander Ark had peppered the site with "This is my original work. Do not copy." Now, RDR Books have made a great play of the fact it's all free for everyone, everyone is allowed to take whatever they'd like. Except anyone who read the Lexicon online, because Mr. Vander Ark has decided that no one must copy him. Even though what is on there is all my work. So what happens when I decide that I would like to make reference to my work and my phrases and my encyclopedia. Will Mr. Vander Ark sue me?

Q. Ms. Rowling, switching from the consequences to you as an author, do you see any consequences from the publication or possible consequences from the publication of the Lexicon to the market for your own Harry Potter encyclopedia?

A. Well, I think there is no doubt whatsoever that if the Lexicon is published, and if it therefore is deemed in law to be acceptable to take this amount of an author's work and add this little to it, then absolutely anyone, I do believe the floodgates must open and this is the quickest and easiest way to make a quick bit of money. I believe my readers will rightly become servitive with this avalanche of dross, and I imagine that by the time my encyclopedia comes limping into the market, everyone will be sick to the back teeth of Harry Potter encyclopedias.

Q. Ms. Rowling, you have a lot of fans. Don't you think your fans will buy your encyclopedia no matter what

A. No. Frankly, no. I don't. I'm not that arrogant. If they've already bought five books expecting to get something new and interesting when they haven't yet seen it, I don't really see why they are going to keep spending money. And it of course is also the case, as I think you mentioned in your opening remarks, that the market for companion books is smaller than the books -- than the market for novels. The Fantastic Beasts and Where To Find Them and Quidditch Through the Ages, they sold very well and the charities were grateful for the

money. But they didn't sell anything like the quantities of the novels. It is a different market.

Q. Turning to -- we talked about consequences to you as a writer and consequences with regard to your planned perhaps encyclopedia. Let's talk about potential consequences if any to the Harry Potter novels themselves. Do you have any concerns about that as a result of potential publication of the Lexicon?

A. I think that I would -- I would quibble very much with the statement that the Lexicon only means anything to someone who has read all of the books. That simply is not true. In all of the longer entries under characters, my plots are abridged. So you're being told exactly what happens to Lord Voldemort's mother and to Harry Potter. Books one through seven. So it is possible, I imagine that someone might decide, well, I don't really need to read books four and five, I might just skip through to book seven. But I think that it needs to be stated that I am not here because -- we all know I've made enough money. This is not -- this is not -- I didn't come here because I thought, uh, I might sell three fewer novels. That is absolutely not why I'm here.

Q. Do you have any concerns about reading in terms of --

A. I absolutely do. Because if there is one thing of which I am enormously proud with regard to the Harry Potter novels, it is that there were children who are not big readers before they read Harry Potter, and that is the most gratifying thing I think an author for children can be told. "I wasn't interested in reading until I found Harry Potter." And I have met numerous times children who have told me that, and who have been very proud of themselves that they finished seven books. Clearly I'm not a big fan of people putting abridged forms of my plots out there. I would rather they read the whole novel. This isn't about selling books. They can get them from the library. I frequently encourage children to take them off the library shelves. It is the reading experience that I think stands to be endangered here.

Q. Ms. Rowling, do you intend to have detailed plot summaries in your encyclopedia if you write it?

A. No. I've already told my stories in the novels. I don't intend to abridge my own books.

Q. Ms. Rowling, do you see any consequences -- we talked about potential harm to you as a writer, to your encyclopedia, to the Harry Potter books, do you see any potential consequences from publication of the Lexicon to your existing Harry Potter companion books, Fantastic Beasts and Quidditch Through the Ages?

A. There is no doubt at all in my mind that there would be no incentive for anyone to buy those two companion books if they owned a copy of this Lexicon. Because effectively, those two books are reprinted within the Lexicon.

Q. Ms. Rowling, do you see any consequences to your Harry Potter licensing program from the publication of the Lexicon?

A. Well, I'm not delighted to have work that I consider to be this shoddy associated with Harry Potter. So to that extent, yes, I would say there is some harm.

Q. You mentioned shoddiness. Do you have a view as the author of the Harry Potter novels as to the quality of the Lexicon manuscript?

A. I think it's dire. I think it is atrocious.

Q. Could you explain why.

A. I think that it is sloppy, I think there is very little research, and I don't think that it -- I don't think it constitutes an original work.

Q. You mentioned that the Lexicon occasionally -- earlier that the Lexicon occasionally contained etymologies.

A. Yes.

Q. I believe you also mentioned that the some of those etymologies were wrong?

A. Hmm-hmm.

Q. Could you give the Court an example.

A. I could give several. But Mr. Vander Ark gives an etymology for alohomora, which is an incantation used within the Harry Potter books to open a locked door by magic. And he asserts that this word was derived from the Hawaiian aloha meaning good-bye. Which is errant nonsense. Alohomora is a Sidiki word from West Africa, and it is a term used in geomancy. It is a figure -- the figure alohomora means in Sidiki "favorable to thieves." Which is obviously a very appropriate meaning for a spell that enables you to unlock a locked door by magic. Later on there is the word alihotsy which came from the same source which is also from Western Africa. And it means lightness of spirit. I used that word for a bush, the leaves of which causes hysteria. But Mr. Vander Ark simply does not explain the etymology of alihotsy, and he makes no attempt to do so.

Q. Now, Ms. Rowling, do you have any concerns about the publication of the Lexicon in terms of your fans?

A. Huge concerns. That is at least half the reason I'm here. I think that this publication of this book, the sale of this book would be exploitive. If would be exploiting a very loyal readership. Or attempting to exploit a very loyal readership.

Q. Why do you believe that?

A. I believe because it is attempting -- I believe that the proposed price is $24.95? For that money, I believe you are being resold the Harry Potter books with a negligible amount of attempted commentary, some of it false, and a lot of facetious comments. I quote, I would like to see Hagrid fit himself into a McDonald's booth. For $24.

Q. Ms. Rowling, do you have any concerns about the online fans who might have helped contribute to the Lexicon at one point in time online?

A. Well, I am certainly confused to see Mr. Vander Ark's name alone, alone on the cover, of the proposed cover of the Lexicon, because it was my understanding that he worked with a team of people. So I don't really understand that.

Q. Do you have any views as to the impact the publication of the Lexicon on your relationship with fan Web sites?

A. Very definitely, that's part of my concerns about fans. I, perhaps naively, I accept that, perhaps naively, I was very keen to maintain an almost entirely hands-off approach to the online fandom where Harry Potter was concerned. And I say "almost" because there are obvious boundaries of decency that occasionally one would not like to see overstepped. But by and large, I simply let it happen. Maybe that was naive, but I saw massive positives in this amount of fan activity. I saw – I saw it as a great global book club with a lot of enthusiasm. I met people who had made real life friendships through posting on Harry Potter message boards, which I thought was a wonderful thing. The fan sites, the fan created fan message boards and the essays and so on, they were all fun. I have never read online fan fiction. It is uncomfortable to see your world restated in that way. But, I never censored it or wanted to censor it. I let it all happen. So, what will happen if it is decided in court that by taking that approach, I effectively gave away copyright, I -- well, I know what will happen. Other authors -- I mean, other authors are already much more draconian than I am with their view of the Internet. Of course, other authors will look sideways at what happened to me and say I need to exercise more control. She was an idiot. She let it all go.

Q. Ms. Rowling, do you want the Court to enjoin the book?

A. Yes, I do.

CROSS EXAMINATION BY MR. HAMMER (attorney for RDR Books):

Q. Ms. Rowling, good afternoon.

A. Good afternoon.

Q. My name is David Hammer and I believe that I'm one of the esteemed and learned counsel that the lawyer was referring to. Perhaps we will find out. The first thing I want to discuss with you is the Vander Ark time line. Now, you said -- I believe you said twice that Vander Ark was demanding extortionate sums from Warner Brothers for use of that time line, is that correct?

A. That was my belief, yes.

Q. Yes. That was your testimony, isn't that correct?

A. Yes, that's what I said.

Q. I would like to show, perhaps, if we could, what you call the cease and desist letter? So, this is a letter that you are referring to dated October 11, 2007 that Mr. Rapoport in fact wrote to Warner Brothers; isn't that correct?

A. I never saw this letter before this case but that's how it appears, yes.

Q. Well, it is a letter that you testified about, isn't that true?

A. No.

Q. This morning, this morning in your testimony --

A. No. My belief that Mr. Vander Ark was looking for financial recompense for what he represented as original work on the time line was not based on ever having seen this letter. It was information that I believe I got from Neil Blair, my lawyer.

Q. This letter was in fact displayed to you this morning, isn't that true?

A. Yes, that's true.

Q. Okay. And you were asked to read from that letter this morning by your lawyer Ms. Cendali, isn't that true?

A. Yes, that's true.

Q. And, in this letter at the end of this letter Mr. Rapoport says to Warner Brothers, You will surely agree it is only fair and just that he -- that is Mr. Vander Ark – receive acknowledgment and tangible rewards for his contribution. Isn't that true?

A. Yes.

Q. Okay. So acknowledgement, that's not in itself an extortionate sum, is it?

A. No.

Q. And tangible reward is not an extortionate sum, is it?

A. Well, I don't know what Mr. Rapoport meant by tangible reward so I can't judge.

Q. And Vander Ark has never asked you or your representatives for a penny, has he?

A. Well, that's not quite true. He proposed himself as my new editor in an e-mail that I believe was submitted in this case so --

Q. He asked to work for you and be paid for his work. That's usually how it is done when you work for someone, isn't it?

MS. CENDALI: Your Honor, I object to Mr. Hammer not letting Ms. Rowling get to answer his question before he starts the next one.

THE COURT: Do you wish to add more to your answer?

THE WITNESS: Yes, please, your Honor. I think your question was had he ever asked me for a penny. Well, he certainly was asking me to pay him for his services so he was asking for more than a penny, I would imagine.

Q. That's not illegitimate, is it, for someone to be asked to be paid for his services?

THE COURT: Let me just understand. He hadn't performed any services?

THE WITNESS: No.

BY MR. HAMMER:

Q. He never asked you for a penny for the time line, isn't that true?

A. I don't believe that he did, although the impression given to me by my lawyer who had met with Mr. Vander Ark was that Vander Ark was very keen to receive recompense in some form for the time line. And I -- the impression I received is that he was -- was that he was not fussy about where the recompense came.

Q. You have never seen a letter or other document other than this letter in which in request is made of anyone on earth for money from that time line, have you?

A. Well, no. It is correct but I did hear about conversations, several of them, that Mr. Vander Ark had with Neil Blair.

Q. You complained that Mr. Vander Ark's etymology is sometimes inaccurate, is that so?

A. Yes, that is so.

Q. And one of the examples you gave was to spell "alohomora"?

A. That is correct, yes.

Q. And Mr. Vander Ark's derivation of alohomora came from the Hawaiian word "aloha," correct?

A. Yes.

Q. And you disparage that because in fact you coined that word from something in a West African dialect, right?

A. No. I didn't coin it. I used a term that's used in a form of West African geomancy.

Q. You derived it from a West African geomancy you say?

A. Yes.

Q. That's not in the book in which "alohomora" appears, is it?

A. No.

Q. You have never given an interview in which you identify that as the source of alohomora, did you?

A. I'm not sure that's true, actually, Mr. Hammer. I may well have told a fan or two that fact but I don't believe that I've ever said it on television.

Q. Mr. Vander Ark is not privy to every conversation that you had have with a fan, correct?

A. Of course not.

Q. So there is no way that he could have known that you had told a fan that alohomora derived from a word in a West African language, correct?

A. Well, they said there is a much easier way to find out where alohomora comes from and that's to do some actual research.

Q. You never sent in to the Lexicon website a correction saying: You've got this wrong, Steve. It doesn't come from "aloha," did you?

A. Well, the answers on the Lexicon made it rather useful for me to know what fans thought they knew so I wasn't in the business of correcting Mr. Vander Ark's work. I was too busy writing my own novels.

Q. But now you have some free time and you are willing to correct his work?

A. I have no intention of correcting his work. I'm busy on my own encyclopedia.

Q. In fact, when you write there are meanings that are subconscious that are attached to terms that you use; isn't that true?

A. Well, if they're subconscious I don't know how I would know that.

Q. That's what we hope to go through here, the process of therapeutic disclosure.

A. Oh.

Q. Sometimes things were pointed out to you about your work that you didn't realize yourself, isn't that true?

A. It is true that a friend of mine, on one occasion, said to me, Do you not remember that we saw a plant called Hogwarts? And I took her word for it. I don't remember but that could well could have been a subliminal memory. So, if you are talking about something like that, then I suppose so.

Q. But, it often happens in doing etymologies that people suggest different sources for an unusual word, isn't that so?

A. Well, I would take issue with that really because in the case of many of my made up words they have -- they are derived from existing languages so it is not such a stretch to find out what the underlying meaning is. It is not as though I threw Scrabble letters up in the air and took what was formed there. There is usually an underlying meaning.

Q. Let's turn to the example you gave of death. You complained that Vander Ark's discussion of death was too short, correct?

A. I think it is -- if this book is purported to be a guide, a reference guide of any kind, then I think that that's one particularly lamentable example of no commentary, true.

Q. Because death is in fact a major theme of your works, correct?

A. Yes, that's true.

Q. But Vander Ark wasn't talking about the process of dying in the Lexicon, was he? The entry that you displayed was about a character named Death in one of your books, isn't that true?

A. I don't exactly understand your question.

Q. Simple question. There are two meanings to death: One is a character in one of your books, one is the process of dying we all go through.

A. I would actually say there are many more meanings of death than just two.

Q. Well, fine. But the one I'm trying to hone in on that Mr. Vander Ark referred to was the character Death in one of your novels. Isn't that so?

MS. CENDALI: Objection. Objection.

THE COURT: Objection overruled.

A. He was undoubtedly destroyed by Death as a character as a story within my story, of course, but --

Q. So, there is much more to talk about than the process of dying than a -- it is not really criticism about his entry about a character?

A. Mr. Hammer, I don't think you have shown great familiarity with my book. It is not that I am complaining that he doesn't explain to the reader what it means for someone to die. That's not my complaint in the slightest.

Q. Perhaps I misunderstood your testimony, Ms. Rowling. I would like to go now to what you said about the fan site. I think you said on several occasions that the fan site was not useful to you at all; is that true?

A. No, that's not true. I --

Q. Sorry. I don't mean to interrupt.

A. The fan site, the website, the Lexicon did have a use to me but not the use I think that Mr. Vander Ark thinks it had to me.

Q. I think you said this morning that the only reason you gave it an award was that you were giving it an A for effort; isn't that true?

A. Well, if you are talking about the fan site award, then that is substantially the reason I gave for --

MS. CENDALI: Again, your Honor .

THE COURT: Please don't interrupt the witness, Mr. Hammer.

MR. HAMMER: Forgive me. If you want to repeat the answer, please do.

A. It is true that the main reason I gave the fan site award to the Lexicon was because I felt that it represented something in terms of effort, yes.

Q. And, in fact, you disparaged the quality of the Lexicon, isn't that true; the website Lexicon this morning in your testimony?

A. Yes.

Q. And I believe if you will think back you did say on two occasions that it was of no use to you, isn't that so?

A. I can't remember. I would need to see a transcript but I would stand by the statement that it was not a useful reference tool for me.

Q. Now, in 2004 I believe you testified you gave it a fan site award, is that true?

A. I testified this morning that I gave it an award in 2004, yes.

Q. And I would like you to look at that demonstrative on the wall, I believe that contains the language from your website. Is that correct?

A. That's absolutely correct, yes.

Q. And what you say in that award is this is such a great site that I have been known to sneak into an Internet cafe while out writing and check a fact rather than go into a book store and by a copy of Harry Potter, which is embarrassing. A website for the dangerously obsessive; my natural home. That's your language, correct?

A. That's my language.

Q. That wasn't written by Mr. Vander Ark, was it?

A. Well, it probably will be at some point, but no, he hasn't done it yet.

Q. But, in fact, aside from the witness it was written by you? Not by Ms. Cendali or any lawyer but by you? And what you are saying there is that as you are writing -- were you referring to writing your novels in an Internet cafe?

A. No, I don't write in an Internet cafe but I -- I would be out in Edinburgh in a cafe writing.

Q. And what would be the nature of a fact that you would want to investigate at that stage?

A. Well, the truth is that I think -- I think twice I did go into an Internet cafe and I used the Lexicon but I used the Lexicon so I could say I had used it, Mr. Hammer, because the fact is that Harry Potter is so ubiquitous on the Internet that a Google search engine will give you the kind of information that I was

checking; which I know on one occasion was the Christian name of an incidental character. I didn't need the Lexicon specifically to tell me that. I could have simply Googled it but because I knew of the existence of the Lexicon. And because I had seen it and glanced at it, I wanted to say I had used it because I wanted to do a nice thing and give him the award. Do I now regret that? Yes, bitterly.

Q. Is that not in fact something that a fan could find useful if he wanted to look up the Christian name of a minor character, to use the Lexicon?

A. He could Google it the same as I did so I strongly suggest the Lexicon was not necessary for that.

Q. If you had a lexicon book could he not use it in precisely the way you used it, to look up the name of a minor character?

A. But, again, he would be much better advised getting a book that had commentary in it rather than regurgitation of Harry Potter.

Q. The book that you picked up in fact is not a comprehensive encyclopedia of Harry Potter, is it?

A.. If we define comprehensive Harry Potter encyclopedia, which is inasmuch as I have gotten then, no, sir, David Colbert is not.

Q. That's not how I was defining it.

A. Can you rephrase?

Q. I was defining encyclopedia of all the characters, major and minor, in Harry Potter. Is that not such a book?

THE COURT: What is not such a book?

MR. HAMMER: The book by David Colbert that you just picked up.

MS. CENDALI: Objection to the form.

THE COURT: Of which book? Which book? Just so we have -- we are talking about The Magical World of Harry Potter.

BY MR. HAMMER:

Q. Magical World of Harry Potter is not a comprehensive encyclopedia of all the characters in Harry Potter, is it?

A. Well, I don't know it well enough to say whether it has all my characters in it.

Q. What was the name of the character that you looked up that day in the Internet cafe?

A. I can't remember. But it was a -- I can't remember. But it was a very incidental character, like a -- I think it was a member of the Order of the Phoenix.

Q. None of the books that you mentioned today -- books that you did not challenge -- are comprehensive encyclopedias of the characters of Harry Potter, are they?

A. Well, I don't have enough familiarity with these books to say that.

Q. Well, you have enough familiarity to say that you approve of them, that they're fine books; isn't that true?

A. I have enough familiarity to see that there is masses of commentary there but I haven't -- I haven't combed them to see whether every one of my characters is mentioned.

Q. Well, it doesn't take a long time to open those books and see if they're a comprehensive listing of every character in the Harry Potter novels, why don't you do that; take them one by one?

A. You would like me to do that now on the stand?

Q. Yes, I would like you to do that, please.

MS. CENDALI: Objection.

THE COURT: Objection overruled.

A. I have done one. Do you want me to do the rest?

Q. Well, I would like you to answer the book that you have done. Would you identify it for us?

A. The Magical World of Harry Potter.

Q. Who is the author of that book?

A. David Colbert.

Q. That book does not in fact contain listings for all the entries in the Harry Potter novel, isn't that true?

A. No, it doesn't.

Q. Now, why don't you go through the Idiot's Guide because you like it so much.

A. I no longer have the Idiot's Guide with me. Sorry, I don't have that one here on the stand.

MR. HAMMER: Your Honor, may I give this to the witness?

THE COURT: Yes.

THE WITNESS: Thank you.

BY MR. HAMMER:

Q. That book also, the Idiot's Guide also is not a comprehensive listing of all the characters in your novels, correct?

A. I would agree.

Q. Nor of the spells in your novels, correct?

A. I didn't check the spells. Would you like me to go back through and look at the spells?

Q. Nor of the -- how about this, how about the beasts in the books? That might be easier.

A. Well, it has a section on beasts. I don't know whether it has every beast. I don't know.

Q. In fact, the encyclopedia sections of these books are a lot shorter than the encyclopedia section of -- I'm sorry, Judge -- the encyclopedia section of the Lexicon, isn't that true?

A. Yes.

Q. There are many fewer entries. So, it is not -- because the encyclopedia sections are shorter it is understandable that each individual entry might be longer than the entries in the Lexicon, isn't that true?

MS. CENDALI: Objection. Argumentative.

THE COURT: Objection sustained – objection overruled. I'm sorry.

A. Mr. Hammer, to me you seem to be suggesting that what Mr. Vander Ark has produced is an index, a simple listing of everything in my books.

Q. No, I'm not. I'm suggesting that it's -- I don't want to get into an argument with you. The Lexicon describes itself as an encyclopedia about the Harry Potter books, is that correct?

A. I know it describes itself that way, yes.

Q. And it has more than simply an index of names, isn't that true?

A. It lifted my work wholesale, that's very true.

Q. Please, Ms. Rowling. Just say yes or no.

A. No, that wasn't a yes or no, Mr. Hammer.

Q. The Lexicon has entries under each listing in the text, correct?

A. It has verbatim copying from my work under each entry.

Q. So you are saying that the entire Lexicon has simply example of Xerox copying of the Harry Potter novels?

A. It is very slightly more than that.

Q. In any event it has text wherever the source of the text is for every one of the characters of the Potter novels, as far as you know, isn't that true?

A. Yes. And is that the best you can say for The Lexicon? It has text?

Q. What I'm getting at now is that that amounts to hundreds and hundreds and hundreds of entries within one book. Isn't that true?

A. Yes. It was a lot of work. I remember doing it.

Q. Many times the number of entries in either of the books that you have just looked at?

A. But --

Q. Isn't that true?

A. Yes.

Q. That's all I'm asking, a simple quantification question.

A. Yes, but quantity is no guarantee of quality, is it?

Q. No, it certainly isn't, but quantity is an explanation why individual entries might be shorter than individual entries in a book with fewer entries; isn't that so?

A. I'm afraid I don't think that follows at all.

Q. In fact, there have been two other comprehensive encyclopedias about Harry Potter and you've forced them both off the market, haven't you? I would like to show you --

THE COURT: Do you want an answer to that question or not?

MR. HAMMER: I do, your Honor. Thank you.

A. I'm not sure what books you are talking about. I would need to see --

Q. Well, first let's look at 527, Exhibit 527, which is the J.K. Rowling Encyclopedia by Connie Ann Kirk.

A. Thank you.

Q. Have you seen that book before?

A. I have seen it recently in the context of this lawsuit.

Q. It is about a 350-page book, is it not?

A. Yes.

Q. It seems to be --

A. Appears to be.

Q. Seems to be the comprehensive encyclopedia of Harry Potter novels, does it? A lot of entries?

A. I haven't read it so at a glance it looks very lexicon-like in the sense it looks rather like the book we are here to discuss.

Q. Now, in fact, when you looked at this book were you told that your lawyers had forced this book to be withdrawn from the market?

A. I was --

MS. CENDALI: Objection. Privilege.

THE COURT: I don't know in what context she looked at the book from whom so I can't rule on that objection.

BY MR. HAMMER:

Q. Are you aware, Ms. Rowling, that your lawyers wrote a letter to the publisher of that book demanding it be taken out of circulation?

A. I have not seen the letter but I am aware that my representatives took action on this book.

Q. And I would like to read from the letter they wrote and ask you whether or not you agree with the propositions that are contained in it. It is Defendant's Exhibit 574, it is a letter written by Ms. Cendali to the publisher of Greenwood Publishing Group. And it says: The book appears to contain unauthorized derivative material in violation of our client's intellectual property rights. For example, the book purports to contain an alphabetical glossary of fictional facts from the Potter books, presumably with little or no independent analysis or commentary, e.g. hundreds of alphabetically arranged entries on Rowling's characters, themes, settings, motifs, spells, positions, etc. Then it goes on to say that this type of infringement is particularly troublesome and inappropriate as Ms. Rowling has long stated that she wants to create a companion book to the series and perhaps donate such proceeds to charity. Now, the proposition in that letter is that an alphabetical glossary of characters, themes, is itself a violation of your copyrights? Is that a proposition that you agree with?

A. It is not a proposition. I don't think that's what Ms. Cendali was saying, that an alphabetical arrangement is, per se, damaging to me or anyone else. It so happens -- and I think I testified this morning -- that an alphabetical rearrangement is the laziest way to rearrange and sell my work.

Q. Well, it is a lazy way but it is a very useful way to readers, isn't it?

A. In what way?

Q. It is easy to get information in alphabetical listing, isn't it?

A. I don't understand. Why -- how would I -- I don't understand how I would use this book as a reader.

Q. Have you ever used a dictionary, Ms. Rowling?

A. You are telling me Mr. Vander Ark is going to teach me how to spell?

Q. I'm telling you the dictionary uses A to Z listings.

A. Yes, but I think that's slightly different.

Q. Talking simply about the purpose of an A to Z listing. You say you think it is a lazy way to arrange things. I'm asking isn't that a useful way to arrange things? It is what the dictionary uses, isn't that true?

A. Yes.

Q. It is what the Encyclopedia Britannica uses, isn't that true?

A. Definitely what the encylcopedia Britannica uses.

Q. And that is because it is an easy way for ordinary reader to access information?

A. To access information, yes.

MS. CENDALI: Objection, your Honor. Would Mr. Hammer please let Ms. Rowling finish her answers before he starts asking?

THE COURT: Please, let her finish.

MR. HAMMER: Yes.

A. Mr. Hammer, you said to access information. I think that's what -- part of

the reason we are all here, isn't it? What are you accessing in these A to Zs? You are accessing my words lifted verbatim. And you, on the Harry Potter books, aren't you being suckered out of your hard-earned cash?

Q. You feel that it is your responsibility to prevent people from paying their hard-earned cash for things you don't like?

A. Absolutely not.

Q. But you don't like the Lexicon, correct?

A. I don't like it.

Q. You don't think it is a good book?

A. Correct.

Q. You think the etymologies could have been better done?

A. To say the least.

Q. You could have simply said on the publication of the Lexicon I don't like this book, couldn't you?

A. It is not only about that, Mr. Hammer, and you know that. This is -- this is theft. This is, wholesale, is theft. This is -- of course it is nonsensical to suggest that I think I have the right to stop a book because I might not like it. There are -- there are books out there that I – I don't agree with conclusions and I think that they could have been done better but, of course, they're not infringing my rights. I have made no attempt to stop them being published.

Q. Okay. Is it true that you had your lawyers stop the publication of a book by the staff of Mugglenet this last year?

A. I know that my -- I know that my lawyers asked them to, I think, not to proceed with plans to produce a book very like the Lexicon.

Q. And that was a book that hadn't even been written yet, isn't that true?

A. Yes, it was. And Mugglenet had done us the courtesy I think of -- I may be wrong, but I believe that we have already had -- always had a very good relationship with Mugglenet. They have already published one Harry Potter book that was very good. And they were very open about their plans and I believe my representatives said it sounded like an infringing book and that was the end of it.

Q. I think your testimony was, though, that you don't see it as your role to tell people not to write books just because you don't like them. Isn't that so?

A. That's so.

Q. I would like you to turn to Exhibit 567 -- Defendant's Exhibit 567, which is a letter that Ms. Cendali wrote to an attorney for the publisher of that Mugglenet book.

THE COURT: Can we have dates on these letters?

MR. HAMMER: Yes, sir. That letter is dated June 20th, 2007.

Q. The letter starts off as noting that, We are writing in response to your letter -- that is, the lawyers for Mugglenet's letter -- confirming that your client Ulysses Press is considering the publication of a new work of commentary and criticism. So, the first paragraph starts off by noting that the Mugglenet people said this was going to be a work of commentary and criticism. Is that true?

A. Yes.

Q. Now, commentary and criticism, normally you would agree, is acceptable; correct?

A. I would, yes.

Q. The letter then goes on in the third paragraph to state: We reiterate that the issue of Harry Potter companion books is particularly troubling to Ms. Rowling who has publicly stated that it is her intention to write a definitive companion book with commentary herself and to donate the proceeds from the sale of such book to charity. Then on the next page: As a result, not only is Ms. Rowling concerned that the book may be an infringement of her rights, but that it might be quite similar to her intended companion book and may, therefore, diminish its charitable proceeds. She therefore requests that regardless of any discussion of the respected legal positions, as a courtesy to her and out of respect to her wishes (and charitable design), Ulysses Press and the authors refrain from publishing the book. So, here is an example in which you asked these people not to write a book simply because you didn't want them to write the book?

MS. CENDALI: Objection. Foundation.

MR. HAMMER: Foundation. It has just been read out.

MS. CENDALI: She hasn't even seen the letter.

THE COURT: Isn't the letter displayed in front of her?

THE WITNESS: It is. It is, your Honor.

MS. CENDALI: I meant before.

THE COURT: I'm sorry. It is displayed, Ms. Cendali.

BY MR. HAMMER:

Q. When Ms. Cendali said that, "Ms. Rowling requests," had she spoken to you and asked if that was your request?

A. Not directly, no.

Q. So she simply invented the notion that that's what you wanted her to do?

A. Mr. Hammer, I'm --

THE COURT: Just a yes or no answer.

THE WITNESS: No, she did not invent it but, your Honor, I --

BY MR. HAMMER:

Q. Is Ms. Cendali empowered on her own to force books or demand that books be taken off the market without consulting you first?

A. My representatives do not consult me every time such a matter comes up, Mr. Hammer.

Q. Is she empowered to say that you have personally said that you want such a book taken off the market without asking if that's what you said?

A. Is she -- sorry. Could you repeat that question?

Q. The letter says Ms. Rowling wants this. Is she empowered, Ms. Cendali empowered?

THE COURT: Are you going to repeat the question or --

Q. The letter states that: Ms. Rowling requests that regardless of any discussion of the respective legal positions, as a courtesy to her and out of respect for her wishes (and charitable designs), Ulysses Press and the authors refrain from publishing the book. Now, in that sentence Ms. Cendali has attributed certain desires and certain requests to you, is that correct?

A. Yes. Yes, that is correct. Yes.

Q. And you say that she had not in fact spoken to you when she wrote that letter?

A. She didn't need to speak to me. It is absolutely the case that I would have -- had I spoken directly to Mugglenet I would have said to them -- not in legalese -- but I would have said you know that I want to do my own encyclopedia, please -- please, don't do this. I would have said that directly to them.

Q. So, have you given Ms. Cendali guidelines to follow in determining what books to demand be removed from the market?

A. I haven't given her guidelines. She follows the law. Those are the guidelines. I said it is not --

Q. In that letter Ms. Cendali states that you requested that the Mugglenet manuscript not be published, correct?

A. Correct.

Q. You say that you did not discuss this with Ms. Cendali, correct?

A. Correct. Although I -- I'm sorry, Mr. Hammer, but to, the only lawyer with whom I have regular contact is --

THE COURT: Just answer the question yes or no if you possibly can, Ms. Rowling.

A. It is, no, I didn't discuss it with Ms. Cendali.

Q. So Ms. Cendali, on her own, decided to simply write to these people saying you wanted them to remove that book from the market?

A. Well, I can't -- I can't answer for what Ms. Cendali was thinking, but it is my belief that my representatives, as a matter of course, would protect my copyright.

Q. Well, this was a book on commentary and criticism, isn't this true?

A. Well, I never saw it so I don't know that it is described thus in this letter.

Q. And commentary and criticism, I believe you will concede, is fair use?

A. Genuine commentary and criticism is fair use.

Q. So that book would not be an infringement of your copyright, correct?

A. Well, I don't know because it never existed so how can I judge that.

Q. So you demand that all possible books be suppressed because one of them may conceivably violate your copyright?

A. No, Mr. Hammer.

Q. Why did you not wait until the book did exist to decide if it infringed a copyright?

A. I don't really know how to answer that. Ms. Cendali approached Mugglenet and we have seen and asked them courteously to not proceed with what she felt would be an infringing book -- and they were kind enough to do so.

Q. Isn't it true that in fact what Ms. Cendali's brief is, is to force the removal of any book that might conceivably compete with a companion book that you one day might want to write?

A. Absolutely not. We have seen there are a hundred books out there. Some of them are guides, encyclopedias. Some of them are great. Some of them, in my view, are less great, but they're all legitimate and they've been published. And, Mr. Hammer, we have seen what's published in the states. Worldwide it amounts to thousands of books about Harry Potter that have not been, in your words, forced off the market by anyone.

Q. We saw this morning some titles like Harry Potter and the Talmud, correct?

A. And the?

Q. Talmud.

A. Yes, yes.

Q. You were never going to write a book on Harry Potter and Judaism, right?

THE COURT: And what?

Q. It was never her intention to write a book about Harry Potter and the Talmud, isn't that correct?

A. I regret to say that is the case.

Q. So that book, in fact, was not going to compete with any books that you intended to write; true?

A. True.

Q. So, the fact that you allowed that book to be published doesn't indicate anything at all about whether or not you tolerate books that may be in competition with yours?

A. Mr. Hammer, you are a lawyer so of course you're going to pick that example, but a looking at The Magical World of Harry Potter is a guide of precisely the same type as the one that I intend to write and I think is a good one.

Q. Actually, Ms. Rowling, you picked that example.

A. I picked which example.

Q. Harry Potter and the Talmud. That's how I saw it, it was up on your screen.

THE COURT: I'm sorry. Have you got a question or is that just a commentary?

MR. HAMMER: That was just a snide remark.

Q. All right, I would like to show you a book by Fionna Boyle. May I, your Honor? It is 521.

THE COURT: We don't have that.

BY MR. HAMMER:

Q. Have you seen that book before, Ms. Rowling?

A. I don't think I have.

Q. Very well. I don't have any questions about it. I would like to go over some of the display material that you showed this morning. The first one, you made a display of the Brain Room. We have presented a display which shows both the text from the Harry Potter novel, the text from your chart that you say overlaps with the text from the novel, and then the large text of the entire lexicon. So, if you would look at that and if you want to have the Lexicon by hand to check if we have accurately displayed the entire text of the Lexicon, you may. Do you have the Lexicon? Do you have a copy there of your own?

A. I do. I have a Lexicon here, yes.

Q. If you want to check on the Brain Room entry you can, but the one on the right-hand side is the entire text of the Lexicon. This morning you pointed out that the entry in – part of the entry in the Lexicon seemed to overlap with language from the Order of the Phoenix and the language in the Order of the Phoenix that you quoted was: "What looked like ribbons of moving images flew from it unraveling like rolls of film," correct?

A. Yes, correct.

Q. And the portion you said that left -- was highlighted and it goes, "the brains fly out of the tank unspooling ribbons of thought like strips of film." So that phrase, "unspooling ribbons of thought like strips of film," is the overlapping phrase, correct?

A. There is more than that phrase in that entry.

Q. Okay. But, in fact, there is more to that entry than simply that phrase?

A. It is lifted. May I show you where? I'm ready --

Q. You may.

A. "A long rectangular room," my language. "Low-hanging lamps," my language. "Huge tank of greenish liquid," my language. At -- towards the end of the entry, "which Wrap themselves around the summoner and cause quite a bit of damage," that's not my language. And then, "As Pomfrey says, thoughts can leave deeper scarring than almost anything else," my language. So, in fact, I highlighted just the one phrase that I thought was particularly -- a particularly shameless example of copying because it was an unusual image but, in fact, nearly all of that entry is taken, Mr. Hammer, from my work.

Q. You say that "long rectangular room" is your language?

A. Well --

Q. Well that's what you just said, isn't it?

A. It is, yes.

Q. You find that a particularly distinctive phrase?

A. No. That's why I didn't copy it into the chart. But you are claiming that long rectangular room adds value.

Q. You don't know what I'm claiming. I haven't asked you a question.

A. Please ask me a question.

Q. I'm claiming that the phrase that you said quoted definitive J.K. Rowling language is highlighted, correct?

A. One of the --

Q. You did not include the rest of the that section, is that correct?

A. I literally did not have time. I didn't include it because I didn't have time. If I listed every example of Mr. Vander Ark lifting or minimally paraphrasing my work my daughter and would I have had to sit at the dining room table for a week. I did not have the time.

Q. May we show the next one? This is armor, goblin-made armor. And we have in your testimony you complain that the highlighted phrase on the right had not been placed in quotation marks? Once again we have in the middle section the text that you quoted in your Exhibit 47 from your own novels. The right-hand section highlighted the text that you complained about from the Lexicon? I believe that you complained this morning that the highlighted portion of that text, "goblin-made armor does not require cleaning because goblin silver repels mundane dirt, imbibing only that which strengthens," this had not been placed in quotation marks is that true?

A. Yes. Yes, sir that true.

Q. In fact, the portion of the Lexicon that you did not include in your entry states: According to Phineas Nigellus, goblin-made armor does not require cleaning. Isn't that true?

A. No, sir, that's so -- that's a trick that Mr. Vander Ark uses quite a lot. He thinks that putting in 'according to a fictional character' means that anything that follows that does not need to be in quotation marks.

Q. Is that the slightest doubt in the mind of a reader? Do you think that that is a quotation when it is preceded that way, "As according to Phineas Nigellus"?

A. I definitely think that there is a doubt. Just because it says "According to" there is -- unless there are quotation marks around it why would any reader not think that the phrase is Mr. Vander Ark's rather than mine?

Q. Why would you leave out "According to Phineas Nigellus" in trying to list this, that one, without quotation marks?

A. Mr. Hammer, I didn't have time. If I listed literally every sample of copying I would not -- I would have been a week at this job.

Q. You did not have time to write those four words: "According to Phineas Nigellus?"

A. Do you really think that makes a difference?

Q. I certainly do. It makes it an indirect quotation.

THE COURT: Please, let's go on. Let's not have an argument.

MR. HAMMER: Can I just have a second?

THE COURT: Sure.

Q. Can we show the Voldemort exhibit that you looked at this morning? Now, Ms. Rowling, you complained that the entry on Voldemort was a plot summary, correct?

A. Yes.

Q. Voldemort, by the way, is one of the major figures in the Potter novels?

A. Correct. Yes.

Q. So, on its face it is not surprising that one of the longest entries in the Lexicon should be devoted to Voldemort, correct?

A. I would expect one of the longer entries to be on Voldemort, that's correct.

Q. Now, the first paragraph of the entry on Voldemort goes: Tom Marvolo Riddle was the son of Merope Gaunt, a descendent of the Salazar Slytherin and Tom Riddle, a handsome, wealthy Muggle from Little Hangelton who Merope ensnared with a love potion. When her husband found out she was a witch, he abandoned her while she was pregnant. And that is -- what the heck is (HBP 10)? Half-Blood Prince? Okay. Chapter 10. She died shortly after giving birth to Tom. Half-Blood Prince is what? Is the sixth book in the series?

A. That's correct.

Q. Voldemort appears, what, in the second book in the series?

A. He appears in the first book.

Q. In the first book. So if this were simply a plot summary, it would be arranged by the order that the stuff arises in the plot, isn't that correct? It would start with, as plot summaries do, with Book 1, Voldemort first appears.

A. Mr. Hammer, I truly -- of course a summary doesn't have to be chronological.

Q. Isn't a plot summary, in fact, usually a tracking of the plot? If you buy a pony, for example, in a store that talks about the plot of War and Peace, doesn't it usually start with the first scene in War and Peace?

A. Yes, but that's describing a book. As he's describing a character, he has, of course, rearranged -- which is all he ever does -- rearrange my fictional facts chronologically in terms of the character's history.

Q. And doesn't that, in fact, turn it into other than a plot summary?

A. What does it turn it into?

Q. Into a character description.

A. This doesn't describe a character; it simply says what a character did. There's no --

Q. But it rearranges the plot in order to do that, isn't that true? It starts with something that happens in the sixth book, not the first book.

A. Please show me in the century where he discusses the psychology, the mythology, the archetype, please show me in the century where he does any of those things except just say Voldemort did this and this and this and this.

Q. Ms. Rowling, my question was only isn't this different than a simple plot summary, isn't that true?

A. You believe so, but I don't.

Q. This starts with nearly the end of the series; that is not what a plot summary usually does, is it?

A. It so happens in Book 6 for the first time you have Voldemort's pre-story; therefore, he has chosen to start, predictably, with a pre-story. Subsequently, he goes through Books 1 to 7.

MR. HAMMER: I have no further questions of Ms. Rowling, your Honor.

DIRECT EXAMINATION BY MS. CENDALI:

Q. Ms. Rowling, there was a lot of discussion about a letter that I sent. Who normally instructs me on your behalf?

A. Neil Blair, who works at my literary agency.

Q. And as far as you know, have you ever acted in any way to stop a book that did not infringe your copyrights?

A. Definitely not.

Q. Now, counsel asked you some questions about usefulness and whether the lexicon could be useful in some sort of a way. What is your view of that?

A. If you've already read the Harry Potter books, then I do not believe that the lexicon gives you anything of value. It simply tells you what you will already know, because you read the Harry Potter books.

Q. Now, what does the lexicon do, if anything, in terms of letting you find where characters appear in your books?

A. It is useless as a serious tool. For example, if you look up a character to discover where they first appear, you will frequently not find that information. Gilderoy Lockhart, the entry of Gilderoy Lockhart is a prime example. He is a character who appears throughout the second book, Chamber of Secrets, and only once subsequently in the series. And Chamber of Secrets isn't mentioned once in his entry. So it's not only it's not exhaustive, it doesn't tell you every place that a person appears. It doesn't mention the first place frequently that a person appears, which people might want to look up, I suppose. And it occasionally misleads.

Q. Does it give you the page numbers where --

A. No page numbers. Only refers to the chapters.

Q. And you mentioned errors. You were asked about the Alohomora entry. Are there other errors in the lexicon that you noticed?

A. There are many, actually. And some of them are mistranslations. For example, patronus the Latin word patronus is mistranslated. I think Mr. Vander Ark says it means patron saint; it means guardian, protector. And it also has an association, which one of these books has picked up on, with the word pater, father, which is relevant to Harry, as he has the same guardian as his father. But there are more serious, to me, more serious mistakes in the Lexicon. On the few places where Mr. Vander Ark cannot simply copy and attempt to explain a concept, a larger concept that cannot be lifted from the few lines in the book, I counted, I think, four or five places where he attempts to do that. And on every occasion he gets it wrong. He literally has not understood -- for example, he does not understand how Harry survived the final dual with Voldemort, which I think is a very serious error. This is not a small matter of an etymology that he's mistakenly ascribed as Hawaiian.

Q. What did he get wrong?

MR. HAMMER: This is not redirect. None of this was touched upon in cross.

MS. CENDALI: You asked about it error.

MR. HAMMER: I asked about specific errors; nothing that you're now eliciting.

THE COURT: It does seem to be beyond the scope.

MS. CENDALI: You asked about errors in the Lexicon. I'll move on, your Honor, but I'd like you to at least tell us what he got wrong; I think everyone is interested in hearing.

THE COURT: All right. I'll allow you to go ahead.

A. Mr. Vander Ark asserts that Harry survived the final dual with Voldemort because Voldemort's wand wouldn't work against him. This is not correct. He's missed the key point. The key point is that Voldemort is keeping alive in his own body the sacrifice that Harry's mother made for him 17 -- 16 years previously. I could go into detail, but I think that...

Q. Thank you. Mr. Hammer occasionally interrupted you, Ms. Rowling. Is there anything else that you wanted to say that you did not have a chance to respond to?

A. I don't think so. I think I've said my piece.

MS. CENDALI: Thank you, your Honor.

MR. HAMMER: Nothing further, your Honor.

THE COURT: Thank you very much.

THE WITNESS: Thank you.

(Witness excused)

REBUTTAL TESTIMONY GIVEN ON APRIL 16, 2008

[Much of J.K. Rowling's rebuttal testimony concerns statements given the previous day by witnesses for defendant RDR Books]

MS. CENDALI (attorney for J.K. Rowling): Plaintiffs call, in rebuttal, J.K Rowling.

THE COURT: Ms. Rowling, you are reminded that you are under oath. And, no one is to draw any inferences from the fact that I remind the witness that she is still under oath. I am required, as a matter of court procedure, to give that instruction to the witness when they resume the stand on a subsequent day.

JOANNE ROWLING, called as a witness by the Plaintiff, in rebuttal, having been first duly sworn, testified as follows:

DIRECT EXAMINATION BY MS. CENDALI:

Q. Ms. Rowling, good afternoon.

A. Good afternoon.

Q. You've been here through the whole trial, haven't you?

A. I have.

Q. And you have listened to the different testimony of the different witnesses, correct?

A. Yes, I have.

Q. Now, Ms. Rowling, you heard from Mr. Vander Ark and you heard Mr. Vander Ark and Dr. Sorensen testify about the amount of your work that was copied and whether it was necessary in order to do that in order to make a guide to the Harry Potter series. Do you have a view as to that?

A. Yes, I do. I -- I have a very strong view and my view -- my view is that it is analogous to me making a cake and that in the creation of this Lexicon, all the plums in my cake, as it were, all the highlights of my work, in other words character's secret history, the jokes certainly, certain exciting narrative twists, all the things that are the highlights of my stories and my books have been taken and put into the Lexicon for their entertainment value. The --

MR. HAMMER (attorney for RDR Books): I'm just going to object. This is not rebuttal testimony, this is simply a restatement of her original testimony.

THE COURT: I'm going to overrule.

Q. Ms. Rowling, does the fact that your work contains fictitious facts in your mind change how much the Lexicon should be allowed to copy from your work?

A. It very -- it, to my mind, it very much changes that, yes. And the reason is, as I believe I stated before in my previous testimony, that these things have no existence outside my specific language, my turns of phrase. And I think that those people who are familiar with the seven Harry Potter books would see very easily how much of my distinctive phrasing has been lifted and replicated. And, I find it frankly unbelievable that anyone could argue that this was necessary. I simply don't see why that was necessary unless it is the argument that Mr. Vander Ark does have the right to resell my work for its entertainment value. Because these narrative twists and these very distinctive phrasings are not -- well, firstly, they're rarely quoted within quotation marks so I am not even being credited with having invented these things -- but, they're not being used in support of anything. He's not making an argument, he is simply restating. He is not discussing, he is simply restating. I believe in the overwhelming majority of this book so-called, this Lexicon, he simply restates in my exact words. That remains my belief.

Q. Well, what about Mr. Vander Ark's argument that the book is a memory aid or something like that. Doesn't that justify the taking of your work?

A. In my view, absolutely not. I completely accept that a reader of whatever age may, at some point, want to glance at what Mr. Vander Ark calls a ready reference guide. I know what such a guide looks like. What I find absolutely baffling is that, first of all, if it's a ready reference guide then it must be used

concurrently with reading my novels. Yes, I think that that is clear because a reader, let's say our hypothetical 9-year-old reader comes across Peeves the poltergeist and thinks: I don't remember who he is -- I find that unlikely because he is normally floating along in mid-air so I think he is unlikely to be confused with many other characters -- but, let's say they have forgotten that. Of course I would never, for a second, say that no work should be produced that could not give a quick reference but that, of course, such a ready reference guide would be something that would be read along with the novels. Therefore, when the 9-year-old, our hypothetical 9-year-old looks up Peeves, in the Lexicon it is my belief that he received -- he or she receives far more information than is necessary simply to place that character, simply to jog the memory. And, in the case of many of my characters, your Honor, particularly key characters, the hypothetical 9-year-old looking up Sirius Black, for example, the first time he is mentioned in my novels, turned to such a memory jogging work, if that work were the Lexicon he would receive, or she would receive, everything that happens to Sirius the first time he turns up. He wouldn't receive the information: Sirius Black is Harry's godfather. He was -- and at the beginning of the book he is in Azkaban. He will receive pages of information leading up to the fact that he is murdered. So, it is not a memory-jogger at all. But then, it seems to me that the defendant's --

MR. HAMMER: I'm sorry, your Honor, but this is pure narrative. If we are going to have questions on this, let's have questions and answers.

THE WITNESS: Mr. Hammer, that is my answer.

MR. HAMMER: I know, ma'am, but I would like to have a question.

THE COURT: Well, it does make it difficult in order to frame the cross-examination when an answer goes on --

THE WITNESS: I apologize.

THE COURT: -- at length but I think you are entitled to give examples --

THE WITNESS: Thank you.

THE COURT: -- of what you mean because --

BY MS. CENDALI:

Q. Can you give me other examples, Ms. Rowling, of entries in the Lexicon where you believe go on for too long and give information away to readers?

A. Your Honor, it is my belief that this applies to virtually every entry. If the justification for this book is as an aid to memory --

THE COURT: Let me ask you something.

THE WITNESS: Yes.

THE COURT: You call it entertainment value.

THE WITNESS: Yes.

THE COURT: Can you imagine anyone reading this Lexicon for entertainment value, really?

THE WITNESS: Honestly, your Honor, no. But, if I may say it without being arrogant or vain, I think there are funny things in there and I wrote them. So, I think the entertaining parts of it buried within it are my entertaining facts or my entertaining jokes.

THE COURT: I see what she is saying. All right.

BY MS. CENDALI:

Q. Ms. Rowling, do you have any concerns about your companion books, Quidditch Through the Ages and Fantastic Beasts, in particular?

A. My concerns regarding those two companion books have not changed a jot since we entered this courtroom. I believe that the contents of those books have been plundered, taken wholesale, and repeated in the Lexicon.

Q. Now, you heard Mr. Harris, the marketing expert for RDR testify that you would not be hurt if the Lexicon were published because you are so popular. What is your reaction to that?

A. Frankly, outraged. Because it seems to me that that argument says because your work was popular, because your work was interesting to so many people you don't have the right -- you don't have rights over your work anymore; that somehow because -- because my work

was successful I have weakened my own right to protect my copyright. I don't understand how that holds. Your Honor, I do accept that Mr. Harris was talking very specifically about would this specific book cause harm to my sales. And I can only repeat my previous testimony. I did not fly here because I thought that I would lose some sales. This is not why I am here. I am here because I passionately believe that this is a case that is about an author's right to protect their creation -- their creation. And, I believe that if this book is allowed to be published, the flood gates will open and the precedent is established that anyone can lift an astonishingly large portion of an author's work and present it as their own.

Q. Do you believe Mr. Harris when he discussed, when he gave his testimony, discussed or took into account appropriately the issue of not just sales of this particular book but other books that would follow?

MR. HAMMER: Just objection on every ground an objection can be made. This is first, leading, and we are being asked about what her beliefs are, not about any facts at all. And, I object to the form of these questions. If they want to ask questions about specific factual disagreements with testimony, that's fine.

THE COURT: I have to hear the question back. (Record read)

THE COURT: I'm not sure I understand the question.

THE WITNESS: I may need it rephrased just because I didn't understand that.

BY MS. CENDALI:

Q. I will rephrase the question. Ms. Rowling, you heard Mr. Harris testify?

A. Yes.

Q. Do you -- what do you believe the harm would be from publication of the Lexicon book?

A. As I have previously stated, I believe that this would inevitably -- inevitably lead to a slippery slope. I believe the flood gates would open. And it is, of course, not just -- not just my work that therefore is endangered. If authors, any authors including much less successful authors than I am cannot protect their work -- and that goes to term papers on the Internet, that goes to -- I see this as an incredibly important case. Are we or are we not the owners of our own work.

Q. Ms. Rowling --

THE COURT: How long does it -- do you have any idea -- each of these books are how long?

THE WITNESS: Of my novels?

THE COURT: Yes.

THE WITNESS: They vary in length, your Honor. The first book is 95,000 words but the longest one, I believe, is nearly 200,000 words.

THE COURT: Pages I was thinking.

THE WITNESS: Pages. Oh, pages.

THE COURT: I'm talking about the novels.

THE WITNESS: In the American edition I believe the longer ones would be six-hundred-and-something pages.

THE COURT: And they came out periodically?

THE WITNESS: Yes.

THE COURT: How far apart were they published?

THE WITNESS: The first four novels were published a year apart, annually in the U.K. anyway, and there was a three-year gap between the novels, but during that time the two companion books were written and published. And then the last three novels in the series were published two years apart.

THE COURT: So, they were published over a period of time?

THE WITNESS: Yes.

THE COURT: I don't know how long it would take children to read. I know how long it would take adults to read, too, that's the matter of time the adults have, not the time the children have. So, I guess I won't ask you any further questions, but.

BY MS. CENDALI:

Q. Ms. Rowling, is this case being driven by Warner Brothers?

A. Absolutely not. Not at all. Any representation that Warner Brothers has in this case is for entirely -- I don't even know the correct legal terms, but they're licensees. I have licensed them certain rights in the Harry Potter property to enable them to make their film adaptations. But, I am here on my own account. I am not a corporation driving this, I am an author who is here to stand up for what I believe is an important principle on behalf of creators. Those who create from nothing.

Q. Mr. Hammer, in some of his questions to you and to Dean Johnson and to Dr. Sorensen used the word "suppression." Are you opposed to Harry Potter guidebooks, in general?

A. I am not only not opposed to Harry Potter guides, I am flattered by their existence. I think that they vary in quality but I don't think that that matters. All I care about -- all I care about is that they don't infringe my copyright. That's all I care about. I think some of them are very good. I think some of them are really not so good. I would even go as far as to agree with Dr. Sorensen that it all contribute to a discussion of a literary property. The Harry Potter novels are some of the most banned of the late 20th, early 20th -- First Century. I am vehemently anti-censorship. I have never wanted -- your Honor, I think it is highly relevant before this case ever came into litigation, I attempted to reach out to Mr. Vander Ark and I have to say that I believe --

MR. HAMMER: Your Honor, that really I do object to, your Honor.

THE WITNESS: It is highly relevant, your Honor.

MR. HAMMER: It may be, but it is also settlement negotiations that I asked --

THE WITNESS: No, no, no. Mr. Hammer, I am not talking about that at all, I promise you.

THE COURT: All right, but.

THE WITNESS: I am trying to express that --

THE COURT: But it really doesn't go to -- unless it goes to something that is germane to the issues here I don't think that I should be hearing what discussions were had between.

BY MS. CENDALI:

Q. I'm not sure, but I think, Ms. Rowling, are you talking about the pre-litigation cease and desist communications --

A. Yes, I am.

Q. -- with RDR --

A. Yes, I am.

Q. -- and Mr. Hammer? Do you feel that you --

MR. HAMMER: And unless that's rebuttal for something that was stated -- well, but I want to --

MS. CENDALI: Are you trying to suppress Ms. Rowling, Mr. Hammer?

MR. HAMMER: No, that seems to be impossible. I'm just trying to state that unless that is rebuttal to something that was stated by Mr. Vander Ark, that it really should not come in on that ground and also on the grounds that it seems to be associated with some sort of settlement offer.

BY MS. CENDALI:

Q. Ms. Rowling, you heard the testimony of Mr. Rapoport?

A. Yes.

Q. And Mr. Vander Ark, correct?

A. Yes.

Q. And you heard them testify about the cease and desist letters and communications they received from your representatives prior to starting this case?

A. Yes, I did.

Q. Was litigation your first choice, Ms. Rowling?

A. It was my absolute last resort.

MR. HAMMER: Really, I just object to that. This is not relevant to the underlying questions that are before this Court.

THE COURT: I don't see what it's rebuttal to, Ms. Cendali.

Q. Isn't it true, Ms. Rowling, that -- do you agree that with their testimony -- do you disagree with any of their testimony with regard to the prefiling communications in this case?

MR. HAMMER: The question is is the book fair use or not. The question is not whether or not beforehand we ignored a cease and desist letter or we should have followed -- I mean I'm speechless. I am

suppressing myself. I do not think that this testimony is relevant to this case.

Q. Ms. Rowling, why are you opposed to this book?

A. It takes too much from me, and I think the justification for doing that is next to nonexistent. But I never, ever once wanted to stop Mr. Vander Ark doing his own guide, never. Never. All I ever said through my representatives repeatedly, and I think beyond the point where some of this would have lead to litigation, I repeatedly tried to say to Mr. Vander Ark, Do your book, but please change it so it does not take as much of my work.

MR. HAMMER: I'm sorry. This is exactly what was objected to. There is no evidence in the record that this is responding to -- this is something that --

MS. CENDALI: You're accusing Ms. Rowling of unclean hands and copyright misuse. She has a right to defend herself, Mr. Hammer.

MR. HAMMER: Why didn't she say this in her direct testimony? There is nothing that is rebutting. We then could have followed with our testimony.

MS. CENDALI: Cross-examine her.

MR. HAMMER: No, ma'am. I'd like to do this according to the normal rules.

THE COURT: I don't think it's appropriate for you -- I don't think you should be asking these questions, Ms. Cendali, because if you know what the -- what you're getting at because -- I'm a little troubled because I worry that -- because I said I thought and was afraid yesterday that this case might be lawyer-driven. I'm not referring to either counsel. Counsel in cases get cases. And they get looking at the legal aspects of it and they charge no holds barred in some cases. And that's considered -- I've seen lawyers brag about it in this country. And I think that that happens in cases. And what I was really concerned about is because this case is in a murky state of the law, it's not a clear statement of law. Judge Havell has written two Law Review articles about this whole area. And he has gotten his share of reversals in this area before he went up to the Circuit Court. Now, it's a murky area. And what I was trying to make clear is that that was the fact. And because that was the fact, and because of the time element that I see in this case, that it made a lot of sense, you just said it, a lot of sense, and that's why I raised the question. And I've listened to the parties and heard them. I'm not sure that you still couldn't settle it if you listen to what people said on the stand.

MS. CENDALI: I have no further questions, Ms. Rowling.

THE WITNESS: Thank you.

MR. HAMMER: I have no cross, your Honor.

THE COURT: All right. Thank you very much.

THE WITNESS: Thank you.

(Witness excused)

THE COURT: No more witnesses?

MR. HAMMER: I think that's it, Judge.

MS. CENDALI: I believe we are done, your Honor.

OPINION AND ORDER OF THE COURT
(JUDGE PATTERSON'S DECISION)

WARNER BROS. ENTERTAINMENT INC. AND
J.K. ROWLING,

                        Plaintiffs,

        -against-

RDR BOOKS and DOES 1-10

                        Defendants.

Case No. 07-09667 (RPP)   Filed: September 8, 2008

On October 31, 2007, Plaintiffs Warner Bros. Entertainment Inc. and
J.K. Rowling commenced this action against Defendant RDR Books, alleging
copyright infringement pursuant to 17 U.S.C. §§ 101 *et seq.*, as well as several
other federal and state claims, and seeking both injunctive relief and
damages. By order dated March 5, 2008, the Court consolidated the
scheduled evidentiary hearing on Plaintiffs' motion for a preliminary
injunction with a trial on the merits pursuant to Federal Rule of Civil
Procedure 65(a)(2). By their pretrial orders, the parties narrowed the claims
and defenses to be tried: Plaintiffs pursued only their claims for copyright
infringement and statutory damages under 17 U.S.C. §§ 101 *et seq.* of the
Copyright Act; Defendant pursued only its defenses and affirmative defenses
of copyright fair use under 17 U.S.C. § 107, copyright misuse, and unclean
hands. The Court held a bench trial on the merits from April 14, 2008 to
April 17, 2008. This opinion constitutes the Court's findings of fact and
conclusions of law pursuant to Federal Rule of Civil Procedure 52(a).

FINDINGS OF FACT
I. The Copyrighted Works
Plaintiff J.K. Rowling ("Rowling") is the author of the highly
acclaimed Harry Potter book series. Written for children but enjoyed by
children and adults alike, the Harry Potter series chronicles the lives and
adventures of Harry Potter and his friends as they come of age at the
Hogwarts School of Witchcraft and Wizardry and face the evil Lord
Voldemort. It is a tale of a fictional world filled with magical spells,
fantastical creatures, and imaginary places and things.

Rowling published the first of seven books in the series, <u>Harry Potter and the Philosopher's Stone</u>, in the United Kingdom in 1997. In 1998, the first book was published in the United States as <u>Harry Potter and the Sorcerer's Stone</u>. Over the next ten years, Rowling wrote and published the remaining six books in the <u>Harry Potter</u> series: <u>Harry Potter and the Chamber of Secrets</u> (1998), <u>Harry Potter and the Prisoner of Azkaban</u> (1999), <u>Harry Potter and the Goblet of Fire</u> (2000), <u>Harry Potter and the Order of the Phoenix</u> (2003), and <u>Harry Potter and the Half-Blood Prince</u> (2005). The seventh and final book, <u>Harry Potter and the Deathly Hallows</u> was released on July 21, 2007. Rowling owns a United States copyright in each of the <u>Harry Potter</u> books. The books have won numerous awards, including children's literary awards and the British Book Award.

The <u>Harry Potter</u> series has achieved enormous popularity and phenomenal sales. The books have won numerous awards, including children's literary awards and the British Book Award. Most gratifying to Rowling is that the <u>Harry Potter</u> series has been credited with encouraging readership among children.

As a result of the success of the <u>Harry Potter</u> books, Plaintiff Warner Bros. Entertainment Inc. ("Warner Brothers") obtained from Rowling the exclusive film rights to the entire seven-book <u>Harry Potter</u> series. Warner Brothers is the exclusive distributor for worldwide distribution of these films. To date, Warner Brothers has released five <u>Harry Potter</u> films, and the sixth is scheduled for a worldwide release in November 2008 [recently postponed until summer 2009]. Each of the <u>Harry Potter</u> films is the subject of a copyright registration. Warner Brothers licensed certain rights to Electronic Arts to create video games based on the <u>Harry Potter</u> books and films, which included a series of "Famous Wizard Cards" that Rowling created and which are the subject of U.S. copyright registrations jointly owned by Warner Brothers and Electronic Arts.

Early on in the publication of the <u>Harry Potter</u> series, Rowling wrote a short series of fictional newspapers entitled "The Daily Prophet," which were published and distributed to fans in the United Kingdom. Rowling owns a U.K. copyright in "The Daily Prophet" newsletters.

In addition, Rowling wrote two short companion books to the <u>Harry Potter</u> series (the "companion books"), the royalties from which she donated to the charity Comic Relief. The first, <u>Quidditch Through the Ages</u> (2001), recounts the history and development of "quidditch," an imaginary sport featured in the <u>Harry Potter</u> series that involves teams of witches and wizards on flying broomsticks. The second, <u>Fantastic Beasts & Where to Find Them</u> (2001), is an A-to-Z encyclopedia of the imaginary beasts and beings that exist in <u>Harry Potter</u>'s fictional world. Both appear in the <u>Harry Potter</u> series as textbooks that the students at Hogwarts use in their studies, and the companion books are marketed as such. Neither of the companion books is written in narrative form; instead each book chronicles and expands on the fictional facts that unfold in the <u>Harry Potter</u> series. The companion books are both registered with the United States Copyright Office. Although the market for the companion books is not nearly as large as the market for the <u>Harry Potter</u> series, Rowling's companion books have earned more than $30 million to date.

Rowling has stated on a number of occasions since 1998 that, in addition to the two companion books, she plans to publish a "<u>Harry Potter</u> encyclopedia" after the completion of the series and again donate the proceeds to charity. Rowling intends that her encyclopedia contain alphabetical entries for the various people, places and things from the <u>Harry Potter</u> novels. While she intends to add new material as well, her encyclopedia is expected to reflect all of the information in the <u>Harry Potter</u> series.

Rowling already has begun preparations for work on the encyclopedia by assembling her materials and requesting from her U.K. publisher its "bible" of <u>Harry Potter</u> materials. The publisher's "bible" is a catalogue of the people, places, and things from the <u>Harry Potter</u> books. Rowling's U.S. publisher has compiled a similar catalogue of elements from the <u>Harry Potter</u> books which Rowling has requested and intends to draw on in creating her encyclopedia. Rowling plans on using an A-to-Z format for her encyclopedia.

II. The Allegedly Infringing Work

Defendant RDR Books is a Michigan-based publishing company that seeks to publish a book entitled "The Lexicon," the subject of this lawsuit. Steven Vander Ark, a former library media specialist at a middle school in Michigan, is the attributed author of the Lexicon. He is also the originator, owner, and operator of "The Harry Potter Lexicon" website, a popular <u>Harry Potter</u> fan site from which the content of the Lexicon is drawn.

A. The Origins of the Lexicon

An immediate fan of the <u>Harry Potter</u> novels, Vander Ark began taking personal notes to keep track of the details and elements that unfold in the <u>Harry Potter</u> world while reading the second book in the series in 1999. After joining an online discussion group about the <u>Harry Potter</u> books, Vander Ark expanded his notes to include descriptive lists of the spells, characters, and fictional objects in <u>Harry Potter</u> to share with fellow fans. These lists included brief descriptions or definitions of the terms.

Vander Ark began work on his website, "The Harry Potter Lexicon" (the "website" or "Lexicon website"), in 1999 and opened the website in 2000. His purpose in establishing the website was to create an encyclopedia that collected and organized information from the Harry Potter books in one central source for fans to use for reference. At its launch, the website featured Vander Ark's descriptive lists of spells, characters, creatures, and magical items from Harry Potter with hyperlinks to cross-referenced entries. In response to feedback from users of the website, Vander Ark developed an A-to-Z index to each list to allow users to search for entries alphabetically.

The website presently features several indexed lists of people, places, and things from Harry Potter, including the "Encyclopedia of Spells," "Encyclopedia of Potions," "Wizards, Witches, and Beings," "The Bestiary," and "Gazetteer of the Wizarding World." In addition to these reference features, the website contains a variety of supplemental material pertaining to Harry Potter, including fan art, commentary, essays, timelines, forums, and interactive data. The website is currently run by a staff of seven or eight volunteers, including four primary editors, all of whom were recruited to help update and expand the website's content after the publication of the fifth book in the Harry Potter series. The website uses minimal advertising to offset the costs of operation. Use of the website is free and unrestricted.

The content of the encyclopedia entries on the Lexicon website is drawn primarily from the Harry Potter series, the companion books, "The Daily Prophet" newsletters, the "Famous Wizard Cards," and published interviews of Rowling. According to Vander Ark, some additional content is drawn from outside reference sources, including Bullfinch's Mythology, Field Guide to Little People, New Shorter Oxford English Dictionary, and online encyclopedias such as Encyclopedia Mythica. Frequently, these sources are not cited in the website's encyclopedia entries. Vander Ark's purpose in including additional information from outside sources or from his own knowledge was to enrich the experience of readers of the Harry Potter series by illuminating "the incredibly rich world and hidden meanings" contained within them.

Vander Ark has received positive feedback, including from Rowling and her publishers, about the value of the Lexicon website as a reference source. In May 2004, Vander Ark read a remark by Rowling posted on her website praising his Lexicon website as follows: "This is such a great site that I have been known to sneak into an internet café while out writing and check a fact rather than go into a bookshop and buy a copy of Harry Potter (which is embarrassing). A website for the dangerously obsessive; my natural home." In July 2005, Vander Ark received a note from Cheryl Klein, a Senior Editor at Scholastic Inc., American publisher of the Harry Potter series, thanking him and his staff "for the wonderful resource [his] site provides for fans, students, and indeed editors & copyeditors of the Harry Potter series," who "referred to the Lexicon countless times during the editing of [the sixth book in the series], whether to verify a fact, check a timeline, or get a chapter & book reference for a particular event." In September 2006, Vander Ark was invited by Warner Brothers to the set of the film <u>The Order of the Phoenix</u>, where he met David Heyman, the producer of all the <u>Harry Potter</u> films. Heyman told Vander Ark that Warner Brothers used the Lexicon website almost every day. Finally, in July 2007, Vander Ark visited the studios of Electronic Arts, the licensed producer of the <u>Harry Potter</u> video games, where he observed printed pages from the Lexicon covering the walls of the studio.

Prior to any discussions with RDR Books about publishing portions of the Lexicon website as a book, Vander Ark was aware of Rowling's public statements regarding her intention to write a <u>Harry Potter</u> encyclopedia upon completion of the seventh book in the series. In June 2007, just before the release of the seventh book, Vander Ark emailed Christopher Little Literary Agency, Rowling's literary agent in the United Kingdom, and suggested that he would be "a good candidate for work as an editor, given [his] work on the Lexicon," should Rowling start working on an encyclopedia or other reference to the <u>Harry Potter</u> series. The literary agency advised him that Rowling intended to work alone and did not require a collaborator.

B. RDR Books' Acquisition and Marketing of the Lexicon

Roger Rapoport is the president of Defendant RDR Books. Rapoport learned of Vander Ark and the Lexicon website when he read an article in his local newspaper dated July 23, 2007, profiling Vander Ark as a well known figure within the <u>Harry Potter</u> fan community and the proprietor of the Lexicon website who "holds the key to all things 'Harry Potter.'" Recognizing a publishing opportunity, Rapoport contacted Vander Ark on August 6, 2007 about the possibility of publishing a <u>Harry Potter</u> encyclopedia based on some of the materials from the Lexicon website. Rapoport denies seeing any coverage by national news outlets of Rowling's appearance on NBC's Today Show on July 25, 2007, where Rowling stated that she intended to write a <u>Harry Potter</u> encyclopedia.

At his first meeting with Rapoport in August 2007, Vander Ark raised his concerns regarding the permissibility of publishing the Lexicon in view of Rowling's plan to publish an encyclopedia and her copyrights in the <u>Harry Potter</u> books. Prior to August 2007, Vander Ark had developed and circulated the opinion that publishing "any book that is a guide to [the <u>Harry Potter</u>] world" would be a violation of Rowling's intellectual property rights. Vander Ark had even stated on a public internet newsgroup that he would not publish the Lexicon "in any form except online" without permission because Rowling, not he, was "entitled to that market." Vander Ark changed his mind about publishing the Lexicon after Rapoport reassured him that he had looked into the legal issue and determined that publication of content from the Lexicon website in book form was legal. Rapoport agreed to stand by this opinion by adding an atypical clause to the publishing contract providing that RDR would defend and indemnify Vander Ark in the event of any lawsuits.

Rapoport and Vander Ark agreed that the content of the book would be limited to the encyclopedia sections of the Lexicon website that presented descriptions of the persons, places, spells, and creatures from the Harry Potter works. They conceived of the book as an encyclopedia organized in the A-to-Z format, rather than by topic as the Lexicon website is organized, to allow the user to find information as quickly as possible. The idea was to publish the first complete guide to the Harry Potter series that included information from the seventh and final Harry Potter novel. Vander Ark believed that there was an advantage to being the first reference guide on the market to cover all seven Harry Potter books. He also believed that by virtue of it completeness, the Lexicon would be most useful for the purpose it sought to serve, namely helping readers and fans to find information from the Harry Potter novels.

RDR Books intended to have a manuscript of the Lexicon completed within two-to-three weeks of execution of the publishing contract. The plan was to rush the book to market by late-October 2007, in part, to capitalize on the interest generated by the last Harry Potter book and the surge in sales during the holiday season. RDR Books initially planned a print-run of 10,000 copies of the Lexicon, but would undertake subsequent print-runs if the book was successful.

Even before his initial meeting with Vander Ark, Rapoport began working to secure foreign publishers for the proposed Lexicon project and had contacted Methuen Publishing in the United Kingdom to gauge their interest in doing such a project. He marketed the Lexicon to foreign publishers, as well as to U.S. bookstores and book sellers, as the "definitive" Harry Potter encyclopedia. Some of Rapoport's marketing communications mischaracterized Rowling's statements about the Lexicon website, giving the impression that she supported the publication of the Lexicon book. One marketing flyer for the Lexicon prominently displayed Rowling's 2004 statement praising the Lexicon website. As a result of Rapoport's marketing efforts, RDR Books secured oral contracts with foreign publishers for rights to the Lexicon in England, Canada, France, Australia, New Zealand, and China, and an order from Borders bookstore in the United States.

C. Plaintiffs' Objections to Publication of the Lexicon

Rowling's literary agent, Neil Blair of the Christopher Little Literary Agency, first learned of the Lexicon book when he saw an advertisement on www.PublishersMarketplace.com announcing that RDR Books would be publishing the Lexicon, scheduled for release in late October 2007. On September 18, 2007, counsel for Rowling and Warner Brothers forwarded a letter to Vander Ark by email, copying Rapoport, notifying them that the Lexicon appeared to infringe Rowling's copyrights and requesting that RDR Books cease publication of the book. Rapoport replied to Plaintiffs' counsel that he intended to study the various issues with RDR Books' legal advisers and that his work had been interrupted by personal circumstances. Meanwhile he continued to market the Lexicon book domestically and abroad.

On October 3, 2007, after receiving no substantive response from RDR Books, Plaintiffs' counsel wrote again to Rapoport emphasizing their clients' concerns and asking for a prompt substantive response. On October 5, 2007, when pitching the Lexicon to a Brazilian publisher, Rapoport asked for confirmation that the agent would not speak with the local publisher of the Harry Potter novels about the Lexicon. On October 8, 2007, despite having received a cease-and-desist letter and a subsequent letter from Plaintiffs' counsel, Rapoport told a German publisher who raised copyright concerns that a lawsuit was unlikely.

On October 11, 2007, RDR Books sent the chairman of Warner Brothers a cease-and-desist letter claiming that Warner Brothers had violated Vander Ark's rights in the "Hogwarts Timeline" of events from the Harry Potter novels that was featured on the Lexicon website. RDR Books also stated that it was seeking "tangible rewards" for Vander Ark in exchange for Warner Brothers' purported use of the timeline as an extra feature of the DVD versions of the first three Harry Potter films. On October 19, 2007, Warner Brothers responded to RDR Books' letter regarding the timeline with a request for a copy of the "print version" of the Lexicon website referred to by RDR Books to aid its evaluation of any potential claims. RDR Books refused, stating that Warner Brothers could print the material from the Lexicon website.

On October 19 and 24, 2007, Plaintiffs' counsel sent two more letters to RDR Books, asking for a substantive response to their clients' concerns regarding the Lexicon and for confirmation that RDR Books would not publish the Lexicon until it attempted to resolve the matter in good faith. RDR Books' responses deflected the inquiries and stated that Plaintiffs' objections were "unwarranted." On October 31, 2007, Plaintiffs called Rapoport to offer a last chance to agree to cease publication, or at least delay publication, and to provide Plaintiffs with a copy of the manuscript and proposed cover, in effort to resolve the matter. RDR refused to delay publication and refused to provide a copy of the manuscript. Plaintiffs filed suit on October 31, 2007, at which time they also moved by order to show cause for a preliminary injunction.

Since the filing of this lawsuit, RDR Books has revised the front and back covers of the Lexicon. Specifically, RDR Books removed the quotation of Rowling's 2004 statement about her use of the Lexicon website from the back cover of the Lexicon after Plaintiffs presented a survey in this litigation demonstrating that 38% of respondents believed that the appearance of the quote on the proposed book cover meant that Rowling endorsed the book. RDR Books changed the title from "The Harry Potter Lexicon" to "The Lexicon: An Unauthorized Guide to Harry Potter Fiction and Related Materials." Additionally, the final revision of the front cover of the Lexicon displays the following disclaimer:

Harry Potter and the names of fictitious people and places in the Harry Potter novels are trademarks of Warner Bros. Entertainment, Inc. This book is not written, prepared, approved, or licensed by Warner Bros. Entertainment, Inc., Scholastic Corporation, Raincoast Books, Bloomsbury Publishing Plc, or J.K. Rowling, nor is the author, his staff members, www.HP-Lexicon.org or the publisher in any way affiliated with Warner Bros. Entertainment, Inc., Scholastic Corporation, Raincoast Books, Bloomsbury Publishing Plc, J.K. Rowling, or any other person or company claiming an interest in the Harry Potter works.

D. The Content of the Lexicon

The Lexicon is an A-to-Z guide to the creatures, characters, objects, events, and places that exist in the world of <u>Harry Potter</u>. As received by the Court in evidence, the Lexicon manuscript is more than 400 type-written pages long and contains 2,437 entries organized alphabetically. The first few pages contain a list of abbreviations used throughout the Lexicon to cite to the original sources of the material.

The Lexicon manuscript was created using the encyclopedia entries from the Lexicon website. Because of space limitations for the printed work, which seeks to be complete but also easy to use, about half of the material from the website was not included in the Lexicon manuscript. The Lexicon itself makes clear that the only source of its content is the work of J.K. Rowling. The first page of the Lexicon manuscript states: "All the information in the Harry Potter Lexicon comes from J.K. Rowling, either in the novels, the 'schoolbooks,' from her interviews, or from material which she developed or wrote herself." While Vander Ark claims that the Lexicon uses material from outside reference sources, such as Bullfinch's Mythology, Field Guide to Little People, New Shorter Oxford English Dictionary, and online encyclopedias, it is not possible to confirm this claim because, aside from four dictionary citations, no other citations to third-party works appear in the Lexicon.

The Lexicon entries cull every item and character that appears in the Harry Potter works, no matter if it plays a significant or insignificant role in the story. The entries cover every spell (e.g., Expecto Patronum, Expelliarmus, and Incendio), potion (e.g., Love Potion, Felix Felicis, and Draught of Living Death), magical item or device (e.g., Deathly Hallows, Horcrux, Cloak of Invisibility), form of magic (e.g., Legilimency, Occlumency, and the Dark Arts), creature (e.g., Blast-Ended Skrewt, Dementors, and Blood-Sucking Bugbears), character (e.g., Harry Potter, Hagrid, and Lord Voldemort), group or force (e.g., Aurors, Dumbledore's Army, Death Eaters), invented game (e.g., Quidditch), and imaginary place (e.g., Hogwarts School of Witchcraft and Wizardry, Diagon Alley, and the Ministry of Magic) that appear in the Harry Potter works. The Lexicon also contains entries for items that are not explicitly named in the Harry Potter works but which Vander Ark has identified, such as medical magic, candle magic, wizard space, wizard clothing, and remorse. Some of the entries describe places or things that exist in the real world but also have a place in the Harry Potter works, such as moors, Greece, and Cornwall.

Each entry, with the exception of the shortest ones, gathers and synthesizes pieces of information relating to its subject that appear scattered across the Harry Potter novels, the companion books, The Daily Prophet newsletters, Famous Wizard Cards, and published interviews of Rowling. The types of information contained in the entries include descriptions of the subject's attributes, role in the story, relationship to other characters or things, and events involving the subject. Repositories of such information, the entries seek to give as complete a picture as possible of each item or character in the Harry Potter world, many of which appear only sporadically throughout the series or in various sources of Harry Potter material.

The snippets of information in the entries are generally followed by citations in parentheses that indicate where they were found within the corpus of the Harry Potter works. The thoroughness of the Lexicon's citation, however, is not consistent; some entries contain very few citations in relation to the amount material provided, e.g., entry for "Dumbledore, Albus Percival Wulfric Brian" (containing no citations in a five-page entry); entry for "Granger, Hermione Jean" (containing no citations in a three-page entry); entry for "Chamber of Secrets" (containing one citation for nearly two pages of material); entry for "Crouch, Bartemius 'Barty', Sr." containing one citation for nearly a full page of material). When the Lexicon cites to one of the seven <u>Harry Potter</u> novels, the citation provides only the book and chapter number. Vander Ark explained that page numbers were excluded from the citations because the various editions of the <u>Harry Potter</u> books have different pagination, but the chapter numbers remain consistent. The Lexicon neither assigns a letter to each edition nor specifies a standard edition while providing a conversion table for other editions, practices which Plaintiffs' expert Jeri Johnson testified were common for reference guides.

While not its primary purpose, the Lexicon includes commentary and background information from outside knowledge on occasion. For example, the Lexicon contains sporadic etymological references, e.g., entries for "Colloportus," "Lupin, Remus," "Alohamora," "Fidelius Charm"), analogies to characters outside the <u>Harry Potter</u> world such as Merlin, and observations of Rowling's allusions to other works of literature such as "the weird sisters" from Shakespeare's Macbeth. The Lexicon also points to the very few "flints," or errors in the continuity of the story, that appear in the <u>Harry Potter</u> series.

While there was considerable opining at trial as to the type of reference work the Lexicon purports to be and whether it qualifies as such (no doubt in part due to its title), the Lexicon fits in the narrow genre of non-fiction reference guides to fictional works. As Defendant's expert testified, the <u>Harry Potter</u> series is a multi-volume work of fantasy literature, similar to the works of J.R.R. Tolkien and C.S. Lewis. Such works lend themselves to companion guides or reference works because they reveal an elaborate imaginary world over thousands of pages, involving many characters, creatures, and magical objects that appear and reappear across thousands of pages. Fantasy literature spawns books having a wide variety of purposes and formats, as demonstrated by the books about <u>Harry Potter</u> that Plaintiffs entered into evidence. The Lexicon, an A-to-Z guide which synthesizes information from the series and generally provides citations for location of that information rather than offering commentary, is most comparable to the comprehensive work of Paul F. Ford, <u>Companion to Narnia: A Complete Guide to the Magical World of C.S. Lewis's</u> The Chronicles of Narnia, or the unauthorized A-to-Z guide by George W. Beahm, <u>Fact, Fiction, and Folklore in Harry Potter's World: An Unofficial Guide</u>.

At trial, Rowling testified that the Lexicon took "all the highlights of [her] work, in other words [her] characters' secret history, the jokes certainly, certain exciting narrative twists, all the things that are the highlights of [her] stories." She compared this taking of her work to plundering all of the "plums in [her] cake." At trial, the testimony of Rowling and the expert opinion of Johnson [Plaintiff's expert Jeri Johnson] focused at length on the Lexicon's verbatim copying of language from the <u>Harry Potter</u> works. Johnson testified that in particular, entries that deal with invented terms, creatures, places and things from the <u>Harry Potter</u> books use "again and again the specific, very colorful, idiosyncratic…nouns and phrases of Ms. Rowling."

Although it is difficult to quantify how much of the language in the Lexicon is directly lifted from the <u>Harry Potter</u> novels and companion books, the Lexicon indeed contains at least a troubling amount of direct quotation or close paraphrasing of Rowling's original language. The Lexicon occasionally uses quotation marks to indicate Rowling's language, but more often the original language is copied without quotation marks, often making it difficult to know which words are Rowling's and which are Vander Ark's.

For example, in the entry for "armor, goblin made," the Lexicon uses Rowling's poetic language nearly verbatim without quotation marks. The original language from <u>Harry Potter and the Deathly Hallows</u> reads:

Muggle-borns," he said. "Goblin-made armour does not require cleaning, simple girl. Goblins' silver repels mundane dirt, imbibing only that which strengthens it."

The Lexicon entry for "armor, goblin made" reads in its entirety:

Some armor in the wizarding world is made by goblins, and it is quite valuable. According to Phineas Nigellus, goblin-made armor does not require cleaning, because goblins' silver repels mundane dirt, imbibing only that which strengthens it, such as basilisk venom. In this context, "armor" also includes blades such as swords.

Although the Lexicon entry introduces Rowling's language with the phrase, "According to Phineas Nigellus," it does not use quotation marks.

The Lexicon entry for "Dementors" reproduces Rowling's vivid description of this creature sometimes using quotation marks and sometimes quoting or closely paraphrasing without indicating which language is original expression. The original language appears in Chapters 5 and 10 of <u>Harry Potter and the Prisoner of Azkaban</u> as follows:

> . . . Its face was completely hidden beneath its hood. . . . There was a hand protruding from the cloak and it was glistening, grayish, slimy-looking, and scabbed, like something dead that had decayed in water. . . . And then the thing beneath the hood, whatever it was, drew a long, slow, rattling breath, as though it were trying to suck something more than air from its surroundings.
>
> * * *
>
> "Dementors are among the foulest creatures to walk this earth. They infest the darkest, filthiest places, they glory in decay and despair, they drain peace, hope, and happiness out ey can't see them. Get too near a dementor and every good feeling, every happy memory will be sucked out of you. If it can, the dementor will feed on you long enough to reduce you to something like itself . . . soulless and evil. . . ."

The Lexicon entry for "Dementors" reads in its entirety:

> Dementors are some of the most terrible creatures on earth, flying tall black spectral humanoid things with flowing robes. They "infest the darkest, filthiest places, they glory in decay and despair, they drain peace, hope, and happiness out of the air around them," according to Lupin. Dementors affect even Muggles, although Muggles can't see the foul, black creatures. Dementors feed on positive human emotions; a large crowd is like a feast to them. They drain a wizard of his power if left with them too long. There were the guards at Azkaban and made that place horrible indeed. The Ministry used Dementors as guards in its courtrooms as well. There are certain defenses one can use against Dementors, specifically the Patronus Charm. A Dementor's breath sounds rattling and like it's trying to suck more than air out of a room. Its hands are "glistening, grayish, slimy-looking, and scabbed". It exudes a biting, soul-freezing cold.

Another example of verbatim copying and close paraphrase can be found in the Lexicon entry for "Mirror of Erised." The original language from <u>Harry Potter and the Sorcerer's Stone</u> reads:

It was a magnificent mirror, as high as the ceiling, with an ornate gold frame, standing on two clawed feet. There was an inscription carved around the top: Erised stra ehru oyt ube cafru oyt on wohsi.
* * *
. . . "It shows us nothing more or less than the deepest desire of our hearts. You [Harry Potter], who have never known your family, see them standing around you. Ronald Weasley, who has always been overshadowed by his brothers, sees himself standing alone, the best of all of them. However, this mirror will give us neither knowledge or truth. Men have wasted away before it, entranced by what they have seen, or been driven mad, not knowing if what it shows is real or even possible."

The first paragraph of the Lexicon entry reads:

A magnificent mirror, as high as a classroom ceiling, with an ornate gold frame, standing on two clawed feet. The inscription carved around the top reads "Erised stra ehru oyt ube cafru oyt on wohsi," which is "I show you not your face but your heart's desire" written backwards (that is, in what is called 'mirror writing'). When you look into the mirror you see the deepest, most desperate desire of your heart. The mirror has trapped people who can't bear to stop staring into it, unsure if what they see is going to actually happen. Harry sees his family in the Mirror; Ron sees himself as Head Boy and Quidditch champion.

The Lexicon entry for "Boggart" takes strands of dialogue from <u>Harry Potter and the Prisoner of Azkaban</u> and closely paraphrases it in the third person. The original work contains the following bits of dialogue:

"Boggarts like dark, enclosed spaces."
"It's a shape-shifter. . . . It can take the shape of whatever it thinks will frighten us most."
"Nobody knows what a boggart looks like when he is alone, but when I let him out, he will immediately become whatever each of us most fears."

The Lexicon entry begins as follows:

> A shape shifter that prefers to live in dark, confined spaces,
> taking the form of the thing most feared by the person it
> encounters; nobody knows what a boggart looks like in its
> natural state.

An example of particularly extensive direct quotation is found in the
Lexicon entry for "Trelawney, Sibyll Patricia," the professor of Divination at
the Hogwarts School who tells two important prophecies in the story. The
Lexicon not only reproduces her prophecies word-for-word in their entirety,
but in doing so, reveals dramatic plot twists and how they are resolved in the
series. For example, the first prophecy reads:

> "The one with the power to vanquish the Dark Lord
> approaches. . . . Born to those who have thrice defied him,
> born as the seventh month dies . . . and the Dark Lord will
> mark him as his equal, but he will have power the Dark Lord
> knows not . . . and either must die at the hand of the other
> for neither can live while the other survives. . . . The one with
> the power to vanquish the Dark Lord will be born as the
> seventh month dies. . . ."

The Lexicon entry reproduces this prophecy exactly but in italics and
indented. The Lexicon entry continues by discussing what happens as a
result of this prophecy: "Severus Snape was eavesdropping on this
conversation and he reported the first part of the Prophecy to the Dark
Lord. Voldemort immediately began searching for this threat, and centered
his attention on the child of Lily and James Potter. The entry then quotes
the second prophecy, but without a citation to where it appears in the Harry
Potter series.

A number of Lexicon entries copy Rowling's artistic literary devices
that contribute to her distinctive craft as a writer. For example, the Lexicon
entry for "brain room," uses Rowling's evocative literary device in a very
close paraphrase. The original language from Harry Potter and the Order of
the Phoenix reads:

> For a moment it seemed suspended in midair, then it soared
> toward Ron, spinning as it came, and what looked like
> ribbons of moving images flew from it, unraveling like rolls
> of film.

The Lexicon entry reads in part:

> . . . When Summoned, the brains fly out of the tank,
> unspooling ribbons of thought like strips of film, which wrap
> themselves around the Summoner and cause quite a bit of
> damage . . . .

The Lexicon entry for "Clankers" copies a vivid simile created by Rowling and reproduces a thought in the mind of Harry Potter as a factual statement using nearly identical wording. The original language from <u>Harry Potter and the Deathly Hallows</u> reads:

> Ron passed the bag to Griphook, and the goblin
> pulled out a number of small metal instruments that when
> shaken made a loud, ringing noise like miniature hammers on
> anvils. . . .
> . . . Harry could see [the dragon] trembling, and as
> they drew nearer he saw the scars made by vicious slashes
> across its face, and guessed that it had been taught to fear hot
> swords when it heard the sound of the Clankers.

The Lexicon entry reads:

> A number of small metal instruments, which when shaken
> make a loud, ringing noise like tiny hammers on anvil [sic].
> Anyone visiting one of the high-security vaults at Gringotts
> must carry one of these, shaking it to make noise. The
> dragon guarding those vaults has been conditioned to
> back away at the sound, apparently by being taught to fear
> hot swords whenever it hears the Clankers.

Similarly, the Lexicon entry for "Marchbanks, Madam Griselda" uses an artful simile from the original works to describe this character. Rowling's language in <u>Harry Potter and the Order of the Phoenix</u> reads: . . .

> Harry thought Professor Marchbanks must be the
> tiny, stooped witch with a face so lined it looked as though it
> had been draped in cobwebs; Umbridge was speaking to her
> very deferentially. . . .

The Lexicon entry reads in part:

> . . . Madam Marchbanks in June 1996 was tiny and stooped,
> her face so lined it appeared draped in cobwebs. . . .

The Lexicon's close paraphrasing is not limited to the seven <u>Harry Potter</u> novels, but can be found in entries drawn from the companion books as well. For example, the entry for "Montrose Magpies" uses language from <u>Quidditch Through the Ages</u>. The original language reads:

> The Magpies are the most successful team in the history of
> the British and Irish League, which they have won thirty-two
> times. Twice European Champions . . . . The Magpies wear
> black and white robes with one magpie on the chest and
> another on the back.

The Lexicon entry reads:

> The most successful Quidditch team in history, which has
> won the British and Irish league thirty-two times and the
> European Cup twice. Their robes are black and white, with
> one magpie on the chest and another on the back.

The same close paraphrasing takes place in the Lexicon entries drawing from Rowling's other companion book, <u>Fantastic Beasts & Where to Find Them</u>. For example, the entry for "Chinese Fireball" closely tracks the original language, which reads:

> The only Oriental dragon. Scarlet and smooth-scaled, it has a
> fringe of golden spikes around its snub-snouted face and
> extremely protuberant eyes. The Fireball gained its name for
> the mushroom-shaped flame that bursts from its nostrils
> when it is angered. . . . Eggs are a vivid crimson speckled with
> gold. . . .

The Lexicon entry reads:

> A species of dragon native to China. The Fireball is a scarlet
> dragon with golden spikes around its face and protruding
> eyes. The blast of flame from a fireball forms a distinctive
> mushroom shape. Eggs of a Fireball are vivid crimson,
> flecked with gold.

Instances of such verbatim copying or close paraphrasing of language in the <u>Harry Potter</u> works occur throughout the Lexicon. Rowling provides numerous examples in Plaintiffs' Exhibit 47, "a chart [she] made to show what [she] felt was the constant pilfering of [her] work."

Aside from verbatim copying, another factual issue of contention at trial was the Lexicon entries that contain summaries of certain scenes or key events in the <u>Harry Potter</u> series. Most frequently, these are the longer entries that describe important objects, such as the "Deathly Hallows," or momentous events, such as the "Triwizard Tournament," or that trace the development of an important character, such as Harry Potter, Lord Voldemort, Severus Snape, and Albus Dumbledore. Plaintiffs' expert [Jeri Johnson] testified at length that in her opinion these entries constitute "plot summaries," while Defendant's expert characterized them as character studies or analysis.

Neither of these characterizations is exactly apt. Without endorsing one characterization or another, such entries in the Lexicon do encapsulate elements of the very elaborate and wide ranging plot (sometimes in chronological order, sometimes not) confined to the subject of the entry. In the entries for significant characters, these plot elements are occasionally used to support an observation about the character's nature or development. For instance, the three-and-a-half page entry for "Lovegood, Luna" contains the following paragraph:

> Luna came into her own during her sixth year at Hogwarts. With Harry, Ron, and Hermione gone from school, she joined Ginny and Neville to revive the D.A. and resist the Death Eaters' influence at Hogwarts. She was kidnapped on the Hogwarts Express on her way home for the Christmas holidays because of what Mr. Lovegood had been writing in The Quibbler, and imprisoned in the cellar at the Malfoy Mansion along with Ollivander. She was helpful in their efforts to escape the Malfoy Mansion, and then fought bravely, again, at the Battle of Hogwarts.

But other times, the presentation of plot details, in effect, summarizes a vignette or portion of a scene. In the same entry for "Lovegood, Luna," the Lexicon summarizes a scene on the Hogwarts Express found on pages 185 to 188 of Chapter 10 of <u>Harry Potter and the Order of the Phoenix</u>:

Harry met Luna for the first time aboard the Hogwarts
Express on September 1, 1995. He, Ginny, and Neville
shared a compartment with her on the train. She was reading
a copy of The Quibbler magazine upside down. She
informed the others that her father is the editor of The
Quibbler, a magazine which most in the Wizarding World
consider a joke. She laughed a little too loud; she stared at
the other kids, and generally made an odd traveling
companion. Harry privately thought, when Cho happened by
their compartment to say hello, that he would much rather
have been sitting with "cooler" kids than Luna and Neville.

The entries for the hero and the villain of the Harry Potter series
(Harry Potter and Lord Voldemort) present the closest thing to "plot
summaries," but are more aptly characterized as synopses or outlines of the
narrative revolving around those characters. Because Harry Potter and Lord
Voldemort drive the narrative and because they appear in nearly every
chapter of the series, an encapsulation of the events surrounding them
ultimately yields a synopsis of the primary narrative thread in the Harry
Potter series. The Lexicon entry for "Potter, Harry James" is eleven pages
long and chronicles each year of Harry Potter's life at the fictional Hogwarts
School, providing the reader with all of the main events of the story through
all seven of Rowling's novels, leading up to Harry Potter's final battle with
Lord Voldemort. The nine-page entry for "Voldemort, Lord" begins by
providing the pre-story for the character, which is included in the sixth Harry
Potter novel, giving background into the character as a child. The entry then
proceeds to describe chronologically all of the events surrounding this
character in the Harry Potter story from books one through seven, and also
gives an account of this character's death in the last Harry Potter novel.
Although the entries proceed chronologically and do not use the same plot
structure as do the Harry Potter novels (which structure the plot so as to
create an interesting drama), the entries do provide a skeleton of the plot
elements that hold the story together.

Finally, Plaintiffs established the Lexicon's extensive copying from
Rowling's companion books, Quidditch Through the Ages and Fantastic
Beasts & Where to Find Them, the schoolbooks used by the students
attending the Hogwarts School. These two books are very short, fifty-six
and fifty-nine pages, respectively. They are written in non-narrative form
and present fictional facts without commentary, in a similar way to the
Lexicon. When questioned about his use of these books in creating the
Lexicon, Vander Ark testified:

. . . <u>Fantastic Beasts</u> and <u>Quidditch [Through] the</u> <u>Ages</u> had sections of them which were essentially encyclopedias already which presented quite a problem. We wanted to be complete, but we certainly didn't want to replace Ms. Rowling's encyclopedia content which presented us with quite a challenge of how to do that, how to include information, but not to include all of it. And that was what we decided to do. We said we'll intentionally leave things out and put a very clear note, Please go read her books, which is what we did.

Although the Lexicon sporadically leaves out material, such as some material from the introductory chapters of <u>Quidditch Through the Ages</u>, it essentially takes wholesale from the companion books. When questioned about the Lexicon entry for "Chudley Cannons" and whether there was anything about this quidditch team in <u>Quidditch Through the Ages</u> that he did not put in the Lexicon, Vander Ark admitted, "In that particular case, it looks like we pretty much caught it all." Vander Ark later admitted that although he left out some of the first half of <u>Quidditch Through the Ages</u>, "[w]hen it comes to descriptions of specific things, Quidditch f[oul], for example, there's not a lot of information there to condense, and so there would be more of that included and referenced." Similarly, the Lexicon copies a large part of the descriptions of each beast in the A-to-Z section of <u>Fantastic Beasts & Where to Find Them</u>.

CONCLUSIONS OF LAW
I. Copyright Infringement
To establish a prima facie case of copyright infringement, a plaintiff must demonstrate "(1) ownership of a valid copyright, and (2) copying of constituent elements of the work that are original." <u>Feist Publ'ns, Inc. v.</u> <u>Rural Tel. Serv. Co.</u>, 499 U.S. 340, 361 (1991); <u>Arica Institute, Inc. v. Palmer</u>, 970 F.2d 1067, 1072 (2d Cir. 1992). The element of copying has two components: first, the plaintiff must establish actual copying by either direct or indirect evidence; then, the plaintiff must establish that the copying amounts to an improper or unlawful appropriation. <u>Castle Rock Entm't, Inc.</u> <u>v. Carol Publ'g Group, Inc.</u>, 150 F.3d 132, 137 (2d Cir. 1998); <u>Laureyssens v.</u> <u>Idea Group, Inc.</u>, 964 F.2d 131, 139-140 (2d Cir. 1992). The plaintiff demonstrates that the copying is actionable "by showing that the second work bears a 'substantial similarity' to protected expression in the earlier work." <u>Castle Rock</u>, 150 F.3d at 137 (citing <u>Repp v. Webber</u>, 132 F.3d 882, 889 (2d Cir. 1997)); <u>see Ringgold v. Black Entm't Television, Inc.</u>, 126 F.3d 70, 74-75 (explaining the distinction between actionable copying and factual copying.

A. Ownership

There is no dispute regarding Plaintiff Rowling's ownership of valid copyrights in the seven Harry Potter novels and two companion books, Quidditch Through the Ages and Fantastic Beasts & Where to Find Them. With respect to those works, Plaintiffs introduced evidence of copyright ownership in the form of registration certificates from the U.S. Copyright Office, which constitute prima facie evidence of the works' copyrightability and the validity of the copyrights. 17 U.S.C. § 410(c). Plaintiffs also introduced the declarations and testimony of Rowling concerning her creation of the works and ownership of the copyrights in them.

Defendant disputes, however, that Plaintiffs have established Rowling's ownership of copyrights in "The Daily Prophet" newsletters and Warner Brothers' beneficial ownership of copyrights in the Harry Potter video games that contain the allegedly infringed "Famous Wizard Cards." The only evidence offered at trial to establish Plaintiffs' ownership of these copyrights was Rowling's testimony. Plaintiffs attached to their post-trial brief documents demonstrating Rowling's U.K. copyright in the "The Daily Prophet" and Warner Brothers' joint ownership with Electronic Arts Inc. of U.S. copyrights in Harry Potter videogames. Having taken judicial notice of these documents as public records as permitted by the Federal Rules of Evidence, see Fed. R. Evid. 201(b)(2); Island Software & Computer Serv. v. Microsoft Corp., 413 F.3d 257, 261 (2d Cir. 2005), the Court concludes that Plaintiffs have established ownership of copyrights in "The Daily Prophet" and the "Famous Wizard Cards." Plaintiffs cannot establish infringement of these works, however, because neither work was entered into evidence, and they are not before the Court. Accordingly, Plaintiffs' claims of copyright infringement will be addressed only with respect to the seven Harry Potter novels and two companion guides.

B. Copying

There is no dispute that the Lexicon actually copied from Rowling's copyrighted works. Vander Ark openly admitted that he created and updated the content of the Lexicon by taking notes while reading the Harry Potter books and by using without authorization scanned, electronic copies of the Harry Potter novels and companion books. While acknowledging actual copying, Defendant disputes that the copying amounts to an improper or unlawful appropriation of Rowling's works. Defendant argues that Plaintiffs fail to establish a prima facie case of infringement because they have not shown that the Lexicon is substantially similar to the Harry Potter works. The appropriate inquiry under the substantial similarity test is whether "the copying is quantitatively and qualitatively sufficient to support the legal conclusion that infringement (actionable copying) has occurred." Ringgold, 126 F.3d at 75; accord Nihon Keizai Shimbun, Inc. v. Comline Bus. Data,

Inc., 166 F.3d 65, 70 (2d Cir. 1999); Castle Rock, 150 F. 3d at 138. The quantitative component addresses the amount of the copyrighted work that is copied, while the qualitative component addresses the copying of protected expression, as opposed to unprotected ideas or facts. Ringgold, 126 F.3d at 75.

In evaluating the quantitative extent of copying in the substantial similarity analysis, the Court "considers the amount of copying not only of direct quotations and close paraphrasing, but also of all other protectable expression in the original work." Castle Rock, 150 F.3d at 140 n.6. As the Second Circuit has instructed, "[i]t is not possible to determine infringement through a simple word count," which in this case would be an insuperable task; "the quantitative analysis of two works must always occur in the shadow of their qualitative nature." Nihon Keizai, 166 F.3d at 71. Where, as here, the copyrighted work is "wholly original," rather than mixed with unprotected elements, a lower quantity of copying will support a finding of substantial similarity. Nihon Keizai, 166 F.3d at 71.

Plaintiffs have shown that the Lexicon copies a sufficient quantity of the Harry Potter series to support a finding of substantial similarity between the Lexicon and Rowling's novels. The Lexicon draws 450 manuscript pages worth of material primarily from the 4,100-page Harry Potter series. Most of the Lexicon's 2,437 entries contain direct quotations or paraphrases, plot details, or summaries of scenes from one or more of the Harry Potter novels. As Defendant admits, "the Lexicon reports thousands of fictional facts from the Harry Potter works." Although hundreds pages or thousands of fictional facts may amount to only a fraction of the seven-book series, this quantum of copying is sufficient to support a finding of substantial similarity where the copied expression is entirely the product of the original author's imagination and creation. See Castle Rock, 150 F.3d at 138 (concluding that a Seinfeld trivia book that copied 643 fragments from 84 copyrighted Seinfeld episodes "plainly crossed the quantitative copying threshold under Ringgold"); Twin Peaks Prods., Inc. v. Publ'ns Int'l, Ltd., 996 F.2d 1366, 1372 (2d Cir. 1993) (upholding the district court's conclusion that "the identity of 89 lines of dialogue" between Twin Peaks teleplays and a guide to the television series constituted substantial similarity); see also Harper & Row, 471 U.S. at 548-49 (stating that "lifting verbatim quotes of the author's original language totaling between 300 and 400 words and constituting some 13% of [the defendant's] article" was sufficient to constitute copyright infringement).

The quantitative extent of the Lexicon's copying is even more substantial with respect to Fantastic Beasts and Quidditch Through the Ages. Rowling's companion books are only fifty-nine and fifty-six pages long, respectively. The Lexicon reproduces a substantial portion of their content, with only sporadic omissions, across hundreds of entries.

As to the qualitative component of the substantial similarity analysis, Plaintiffs have shown that the Lexicon draws its content from creative, original expression in the Harry Potter series and companion books. Each of the 2,437 entries in the Lexicon contains "fictional facts" created by Rowling, such as the attributes of imaginary creatures and objects, the traits and undertakings of major and minor characters, and the events surrounding them. The entry for "Boggart," for example, contains the fictional facts that a boggart is "[a] shape shifter that prefers to live in dark, confined spaces, taking the form of the thing most feared by the person it encounters; nobody knows what a boggart looks like in its natural state," and that "Lupin taught his third year Defence Against the Dark Arts class to fight [a boggart] with the Riddikulus spell, and used a boggart as a substitute for a Dementor in tutoring Harry. In Castle Rock Entertainment, Inc. v. Carol Publishing Group, Inc., the Second Circuit explained that such invented facts constitute creative expression protected by copyright because "characters and events spring from the imagination of [the original] authors." 150 F.3d at 139; see also Paramount Pictures Corp. v. Carol Publ'g Group, 11 F. Supp. 2d 329, 333 (S.D.N.Y. 1998) (stating that "[t]he characters, plots and dramatic episodes" that comprise the story of the "fictitious history of Star Trek" are the story's "original elements," protected by copyright). The Castle Rock court held that a trivia book which tested the reader's knowledge of "facts" from the Seinfeld series copied protected expression because "each 'fact' tested by [the trivia book] is in reality fictitious expression created by Seinfeld's authors." Id. It follows that the same qualitative conclusion should be drawn here, where each "fact" reported by the Lexicon is actually expression invented by Rowling.

Seeking to distinguish Castle Rock, Defendant argues that the qualitative similarity between the Lexicon and the Harry Potter works is significantly diminished because "the Lexicon uses fictional facts primarily in their factual capacity" to "report information and where to find it," unlike the Seinfeld trivia book, which used fictional facts "primarily in their fictional capacity to entertain and 'satisfy' the reader's 'craving' for the Seinfeld television series." While this distinction is important, Defendant's argument goes to the fair use question of whether the Lexicon's use has a transformative purpose, not to the infringement question of whether the Lexicon, on its face, bears a substantial similarity to the Harry Potter works. The court in Castle Rock addressed these two inquires separately and found that the Seinfeld trivia book not only bore a substantial similarity to the Seinfeld series but also lacked a transformative purpose. See Castle Rock, 150 F.3d at 138-39, 141-43. What matters at the infringement stage of this case is that the copied text is expression original to Rowling, not fact or idea, and therefore is presumptively entitled to copyright protection. See Harper & Row, 471 U.S. at 547; Feist, 499 U.S. at 344-46. Even if expression is or can be used in its "factual capacity," it does not follow that expression thereby takes on the status of fact and loses its copyrightability.

Defendant also argues that while a substantial similarity may be found where invented facts are "reported and arranged in such a way as to tell essentially the same story" as the original, "the order in which the fictional facts are presented in the Lexicon bears almost no resemblance to the order in which the fictional facts are arranged to create the story of Harry Potter and the universe he inhabits." Reproducing original expression in fragments or in a different order, however, does not preclude a finding of substantial similarity. See Castle Rock, 150 F. 3d at 139 (finding a substantial similarity even though the allegedly infringing trivia book rearranged fragments of expression from Seinfeld in question-and-answer format); Paramount Pictures, 11 F. Supp. 2d at 333-34 (finding that a book containing brief synopses of major plot lines, histories of major characters, and descriptions of fictional alien species in Star Trek was substantially similar to the Star Trek series even though "the fictitious history is presented in a different order than that in which it appeared in the [original works]"). Regardless of how the original expression is copied, "'the standard for determining copyright infringement is not whether the original could be recreated from the allegedly infringing copy, but whether the latter is "substantially similar" to the former.'" Castle Rock, 150 F.3d at 141 (quoting Horgan v. Macmillan, Inc., 789 F.2d 157, 162 (2d Cir. 1986)). Here, the Lexicon's rearrangement of Rowling's fictional facts does not alter the protected expression such that the Lexicon ceases to be substantially similar to the original works.

Furthermore, the law in this Circuit is clear that "the concept of similarity embraces not only global similarities in structure and sequence, but localized similarity in language." Twin Peaks, 996 F.2d at 1372 (endorsing the taxonomy of "comprehensive nonliteral similarity" and "fragmented literal similarity" from the Nimmer treatise, 4 Nimmer § 13.03[A][2]); see also Ringgold, 126 F.3d at 75 n.3; Arica Institute, 970 F.2d at 1073. In evaluating fragmented literal similarity, or "localized similarity in language," the Court examines the copying of direct quotations or close paraphrasing of the original work. Castle Rock, 150 F. 3d at 140; Paramount Pictures, 11 F. Supp. 2d at 333 ("Fragmented similarity refers to exact copying of a portion of a work."). As determined in the Findings of Fact, the Lexicon contains a considerable number of direct quotations (often without quotation marks) and close paraphrases of vivid passages in the Harry Potter works. Although in these instances, the Lexicon often changes a few words from the original or rewrites original dialogue in the third person, the language is nonetheless substantially similar. See Salinger v. Random House, Inc., 811 F.2d 90, 97 (2d Cir. 1987) (indicating that protected expression is infringed whether it is "quoted verbatim or only paraphrased"); Craft v. Kobler, 667 F. Supp. 120, 124 (S.D.N.Y. 1987) (stating that protected writing is infringed by "direct quotation" or "by paraphrase which remains sufficiently close that, in spite of changes, it appropriates the craft of authorship of the original"); see also 4 Nimmer § 13.03[A][1] ("The mere fact that the defendant has paraphrased rather than literally copied will not preclude a finding of substantial similarity. Copyright 'cannot be limited literally to the text, else a plagiarist would escape by immaterial variations.'" (footnote omitted) (quoting Nichols v. Universal Pictures Co., 45 F.2d 119, 121 (2d Cir. 1930))).

Notwithstanding the dissimilarity in the overall structure of the Lexicon and the original works, some of the Lexicon entries contain summaries of certain scenes or key events in the Harry Potter series, as stated in the Findings of Fact. These passages, in effect, retell small portions of the novels, though without the same dramatic effect. In addition, the entries for Harry Potter and Lord Voldemort give a skeleton of the major plot elements of the Harry Potter series, again without the same dramatic effect or structure. Together these portions of the Lexicon support a finding of substantial similarity. To be sure, this case is different from Twin Peaks, where forty-six pages of the third chapter of a guidebook to the Twin Peaks television series were found to constitute "essentially a detailed recounting of the first eight episodes of the series. Every intricate plot twist and element of character development appear[ed] in the Book in the same sequence as in the teleplays." 996 F.2d at 1372-73 (supporting the Second Circuit's finding of comprehensive nonliteral similarity). Those "plot summaries" were far more detailed, comprehensive, and parallel to the original episodes than the so-called "plot summaries" in this case. Nonetheless, it is clear that the plotlines and scenes encapsulated in the Lexicon are appropriated from the original copyrighted works. See Paramount Pictures, F. Supp. 2d at 334 (noting that Twin Peaks was distinguishable but nonetheless applying its broader holding that "a book which tells the story of a copyrighted television series infringes on its copyright"). Under these circumstances, Plaintiffs have established a prima facie case of infringement.

C. Derivative Work
Plaintiffs allege that the Lexicon not only violates their right of reproduction, but also their right to control the production of derivative works. The Copyright Act defines a "derivative work" as "a work based upon one or more preexisting works, such as a translation, musical arrangement, dramatization, fictionalization, motion picture version, sound recording, art reproduction, abridgment, condensation, or any other form in which a work

may be *recast, transformed, or adapted*." 17 U.S.C. § 101 (emphasis added). A work "consisting of editorial revisions, annotations, elaborations, or other modifications which, as a whole, represents an original work of authorship" is also a derivative work. Id.

A work is not derivative, however, simply because it is "based upon" the preexisting works. If that were the standard, then parodies and book reviews would fall under the definition, and certainly "ownership of copyright does not confer a legal right to control public evaluation of the copyrighted work." Ty, Inc. v. Publ'ns Int'l Ltd., 292 F.3d 512, 521 (7th Cir. 2002). The statutory language seeks to protect works that are "recast, transformed, or adapted" into another medium, mode, language, or revised version, while still representing the "original work of authorship." See Castle Rock, 150 F.3d at 143 n.9 (stating that "derivative works that are subject to the author's copyright transform an original work into a new mode of presentation"); Twin Peaks, 996 F.2d at 1373 (finding a derivative work where a guidebook based on the Twin Peak television series "contain[ed] a substantial amount of material from the teleplays, transformed from one medium to another"). Thus in Ty, Inc. v. Publications International Ltd., Judge Posner concluded, as the parties had stipulated, that a collectors' guide to Beanie Babies was not a derivative work because "guides don't *recast, transform, or adapt* the things to which they are guides." 292 F.3d at 520 (emphasis added).

Plaintiffs argue that based on the Twin Peaks decision "companion guides constitute derivative works where, as is the case here, they 'contain a substantial amount of material from [the underlying work.'" (Pl. Post-trial Br. ¶ 288, at 88-89.) This argument inaccurately states the holding of Twin Peaks and overlooks two important distinctions between the Lexicon and the guidebook in Twin Peaks. First, as mentioned earlier, the portions of the Lexicon that encapsulate plot elements or sketch plotlines bear no comparison with the guidebook in Twin Peaks, whose plot summaries giving "elaborate recounting of plot details" were found to constitute an "abridgement" of the original work. See Twin Peaks, 996 F.2d at 1373 n.2 (reproducing an excerpt of the infringing book containing a high degree of detail). Given that the Lexicon's use of plot elements is far from an "elaborate recounting" and does not follow the same plot structure as the Harry Potter novels, Plaintiffs' suggestion that these portions of the Lexicon are "unauthorized abridgements" is unpersuasive. Second, and more importantly, although the Lexicon "contain[s] a substantial amount of material" from the Harry Potter works, the material is not merely "transformed from one medium to another," as was the case in Twin Peaks. Id. at 1373. By condensing, synthesizing, and reorganizing the preexisting material in an A-to-Z reference guide, the Lexicon does not recast the material in another medium to retell the story of <u>Harry Potter</u>, but instead gives the copyrighted material another purpose. That purpose is to give the reader a ready understanding of individual elements in the elaborate world of <u>Harry Potter</u> that appear in voluminous and diverse sources. As a result, the Lexicon no longer "represents [the] original work[s] of authorship." 17 U.S.C. § 101. Under these circumstances, and because the Lexicon does not fall under any example of derivative works listed in the statute, Plaintiffs have failed to show that the Lexicon is a derivative work.

II. Fair Use

Defendant contends that even if Plaintiffs have shown a prima facie case of infringement, the Lexicon is nevertheless a fair use of the <u>Harry Potter</u> works. An integral part of copyright law, the fair use doctrine is designed to "fulfill copyright's very purpose, 'To promote the Progress of Science and useful Arts,'" <u>Campbell v. Acuff-Rose Music, Inc.</u>, 510 U.S. 569, 575 (1994) (quoting U.S. Const. art. I, § 8, cl. 8), by balancing the simultaneous needs "to protect copyrighted material and to allow others to build upon it." <u>Id.</u> As the Second Circuit has observed, there is an inevitable tension between the property rights [that copyright law] establishes in creative works, which must be protected up to a point, and the ability of authors, artists, and the rest of us to express them – or ourselves by reference to the works of others, which must be protected up to a point. The fair-use doctrine mediates between the two sets of interests, determining where each set of interests ceases to control. <u>Blanch v. Koons</u>, 467 F.3d 244, 250 (2d Cir. 2006). At stake in this case are the incentive to create original works which copyright protection fosters and the freedom to produce secondary works which monopoly protection of copyright stifles—both interests benefit the public. <u>See</u> Pierre N. Leval, <u>Toward a Fair Use Standard</u>, 103 Harv. L. Rev. 1105, 1109 (1990) (noting that on one hand "[t]he monopoly created by copyright . . . rewards the individual author in order to benefit the public," and on the other "[m]onopoly protection of intellectual property that impeded referential analysis and the development of new ideas out of old would strangle the creative process").

The common law doctrine of fair use is codified at Section 107 of the Copyright Act of 1976 as follows:

> The fair use of a copyrighted work . . . for purposes such as criticism, comment, news reporting, teaching (including multiple copies for classroom use), scholarship, or research, is not an infringement of copyright. In determining whether the use made of a work in any particular case is a fair use the factors to be considered shall include —
>
> (1) the purpose and character of the use, including whether such use is of a commercial nature or is for nonprofit educational purposes;
>
> (2) the nature of the copyrighted work;
>
> (3) the amount and substantiality of the portion used in relation to the copyrighted work as a whole, and
>
> (4) the effect of the use upon the potential market for or value of the copyrighted work. 17 U.S.C. § 107.

The evaluation of these factors is "an open-ended and context-sensitive inquiry," Blanch, 467 F.3d at 244; accord Campbell, 510 U.S. at 577 (stating that "the statute, like the doctrine it recognizes, calls for a case-by-case analysis"), and the examples listed in the statute (i.e., criticism, comment, news reporting, and teaching) are illustrative rather than limiting, Campbell, 510 U.S. at 577-78. The four statutory factors may not "be treated in isolation, one from another"; instead they all must "be explored, and the results weighed together, in light of the purposes of copyright." Id. at 578. "The ultimate test of fair use, therefore, is whether the copyright law's goal of 'promoting the Progress of Science and useful Arts,' U.S. Const., art. I, § 8, cl. 8, 'would be better served by allowing the use than by preventing it.'" Castle Rock, 150 F.3d at 141 (quoting Arica Inst., 970 F.2d at 1077).

A. Purpose and Character of the Use

Most critical to the inquiry under the first fair-use factor is "whether and to what extent the new work is 'transformative.'" Campbell, 510 U.S. at 579; see also Bill Graham Archives v. Dorling Kindersley Ltd, 448 F.3d 605, 608 (2d Cir. 2006); Elvis Presley Enters., Inc. v. Passport Video, 349 F.3d 622, 628 (9th Cir. 2003). Specifically, the court asks "whether the new work merely 'supersede[s] the objects' of the original creation or instead adds something news, with a further purpose or different character, altering the first with new expression, meaning, or message." Campbell, 510 U.S. at 579.

The fair use doctrine seeks to protect a secondary work if it "adds value to the original -- if [copyrightable expression in the original work] is used as raw material, transformed in the creation of new information, new aesthetics, new insights and understandings," because such a work contributes to the enrichment of society. Castle Rock, 150 F.3d at 141 (alteration in original) (quoting Leval, supra, at 1111). Courts have found a transformative purpose both where the defendant combines copyrighted expression with original expression to produce a new creative work, see, e.g., Campbell, 510 U.S. at 58283; Blanch, 467 F.3d at 251-51; Suntrust Bank v. Houghton Mifflin Co., 268 F.3d 1257 (11th Cir. 2001), and where the defendant uses a copyrighted work in a different context to serve a different function than the original, see, e.g., Perfect 10, Inc. v. Amazon.com, Inc., 508 F.3d 1146 (9th Cir. 2007); Bill Graham Archives v. Dorling Kindersley Ltd., 448 F.3d 605 (2d Cir. 2006).

The purpose of the Lexicon's use of the Harry Potter series is transformative. Presumably, Rowling created the Harry Potter series for the expressive purpose of telling an entertaining and thought provoking story centered on the character Harry Potter and set in a magical world. The Lexicon, on the other hand, uses material from the series for the practical purpose of making information about the intricate world of Harry Potter readily accessible to readers in a reference guide. To fulfill this function, the Lexicon identifies more than 2,400 elements from the Harry Potter world, extracts and synthesizes fictional facts related to each element from all seven novels, and presents that information in a format that allows readers to access it quickly as they make their way through the series. Because it serves these reference purposes, rather than the entertainment or aesthetic purposes of the original works, the Lexicon's use is transformative and does not supplant the objects of the Harry Potter works. See Elvis Presley Enters., 349 F.3d at 629 (stating that new works are described as transformative "when the works use copyrighted materials for purposes distinct from the purpose of the original material"); see also Bill Graham Archives, 448 F.3d at 609 (concluding that the use of artistic images as historical artifacts is "transformatively different from the original expressive purpose").

The Lexicon's use of Rowling's companion books, however, is transformative to a much lesser extent. Although there is no supporting testimony, the companion books can be used for a reference purpose. Their packaging demonstrates an entertainment purpose: bringing to life the fictional schoolbooks they represent in the Harry Potter novels, the companion books have fictional authors, forewords written by Albus Dumbledore, handwritten notes to Harry from his friends, a game of tic-tac-toe sketched on one page, a library log and warning by the Hogwarts librarian, and a "Property of Hogwarts Library" stamp. In this regard, the companion books serve as playful accessories to the Harry Potter series. At the same time, the content of the companion books takes on the informational purpose of the schoolbooks they represent in the novels. As Vander Ark testified, the companion books are "essentially encyclopedias already." Fantastic Beasts describes the attributes and origins of each beast listed in the alphabetical guide, defines "beast," and explains the place of beasts in the "muggle" and wizard worlds. Quidditch Through the Ages describes the history and development of quidditch, the rules of the game, the teams, and the spread of quidditch internationally. Neither book, however, makes reference to where the beasts or quidditch facts appear in the Harry Potter novels. Although the Lexicon does not use the companion books for their entertainment purpose, it supplants the informational purpose of the original works by seeking to relate the same fictional facts in the same way. Even so, the Lexicon's use is slightly transformative in that it adds a productive purpose to the original material by synthesizing it within a complete reference guide that refers readers to where information can be found in a diversity of sources.

The best evidence of the Lexicon's transformative purpose is its demonstrated value as a reference source. See Am. Geophysical Union v. Texaco Inc., 60 F.3d 913, (2d Cir. 1994) (stating that the "transformative use concept assesses the value generated by the secondary use and the means by which such value is generated"); Leval, supra, at 1111 (stating that for a use to be transformative, "[t]he use must be productive and must employ the quoted matter in a different manner or for a different purpose than the original"). The utility of the Lexicon, as a reference guide to a multi-volume work of fantasy literature, demonstrates a productive use for a different purpose than the original works. The Lexicon makes the elaborate imaginary world of Harry Potter searchable, item by item, and gives readers a complete picture of each item that cannot be gleaned by reading the voluminous series, since the material related to each item is scattered over thousands of pages of complex narrative and plot. The demand for and usefulness of this type of reference guide is evidenced by the publication of similar works such as Paul F. Ford's Companion to Narnia: A Complete Guide to the Magical World of C.S. Lewis's The Chronicles of Narnia. The utility of the Lexicon as a reference guide has been demonstrated to Vander Ark by way of responses to his Lexicon website. This feedback included a remark by Rowling that she has "been known to sneak into an internet café while out writing and check a fact" on the Lexicon website, a remark by David Heyman of Warner Brothers that he used the Lexicon website almost every day while shooting the fifth Harry Potter film, and a glimpse of the walls of the Electronic Arts studios covered with printed pages from the Lexicon website. This feedback supports Defendant's claim that it had good reason to believe that a print version of the Lexicon would serve as a valuable reference source to readers and fans of Harry Potter.

Its function as a reference guide distinguishes the Lexicon from the secondary work at issue in Castle Rock, a 132-page book of trivia about the events and characters depicted in Seinfeld. Despite its specious claims to critique and expose the Seinfeld series, the trivia book served no purpose but "to satiate Seinfeld fans' passion" for the series and simply "repackage[d] Seinfeld to entertain Seinfeld viewers." Castle Rock, 150 F.3d at 142. A statement by the book's creators on the back cover, urging readers to "open this book to satisfy [their] between-episode [Seinfeld] cravings," belied its transformative purpose. Id. By contrast, the Lexicon seeks not to entertain but to aid the reader or student of Harry Potter by providing references about the elements encountered in the series.

The Lexicon's purpose as a reference guide also distinguishes it from the books at issue in Twin Peaks and Paramount Pictures. Those books sought to retell the fictional stories of the Twin Peaks series and the Star Trek series in abridged versions. See Twin Peaks, 996 F.2d at 1372-73, 1375-76 (finding that the book at issue was an "abridgment" because it recounted "precisely the plot details" of the television episodes "in the same sequence" as they appeared in the original series); Paramount Pictures, 11 F. Supp. 2d at 335 (finding that the work at issue "simply retells the story of Star Trek in a condensed version"). Because the books in those cases merely recast the originals in abridged versions, they were held to be derivative works. The Lexicon, on the other hand, has a "further purpose or different character," Campbell, 510 U.S. at 579, that alters the original aesthetic of the Harry Potter series from an intricate narrative to an alphabetized catalogue of elements from the Harry Potter world.

Plaintiffs argue that the Lexicon's use of Rowling's works cannot be considered transformative because the Lexicon does not add significant analysis or commentary. In the opinion of Plaintiffs' expert, the Lexicon contributes nothing new other than occasional facetious phrases and facile jokes that are condescending to children, sporadic and often wrong etymological references demonstrating "no real linguistic understanding," and conclusions that would be obvious to any child reading Harry Potter. The Lexicon, however, does not purport to be a work of literary criticism or to constitute a fair use on that basis; and its lack of critical analysis, linguistic understanding, or clever humor is not determinative of whether or not its purpose is transformative. Cf. Bill Graham Archives, 448 F.3d at 610 (concluding that the defendant's use of copyrighted images "is transformative both when accompanied by referencing commentary and when standing alone" because in either case the images are used as "historical artifacts" for the transformative purpose of "enhancing the biographical information" in the allegedly infringing book). Focusing on what the Lexicon fails to add by way of analysis misses the point that the Lexicon's chief contribution is the function it serves.

Nonetheless, despite Plaintiffs' criticisms, the Lexicon occasionally does offer "new information, new aesthetics, new insights and understandings," Castle Rock, 150 F.3d at 141 (internal quotation marks omitted), as to the themes and characters in the Harry Potter works. The Lexicon's discussion of certain characters, while perhaps not rigorous analysis, contain some reflections on the character, observations of his or her nature, and examples of how that nature is exhibited in the story. For example, the Lexicon observes that "Draco [Malfoy] was constantly frustrated by the attention given to Harry," and gives anecdotal examples from the novels to support this conclusion. Moreover, in some instances, the Lexicon yields insights about an element of the Harry Potter world simply by encapsulating all the fictional facts related to that element in a single entry. When all the fictional facts related to "Hallowe'en" are collected, for example, the entry reveals that this occasion is "an eventful day in Harry's life; on Hallowe'en 1981 his parents were killed and his subsequent years included knocking out a troll, the opening of the Chamber of Secrets, Sirius Black's first break-in to Hogwarts, and Harry's name coming out of the Goblet of Fire." Finally, the Lexicon's etymological references, while occasionally inaccurate, offer one possible interpretation of the meaning and derivation of characters' names, even if not the meaning intended by Rowling. Thus, while not its primary purpose, the Lexicon does add some new insight, of whatever value as to the Harry Potter works.

The transformative character of the Lexicon is diminished, however, because the Lexicon's use of the original Harry Potter works is not consistently transformative. The Lexicon's use lacks transformative character where the Lexicon entries fail to "minimize[] the expressive value" of the original expression. See Bill Graham Archives, 448 F.3d at 611 (finding evidence of transformative use where the defendant "minimized the expressive value of the reproduced images by combining them with a prominent timeline, textual material, and original graphical artwork to create a collage of text and images on each page of the book"). A finding of verbatim copying in excess of what is reasonably necessary diminishes a finding of a transformative use. See Campbell, 510 U.S. at 587 (observing that "whether a substantial portion of the infringing work was copied verbatim from the copyrighted work . . . may reveal a dearth of transformative character" (internal quotation marks omitted)). As discussed more fully in analyzing the "amount and substantiality" factor, the Lexicon copies distinctive original language from the Harry Potter works in excess of its otherwise legitimate purpose of creating a reference guide. Perhaps because Vander Ark is such a Harry Potter enthusiast, the Lexicon often lacks restraint in using Rowling's original expression for its inherent entertainment and aesthetic value. See Elvis Presley Enters., 349 F.3d at 629 (finding that where a film biography of Elvis Presley showed the plaintiffs' copyrighted clips of Elvis's television appearances without much interruption, "[t]he purpose of showing these clips likely goes beyond merely making a reference for a biography, but instead serves the same intrinsic entertainment value that is protected by Plaintiffs' copyrights").

The Lexicon also lacks transformative character where its value as a reference guide lapses. Although the Lexicon is generally useful, it cannot claim consistency in serving its purpose of pointing readers to information in the Harry Potter works. Some of the longest entries contain few or no citations to the Harry Potter works from which the material is taken. In these instances, the Lexicon's reference purposes are diminished.

While the transformative character of the secondary work is a central inquiry, the commercial or nonprofit nature of the secondary work is an explicit part of the first fair-use factor. 17 U.S.C. 107(1); Blanch, 467 F.3d at 253. Given that even the statutory examples of fair use are generally conducted for profit, courts often "do not make much of this point." Castle Rock, 150 F.3d at 141. The real concern behind the commercial nature inquiry is "the unfairness that arises when a secondary user makes unauthorized use of copyrighted material to capture significant revenues as a direct consequence of copying the original work." Blanch, 467 F.3d at 253. Courts will not find fair use when the secondary use "can fairly be characterized as a form of commercial exploitation," but "are more willing to find a secondary use fair when it produces a value that benefits the broader public interest." Id. In this case, Defendant's use of the copyrighted works is certainly for commercial gain. As the testimony of Rapoport and Vander Ark make clear, one of the Lexicon's greatest selling points is being the first companion guide to the Harry Potter series that will cover all seven novels. Seeking to capitalize on a market niche does not necessarily make Defendant's use non-transformative, but to the extent that Defendant seeks to "profit at least in part from the inherent entertainment value" of the original works, the commercial nature of the use weighs against a finding of fair use. Elvis Presley Enters., 349 F. 3d at 628. To the extent that Defendant seeks to provide a useful reference guide to the Harry Potter novels that benefits the public, the use is fair, and its commercial nature only weighs slightly against a finding of fair use.

Finally, in evaluating the purpose and character of a secondary use of a copyrighted work, courts will consider the "subfactor" of whether the defendant acted in good or bad faith. <u>NXIVM Corp. v. Ross Inst.</u>, 364 F.3d 471, 478 (2d Cir. 2004); <u>see also Harper & Row</u>, 471 U.S. at 562-63. Plaintiffs point to several facts in the record to support their argument that Defendant acted with willfulness and bad faith. The Court is not persuaded, however, that the acts of RDR Books, which do not amount to more than intentional delays in responding to Plaintiffs' communications from counsel, constitute acts of bad faith. Based on the reasonable belief that its use of the <u>Harry Potter</u> works constituted fair use, Defendant was entitled to proceed with marketing the Lexicon domestically and abroad and preparing it for publication before competitors released similar books. Vander Ark's use of unauthorized electronic copies of Rowling's works, obtained by improperly scanning each of those works, in preparing the Lexicon manuscript is insufficient proof for the Court to make a finding of bad faith, particularly because Vander Ark did not obtain any material that was not already available to the public. <u>Compare NXIVM Corp.</u>, 364 F.3d at 478 (weighing this factor slightly in favor of plaintiffs because defendants knew they had obtained unauthorized access to the copyrighted manuscript, which was unpublished in the sense it was not available to the general public). In any event, as the Second Circuit has concluded, "a finding of bad faith is not to be weighed very heavily within the first fair use factor and cannot be made central to fair use analysis." <u>Id.</u> At 479 n. 2. This subfactor weighs only slightly in favor of Plaintiffs, as the Court finds that Defendant reasonably believed its use was ultimately fair.

B. Amount and Substantiality of the Use

Plaintiffs contend that the Lexicon's actual use of Plaintiffs' original works far surpasses any purpose as a reference source. They argue, in other words, that the Lexicon takes too much original expression for the use to be fair use. Here, the transformative purpose of Defendant's use and the third statutory factor of fair use -- the amount and substantiality of the use -- must be "explored, and the results weighed together." <u>Campbell</u>, 510 U.S. at 577-78. The question is whether the amount and value of Plaintiffs' original expression used are reasonable in relation to the Lexicon's transformative purpose of creating a useful and complete A-to-Z reference guide to the <u>Harry Potter</u> world. <u>See Campbell</u>, 510 U.S. at 586 (stating that the third factor asks whether the amount and substantiality of the portion used in relation to the copyrighted work as a whole "are reasonable in relation to the purpose of the copying"); <u>Blanch</u>, 467 F.2d at 257 ("The question is whether 'the quantity and value of the materials used,' are reasonable in relation to the purpose of the copying."); <u>see also Chicago Bd. of Educ. v. Substance, Inc.</u>, 354 F.3d 624, 629 (7th Cir. 2003) (stating that "the fair use copier must copy no more than is reasonably necessary . . . to enable him to pursue an aim that the law recognizes as proper"). This inquiry requires the Court to examine not only "the quantity of the materials used, but their quality and importance, too." <u>Campbell</u>, 510 U.S. at 587; <u>Nihon Keizai Shimbun</u>, 166 F.3d at 73. <u>Blanch</u>, 467 F.2d at 257 ("The question is whether "the quantity and value of the materials used," are reasonable in relation to the [transformative] purpose of the copying.").

In undertaking this inquiry, the Court bears in mind that "room must be allowed for judgment, and judges must not police criticism," or other transformative uses, "with a heavy hand." <u>Chicago Bd. of Educ.</u>, 354 F.3d at 629. The Court is hesitant to substitute its own judgment for that of an author in determining how much copying of original material is "reasonably necessary" to create a useful and complete reference work. Nonetheless, the fair use test calls for a court determination on this issue.

To fulfill its purpose as a reference guide to the <u>Harry Potter</u> works, it is reasonably necessary for the Lexicon to make considerable use of the original works. As Vander Ark testified, for a reference work to be valuable and useful, it must be as complete as possible. Similarly, in <u>Ty, Inc. v. Publications International Ltd.</u>, the Seventh Circuit recognized that for a collectors' guide to have enough value "to compete in the marketplace, [it] has to be comprehensive." 292 F.3d at 521. At trial, Plaintiffs questioned Vander Ark and Defendants' expert about whether it was possible to create a reference book that took less of Rowling's work and gave shorter descriptions. While it is *possible* to describe "Albus Dumbledore" or "Bertie Bott's Every Flavor Beans," for example, in a few phrases, such a short entry would not fulfill the Lexicon's purpose of serving as a useful reference guide that provides the reader or student with as complete a picture as possible of the entry's subject.

Weighing most heavily against Defendant on the third factor is the Lexicon's verbatim copying and close paraphrasing of language from the <u>Harry Potter</u> works. In many instances, the copied language is a colorful literary device or distinctive description, as in the Lexicon entries for "Clankers," "Marchbanks, Madam Griselda," "Brain room," and "Dementors." <u>See supra</u> Findings of Fact. This type of language is of great quality and importance; these phrases are, as Rowling testified, the "plums in [her] cake." The Lexicon's verbatim copying of such highly aesthetic expression raises a significant question as to whether it was reasonably necessary for the purpose of creating a useful and complete reference guide. While the exact quantity of verbatim copying and paraphrasing in the Lexicon is difficult to assess, the instances identified by Plaintiffs amount to a substantial enough taking to tip the third factor against a finding of fair use in view of the expressive value of the language. <u>See Harper & Row</u>, 471 U.S. at 564-66 (finding that defendant's verbatim copying, constituting "an insubstantial portion" of the copyrighted work and only 13% of the infringing magazine article, was a substantial appropriation in view of the expressive value of the excerpts and their key role in the infringing work); Salinger v. Random House, Inc., 811 F.2d 90, 99 (2d Cir. 1987) (finding that defendant's biography, in which plaintiff identified 59 instances of verbatim quoting or close paraphrasing (constituting just 40% of defendant's 192-page book), to be so quantitatively significant a taking so as to tip the third factor in favor of plaintiff); Craft v. Kobler, 667 F. Supp. 120, 128-29 (S.D.N.Y. 1987) (concluding that defendant's takings, which constituted approximately 3% of the infringing biography and "the liveliest and most entertaining part" of it, were "far too numerous and with too little instructional justification to support the conclusion of fair use").

Defendant argues that it is impossible to describe an imaginary object that exists only in a fictional world without using some of the language that invented it. Certainly, the Lexicon must be permitted to refer to an object by its invented name and describe some of its invented attributes to fulfill its purpose as a reference work; but again, the use must be reasonable in light of that purpose. The imaginary objects "clankers," for example, can be successfully described without using the original literary device ("like miniature hammers on anvils") and the original turn of phrase ("a number of small metal instruments that when shaken made a loud, ringing noise") that brought them into existence. As the Second Circuit noted in Salinger v. Random House, Inc., a copier is not entitled to copy the vividness of an author's description for the sake of accurately reporting expressive content. 811 F.2d at 96-97. Moreover, in some entries, the Lexicon copies original expression verbatim even when describing objects that are ordinary and exist in the real world. For example, the Lexicon entry for "Mirror of Erised" replicates Rowling's original language from Harry Potter and the Sorcerer's Stone to describe a mirror: "A magnificent mirror, as high as a classroom ceiling, with an ornate gold frame, standing on two clawed feet." (See supra Findings of Fact.) Verbatim copying of this nature demonstrates Vander Ark's lack of restraint due to an enthusiastic admiration of Rowling's artistic expression, or perhaps haste and laziness as Rowling suggested, in composing the Lexicon entries.

Determining how much copying of fictional facts and plot elements from the Harry Potter series is reasonably necessary to create a useful and complete reference guide presents a difficult task. As Vander Ark testified, "[a] reference work of th[is] kind has to have value based on how much information it gives, and so it is difficult sometimes to figure out the balance. And we tried to do the best we could to find a balance between" creating shorter descriptions that take less copyrighted material and creating a valuable entry that is as complete as possible. As to the Harry Potter series, the Lexicon often does demonstrate a significant condensation of narrated events in the novels to bare fictional facts. For example, the entry for "Boggart" encapsulates Professor Lupin's Defense Against the Dark Arts lesson on how to use the Riddikulus spell to defeat a boggart, spanning seven pages of lively narration and dialogue, in one colorless phrase: "Lupin taught his third year Defence Against the Dark Arts class to fight this with the Riddikulus spell." Other times, however, the Lexicon disturbs the balance and takes more than is reasonably necessary to create a reference guide. In these instances, the Lexicon appears to retell parts of the storyline rather than report fictional facts and where to find them. For example, the Lexicon entry for "Trelawney, Sibyll Patricia" not only copies exactly the Divination professor's prophecies about the fates of Voldemort, Harry Potter, and Peter Pettigrew, it then tells how the prophecies are fulfilled, including events that do not involve Trelawney. While it is difficult to draw the line at each entry that takes more than is reasonably necessary from the <u>Harry Potter</u> series to serve its purposes, there are a number of places where the Lexicon engages in the same sort of extensive borrowing that might be expected of a copyright owner, not a third party author.

The Lexicon's use of copyrighted expression from Rowling's two companion books presents an easier determination. The Lexicon takes wholesale from these short books. <u>See supra</u> Findings of Fact. Depending on the purpose, using a substantial portion of a work, or even the whole thing, may be permissible. <u>See, e.g., Perfect 10</u>, 518 F.3d at 1167-68; <u>Bill Graham Archives</u>, 448 F.3d at 613; <u>Nunez v. Caribbean v. Int'l News Corp.</u>, 235 F.3d 18, 24 (1st Cir. 2000). In this case, however, the Lexicon's purpose is only slightly transformative of the companion books' original purpose. As a result, the amount and substantiality of the portion copied from the companion books weighs more heavily against a finding of fair use.

C. Nature of the Copyrighted Work

The second statutory fair use factor, the nature of the copyrighted work, recognizes that "some works are closer to the core of intended copyright protection than others." <u>Campbell</u>, 510 U.S. at 586. It is well settled that creative and fictional works are generally more deserving of protection than factual works. <u>Stewart v. Abend, DBA Authors Research Co.</u>, 495 U.S. 207, 237 (1990) ("In general, fair use is more likely to be found in factual works than in fictional works."); <u>Harper & Row</u>, 471 U.S. at 563 ("The law generally recognizes a greater need to disseminate factual works than works of fiction or fantasy." <u>Castle Rock</u>, 150 F. 3d at 143-144 (finding that the second factor favored plaintiff given the fictional nature of the copyrighted work); <u>Twin Peaks</u>, 996 F.2d at 1376 (stating that the second factor "must favor a creative and fictional work, no matter how successful"); <u>Ty, Inc. v. Publ'ns Int'l, Ltd.</u>, 333 F. Supp. 2d 705, 713 (N.D. Ill. 2004) (recognizing that "creative works are deemed more deserving of protection than works that are more of diligence than of originality or inventiveness." (internal quotation marks omitted)). In creating the Harry Potter novels and the companion books, Rowling has given life to a wholly original universe of people, creatures, places, and things. Such highly imaginative and creative fictional works are close to the core of copyright protection, particularly where the character of the secondary work is not entirely transformative. See Castle Rock, 150 F.3d at 144; Twin Peaks, 996 F.2d at 1376; Paramount, 11 F. Supp. 2d at 336. As a result, the second factor favors Plaintiffs.

D. Market Harm

The fourth statutory factor considers "the effect of the use upon the potential market for or value of the copyrighted work." 17 U.S.C. § 107(4). Courts must consider harm to "not only the primary market for the copyrighted work, but the current and potential market for derivative works" as well. Twin Peaks, 996 F.2d at 1377 (finding that fourth factor favored plaintiff where book about television series "may interfere with the primary market for the copyrighted works and almost certainly interferes with legitimate markets for derivative works"); see also Harper & Row, 471 U.S. at 568. Potential derivative uses "include[] only those that creators of original works would in general develop or license others to develop." Campbell, 510 U.S. at 592. The fourth factor will favor the copyright holder "if she can show a 'traditional, reasonable, or likely to be developed' market for licensing her work." Ringgold, 126 F.3d at 81. In addition to evaluating the particular actions of the alleged infringer, the fourth factor examines "whether unrestricted and widespread conduct of the sort engaged in by the defendant . . . would result in a substantially adverse impact on the potential market for the original." Campbell, 510 U.S. at 590 (omission in original) (internal quotation marks and citations omitted).

Plaintiffs presented expert testimony that the Lexicon would compete directly with, and impair the sales of, Rowling's planned encyclopedia by being first to market. Defendant rebutted this evidence with its own expert who testified that publication of the Lexicon is "extremely unlikely" to affect the sales of any encyclopedia that Rowling might one day publish. This testimony does not bear on the determination of the fourth factor, however, because a reference guide to the Harry Potter works is not a derivative work; competing with Rowling's planned encyclopedia is therefore permissible. Notwithstanding Rowling's public statements of her intention to publish her own encyclopedia, the market for reference guides to the Harry Potter works is not exclusively hers to exploit or license, no matter the commercial success attributable to the popularity of the original works. See Twin Peaks, 996 F.2d at 1377 ("The author of 'Twin Peaks' cannot preserve for itself the entire field of publishable works that wish to cash in on the 'Twin Peaks' phenomenon"). The market for reference guides does not become derivative simply because the copyright holder seeks to produce or license one. Ty, Inc., 292 F.3d at 521; see also Castle Rock, 150 F.3d at 145 n.11 ("[B]y developing or licensing a market for parody, news reporting, educational or other transformative users of its own creative work, a copyrighted owner plainly cannot prevent others from entering those fair use markets"); Twin Peaks, 996 F.2d at 1377.

Furthermore, there is no plausible basis to conclude that publication of the Lexicon would impair sales of the Harry Potter novels. Plaintiffs' expert Suzanne Murphy, vice president and publisher of trade publishing and marketing at Scholastic, testified that in her opinion a child who read the Lexicon would be discouraged from reading the Harry Potter series because the Lexicon discloses key plot points and does not contain "spoiler alerts." Children may be an elusive market for book publishers, but it is hard to believe that a child, having read the Lexicon, would lose interest in reading (and thus his or her parents' interest in purchasing) the Harry Potter series. Because the Lexicon uses the Harry Potter series for a transformative purpose (though inconsistently), reading the Lexicon cannot serve as a substitute for reading the original novels; they are enjoyed for different purposes. The Lexicon is thus unlikely to serve as a market substitute for the Harry Potter series and cause market harm. Campbell, 510 U.S. at 591 (stating that when "the second use is transformative, market substitution is at least less certain and market harm may not be so readily inferred"); see also Castle Rock, 150 F.3d at 145; Bill Graham Archives, 448 F.3d at 614-15. It seems unlikely that a publisher like HarperCollins would produce the Companion to Narnia, which reveals storylines, plot twists, and the ultimate fates of the characters in C.S. Lewis's original works, if it expected the publication would reduce sales and enthusiasm for the original works. Accordingly, the Lexicon does not present any potential harm to the markets for the original Harry Potter works. See Bill Graham Archives, 448 F.3d at 614; Castle Rock, 150 F.3d at 145.

On the other hand, publication of the Lexicon could harm sales of Rowling's two companion books. Unless they sought to enjoy the companion books for their entertainment value alone, consumers who purchased the Lexicon would have scant incentive to purchase either of Rowling's companion books, as the information contained in these short works has been incorporated into the Lexicon almost wholesale. Because the Lexicon's use of the companion books is only marginally transformative, the Lexicon is likely to supplant the market for the companion books. See Campbell, 510 U.S. at 591 (stating that "when a commercial use amounts to mere duplication of the entirety of an original, it clearly 'supersede[s] the objects' of the original and serves as a market replacement for it, making it likely that cognizable harm to the original will occur" (citation omitted)). At trial, Vander Ark himself recognized that although "[t]here's no way that someone's going to take an encyclopedia of [the Harry Potter novels] and think of it as a replacement," using the companion books without "replac[ing] Ms. Rowling's encyclopedia content" presents "quite a challenge." In view of the market harm to Rowling's companion books, the fourth factor tips in favor of Plaintiffs.

Additionally, the fourth factor favors Plaintiffs if publication of the Lexicon would impair the market for derivative works that Rowling is entitled or likely to license. Ringgold, 126 F.3d at 81. Although there is no supporting testimony, one potential derivative market that would reasonably be developed or licensed by Plaintiffs is use of the songs and poems in the Harry Potter novels. Because Plaintiffs would reasonably license the musical production or print publication of those songs and poems, Defendant unfairly harms this derivative market by reproducing verbatim the songs and poems without a license.

* * *

The fair-use factors, weighed together in light of the purposes of copyright law, fail to support the defense of fair use in this case. The first factor does not completely weigh in favor of Defendant because although the Lexicon has a transformative purpose, its actual use of the copyrighted works is not consistently transformative. Without drawing a line at the amount of copyrighted material that is reasonably necessary to create an A-to-Z reference guide, many portions of the Lexicon take more of the copyrighted works than is reasonably necessary in relation to the Lexicon's purpose. Thus, in balancing the first and third factors, the balance is tipped against a finding of fair use. The creative nature of the copyrighted works and the harm to the market for Rowling's companion books weigh in favor of Plaintiffs. In striking the balance between the property rights of original authors and the freedom of expression of secondary authors, reference guides to works of literature should generally be encouraged by copyright law as they provide a benefit readers and students; but to borrow from Rowling's overstated views, they should not be permitted to "plunder" the works of original authors "without paying the customary price" Harper & Row, 471 U.S. at 562, lest original authors lose incentive to create new works that will also benefit the public interest.

III. Injunctive and Statutory Relief

The Copyright Act provides that courts "may" grant injunctive relief "on such terms as it may deem reasonable to prevent or restrain infringement of a copyright." 17 U.S.C. § 502(a). In eBay Inc. v. MercExchange, L.L.C., the Supreme Court made clear that an injunction does not automatically follow a determination that a copyright has been infringed. 547 U.S. 388, 392-93 (2006). A copyright plaintiff seeking a permanent injunction still must satisfy the traditional four-factor test before the district court may use its equitable discretion to grant such relief. The plaintiff must demonstrate: (1) that it will suffer an irreparable injury; (2) that remedies available at law, such as monetary damages, are inadequate to compensate for that injury; (3) that, considering the balance of hardships between the plaintiff and defendant, a remedy in equity is warranted; and (4) that the public interest would not be disserved by a permanent injunction. See Weinberger v. Romero-Barcelo, 456 U.S. 305, 311-13 (1982); Amoco Production Co. v. Gambell, 480 U.S. 531, 542 (1987).

A. Irreparable Injury

Under the law of this Circuit, "generally when a copyright plaintiff makes out a prima facie showing of infringement, irreparable harm may be presumed." ABKCO Music, Inc. v. Stellar Records, Inc., 96 F.3d 60, 66 (2d Cir. 1996). Because Plaintiffs have demonstrated a case of copyright infringement, and because Defendant has failed to establish its affirmative defense to copyright infringement, irreparable injury may be presumed in this case. In view of eBay, which applied the traditional four-part test for injunctive relief in the context of a patent claim, there is some question of whether the presumption of irreparable harm still applies. District courts, however, have continued to apply the presumption post-eBay. See, e.g., Warner Bros. Entm't Inc. v. Carsagno, No. 06 Civ. 2676, 2007 WL 1655666, *6 (E.D.N.Y. June 4, 2007) (finding irreparable harm where plaintiff had demonstrated that without an injunction, its copyrighted work would be subject to continued copyright infringement); UMG Recordings, Inc. v. Blake, No. 06 Civ. 00120, 2007 WL 1853956, *3 (E.D.N.C. June 26, 2007) (stating that irreparable injury is presumed when plaintiff succeeds on the merits).

Regardless, even if irreparable injury is not presumed, Plaintiffs have presented sufficient evidence that such injury would result from Defendant's infringement in the absence of relief. First, Plaintiffs have established that publication of the Lexicon will cause irreparable injury to Rowling as a writer. Rowling testified that if the Lexicon is published, it would destroy her "will or heart to continue with [writing her own] encyclopedia." She further testified that if the Lexicon is published -- giving "carte blanche to . . . anyone who wants to make a quick bit of money" by drawing freely from her works and opening the doors to "a surfeit of substandard so-called lexicons and guides" -- she would have much less incentive to write her own book. By deterring Rowling from writing her planned encyclopedia, publication of the Lexicon would also result in harm to the charitable organizations that would receive the royalties from the sale of the book and the reading public who would be unable to enjoy such a book.

More concretely, publication of the Lexicon would cause irreparable harm to the sales of Rowling's companion books, all the elements of which are replicated in the Lexicon for a similar purpose. Readers would have no reason to purchase the companion books since the Lexicon supersedes their value. Additionally, because the Lexicon engages in considerable verbatim copying of the Harry Potter works, publication of the Lexicon would diminish Rowling's copyright in her own language. Based on evidence of Vander Ark's vigorous claim to his rights in the Lexicon website, publication of the Lexicon may result in conflicting assertions of copyright over the same material by Rowling on one hand and Vander Ark or RDR Books on the other. (In her trial testimony, Ms. Rowling noted her concern that if she published her own encyclopedia, RDR Books would sue her for copyright infringement, claiming that her "paraphrase ran a little too close to [Vander Ark's] paraphrasing."

B. Inadequate Remedies at Law

If an injunction is not issued, Defendant is likely to continue infringing Plaintiffs' copyright in the future. RDR Books has actively marketed the Lexicon domestically and abroad (see supra Findings of Fact) and might gain considerable commercial success as the first Harry Potter reference guide to hit the market after Rowling's completion of the series. In view of the irreparable harm that would flow from Defendant's continuing infringement, including lost sales of Rowling's companion books and the injury to Rowling as a writer, Plaintiffs have shown that money damages alone are an insufficient remedy. See Lauratex Textile Corp. v. Allton Knitting Mills Inc., 519 F. Supp. 730, 732 (S.D.N.Y. 1981) (finding that money damages would not suffice where there was a strong probability that the defendant would continue to infringe plaintiff's copyright).

C. Balance of Hardships

While Plaintiffs have identified their hardships if an injunction were not granted, Defendant identifies no hardship it would suffer if publication of the Lexicon were enjoined. The only possible harm to Defendant is the loss of the chance to sell an infringing book, but the law does not protect this type of hardship. See My-T Fine Corp. v. Samuels, 69 F.2d 76, 78 (2d Cir. 1934) (Hand, J.); see also Concrete Mach. Co. v. Classic Lawn Ornaments, 843 F.2d 600, 612 (1st Cir. 1988); Apple Computer Inc. v. Franklin Computer Corp., 714 F.2d 1240, 1255 (3d Cir. 1983). Thus, the balance of the hardships weighs in favor of Plaintiffs.

D. Public Interest

Issuing an injunction in this case both benefits and harms the public interest. While the Lexicon, in its current state, is not a fair use of the Harry Potter works, reference works that share the Lexicon's purpose of aiding readers of literature generally should be encouraged rather than stifled. As the Supreme Court suggested in Campbell, "[b]ecause the fair use enquiry often requires close questions of judgment as to the extent of permissible borrowing" in cases involving transformative uses, granting an injunction does not always serve the goals of copyright law, when the secondary use, though edifying in some way, has been found to surpass the bounds of fair use. Campbell, 510 U.S. at 578 n.10. On the other hand, to serve the public interest, copyright law must "prevent[] the misappropriation of the skills, creative energies, and resources which are invested in the protected work." Apple Computer, 714 F.2d at 1255. Ultimately, because the Lexicon appropriates too much of Rowling's creative work for its purposes as a reference guide, a permanent injunction must issue to prevent the possible proliferation of works that do the same and thus deplete the incentive for original authors to create new works.

In addition to injunctive relief, Plaintiffs seek statutory damages in this case. Under the Copyright Act, a plaintiff may elect to recover an award of statutory damages for each infringed work "in a sum of not less than $750 or more than $30,000 as the court considers just." 17 U.S.C. § 504. In awarding statutory damages, courts have broad discretion to set the amount of the award within the statutory limits. Fitzgerald Publ'g Co. v. Baylor Publ'g Co., 807 F.2d 1110, 1116-17 (2d Cir. 1986). Since the Lexicon has not been published and thus Plaintiffs have suffered no harm beyond the fact of infringement, the Court awards Plaintiffs the minimum award under the statute for each work with respect to which Plaintiffs have established infringement. Plaintiffs are entitled to statutory damages of $750.00 for each of the seven Harry Potter novels and each of the two companion books.

CONCLUSION

For the foregoing reasons, Plaintiffs have established copyright infringement of the Harry Potter series, Fantastic Beasts & Where to Find Them, and Quidditch Through the Ages by J.K. Rowling. Defendant has failed to establish its affirmative defense of fair use. Defendant's publication of the Lexicon is hereby permanently enjoined, and Plaintiffs are awarded statutory damages of $6, 750.00. IT IS SO ORDERED.

Robert P. Patterson, Jr., U.S. District Judge, September 8, 2008.